More Praise for

THE LOST SONS OF OMAHA

"In *The Lost Sons of Omaha*, Joe Sexton unleashes with disciplined fury a gripping tale of multiple tragedies that reveal layers of prejudice, sadness, loss, and denial. It is a feat of relentless reporting."

—Randall Kennedy, Harvard Law School, author of *Race, Crime, and the Law*

"In an era of instant news, semi-informed social media commentary, and crime-as-entertainment, Joe Sexton has gone in the opposite direction. He's crafted a superb book—both sweeping in scale and incredibly detailed—from years of thoughtful, meticulous reporting. It's a profoundly empathetic endeavor that ranks with the best works of narrative journalism."

—A. C. Thompson, Emmy Award winner for *Documenting Hate: Charlottesville*, PBS *Frontline* correspondent, and *ProPublica* reporter

"It took a brave person to write *The Lost Sons of Omaha*. I sincerely hope that people will take the time to read it. Even if all we do is absorb the meaning of the book's title, it could add a lot to reduce the toxic nature of America's debate."

—Bob Kerrey, former governor and U.S. senator from Nebraska

"Joe Sexton, an old-school reporter, conducts a masterful probe of a heartland tragedy with what is best described as investigative empathy. Gripping. Passionate."

—Errol Louis, Graduate School of Journalism, City University of New York

THE LOST SONS OF OMAHA

Two Young Men in an American Tragedy

Joe Sexton

SCRIBNER

New York London Toronto Sydney New Delhi

Scribner
An Imprint of Simon & Schuster, Inc.
1230 Avenue of the Americas
New York, NY 10020

First Scribner hardcover edition May 2023

Interior design by Davina Mock-Maniscalco

Photograph credits: Part One: Chris Machian/Omaha World-Herald;
Part Two: Z Long/Omaha World-Herald;
Epilogue: Dominic Brockhaus/NOSS Media, LLC

Manufactured in the United States of America

1 3 5 7 9 10 8 6 4 2

Library of Congress Cataloging-in-Publication Data has been applied for.

ISBN 978-1-9821-9834-3
ISBN 978-1-9821-9836-7 (ebook)

A story told straight for the glorious women
who have both had my back and pushed me forward
—Beth, Jane, Lucy, Flynn, and Rowan

Note to the Reader

THIS BOOK IS A WORK OF nonfiction and is based on my research, public records, correspondence, and extensive interviews; certain names have been changed.

★ VETERAN ★
OWNED BUSINESS

PART ONE

"I Hated Fire Watch"

BY NIGHTFALL ON MAY 30, 2020, Jake Gardner was inside his nightclub in Omaha's Old Market district. He had two pistols and a shotgun. One of his regular bartenders soon joined him.

The night before, a Black Lives Matter protest in the streets of Omaha had turned ugly. Police and protesters had skirmished, and there'd been arrests. Some businesses had been damaged. Now a second night of unrest had exploded, and the crowds of protesters were descending on Omaha's downtown. Bricks and Molotov cocktails were being heaved at buildings and at police, and officers in riot gear had responded with tear gas.

Gardner, thirty-eight, had moved to Omaha with his family when he was in middle school. He'd enlisted in the Marines straight out of high school, and won a fistful of medals and combat ribbons as part of one of the very first U.S. Marine Corps units to invade Iraq in 2003.

Gardner had returned from the war to Omaha and made a success of himself running one of the city's more popular downtown nightclubs. For years, the club had been known as The Hive, named after a song by a popular band out of Omaha, 311. The bar was located on the northern edge of the Old Market, a historic district of cobblestone streets and converted warehouses that had been transformed into a revitalized neighborhood of clubs and restaurants, carriage rides and street performers.

In the last year, though, Gardner had reinvented The Hive,

turning it and an adjacent space on Harney Street into The Gatsby, a cocktail bar tricked out to evoke the Roaring Twenties. But the swank of The Gatsby hid what amounted to serious financial troubles for Gardner: he'd been involved in a dispute stemming from a bid to expand into a nearby property and his legal bills were bleeding money from The Gatsby. Worse, the club had been shuttered for weeks amid the global coronavirus pandemic, compounding Gardner's troubles.

With a reopening scheduled for the following week, Gardner by May 30 had stocked his bar full of high-end liquor, some $90,000 in prospective gross profits. The liquor was, in truth, his single most important financial asset.

The protests in Omaha had been ignited by a harrowing national scandal that had been captured on video and broadcast to the world—the killing days earlier of a Black man, George Floyd, by a police officer in Minneapolis, Minnesota. With Floyd on the ground during an attempted arrest, the cop had kneeled on the Black man's neck for close to ten minutes, slowly asphyxiating him. The killing, caught on video by a bystander, triggered nationwide fury, as cities from Atlanta to Portland were convulsed by protests and vandalism.

Omaha, a city of half a million people on the Missouri River, is the hometown of both Warren Buffett and Malcolm X. It is a place of deep-pocketed philanthropy and entrenched segregation in its schools and in its neighborhoods. The Catholic priest Father Edward Flanagan in 1917 founded the famous Boys Town orphanage in Omaha, and fifty years later the Black Panthers set up an office in town, as well. Known as America's biggest small town, Omaha also has an overlooked history of lynchings and race riots. But in a reliably red state, whose Republican Party would pledge its allegiance to Donald Trump, Omaha has come to beat with a faint but durable blue Democratic heart. Both the Jesuit school Creighton University and the University of Nebraska Omaha help give the city a liberal character. Omaha went for Barack Obama in 2008, and again for Joe Biden in 2020.

Gardner—barely five seven with brown eyes, his brown hair

worn to his shoulders and a showman's smile on his face—had for years been something of a known personality in Omaha. The local papers had done feature stories on him and his rise as a nightclub owner in the ever-more-popular Old Market. The Hive had hosted reggae and salsa nights, and Gardner had once attracted notice for an inspired election day promotion: Show you voted, and you got a free drink. Didn't matter who you pulled the lever for.

But Gardner had also been a lightning rod on matters of race and gender. He'd provoked a public outcry over crude remarks he'd made concerning the issue of his bar's bathroom facilities, and whether they adequately served the city's transgender community. Some of the city's LGBTQ advocates never forgave him. The Hive's strict door policy—no hats, no baggy pants, no facial tattoos—had come to be regarded by some as transparently racist. Gardner had also worked on Donald Trump's surprising run for president, and for a while he'd had a cardboard cutout of Trump set up inside his nightclub.

Gardner was no fan of the Black Lives Matter movement. Online, he'd once called it a terrorist organization, one he thought regarded all whites as racists and that was more interested in creating mayhem in America's streets than seeing bad cops punished or real criminal justice reforms instituted. The remark had provoked plenty of blowback, cementing in some people's minds the sense that Gardner's establishments were unwelcoming places for people of color.

On the night of May 30, Omaha Scanner, an online breaking-news outlet, allowed Gardner, holed up inside The Gatsby, to monitor the events unfolding on the streets of Omaha. By 9:00 p.m., protesters were abandoning the scene of the night's initial standoff with police—the intersection of Dodge Street and 72nd Street, Omaha's informal public square—and had made it downtown. Windows at the Douglas County Courthouse, where a Black man named Will Brown had been infamously lynched one hundred years earlier, had been busted out and graffiti painted on the building's walls. The city's cherished Orpheum Theater, just blocks away from Gardner's nightclub, was under assault, as well.

Gardner used his cell phone to text a former Marine and one of his best friends.

"I know this may come as a surprise, but I fucking hated fire watch," Gardner wrote. "Irony is getting out of the Marines to start a company so you are your own boss, then sitting on fire watch all night. Fuck me."

"Fire watch" is a military term for guard duty. Marines eager for combat and adventure tend to hate it—forced to log long hours at night doing something that, while essential to one's unit's safety, most often feels like killing time. Still, the Marine Corps takes the duty dead seriously, and spells out the dozen or so requirements for performing fire watch properly:

> *When on duty as a guard or sentry, you are in charge of your area and have the authority to stop and question any rank who seeks to pass your area; Walk your post in a military manner, keeping always on the alert and observing everything that takes place within sight or hearing; Stay observant with keen attention to details; It is easy to get complacent after many hours on duty—especially if you have not had many people to deal with; But your ability to pay attention to your surroundings will save your life and others; Report all violations of orders you have been instructed to enforce; Be especially watchful at night; Challenge all persons on or near your post, and to allow no one to pass without proper authority. Stay vigilant; Quit your post only when properly relieved.*

Harney Street, where Gardner's club was located, is a wide boulevard, with three lanes for cars and another for bikes. When Gardner was first scouting locations to open his place in the Old Market, he had walked the district's streets with a hand clicker, determining and recording the spots with the greatest foot traffic. Harney Street had won out.

Nearing 10:00 p.m., Gardner got a text from a Marine buddy in town who had been following Omaha Scanner, too. The ex-Marine had been a recruiter in Omaha, and Gardner, once enlisted himself, had been one of the recruiter's best advocates for identifying new prospects. Gardner struck him as both a natural patriot and a persuasive pitchman. The former recruiter and his wife had patronized Gardner's bars over the years, and they were looking forward to going again to The Gatsby when it reopened in the coming days. Now he wrote to Gardner, saying things on the streets were looking "squirrelly." And he fell back on Marine lingo to ask if Gardner wanted him to come get him.

"I asked if he wanted a hot extract," the Marine said.

"No," Gardner wrote back. "I'm good."

The protests ignited by George Floyd's killing grew to be more than just the latest angry reaction to an outrageous police killing. It felt more like a genuine moment of national reckoning. Donald Trump, who had all but sided with white supremacists after the infamous and deadly 2017 rally in Charlottesville, Virginia, was seeking a second term. The COVID pandemic had already begun to take a disproportionate toll among the nation's people of color. Much of the country, then, was out of patience, and motivated like rarely before to take a stand. The notion of defunding the nation's police departments, once a fringe idea, now seemed to many necessary and overdue.

In the days after Floyd's death, hundreds of cities across the country erupted in anger and violence. Curfews were imposed in two hundred of those cities; thousands of arrests were made; some estimates of the damage to property ran to $2 billion.

One of the young protesters making his way along Harney Street was a twenty-two-year-old African American man, James Scurlock. Named for his father, Scurlock was one of more than two dozen siblings, including stepbrothers and stepsisters, blood siblings and informally adopted others, who spent all or parts of their upbringing in North Omaha, the Black and mostly poor corner of Omaha.

"Our own little Detroit," said A. D. Swolley, one of Scurlock's older brothers.

Scurlock had been born in the ambulance racing his mother to the delivery room at the hospital, what would become a funny story about a boy later known for his zest for life and appetite for adventure.

James H. Scurlock Sr. said life for the family could at times be hard.

"Poverty? Yes," he said. "Did my kids miss a meal? No."

The sprawling family had maintained an extraordinary bond over many years. They were fiercely loyal to one another, whether they shared the same set of parents or not.

"Most of us didn't need to have friends," said one of Scurlock's sisters, Qwenyona Evans. "We had each other."

There had, however, been a nomadic quality to Scurlock's childhood. For a while, he and a number of his siblings lived with their grandmother in Denver. He spent time in a homeless shelter with his mother in Norfolk, Nebraska, which once upon a time had been a thriving meatpacking town two hours outside Omaha. When in Omaha, Scurlock attended local schools, at least one of them a magnet school for kids interested in science, and he stayed with a shifting set of mixed households. Family and teachers thought Scurlock had the makings of a promising student—naturally bright, creative, taken with music.

Scurlock had kept an end-of-school-year note from his fourth-grade teacher.

"I will truly miss that cute little smile of yours," the teacher wrote. "I admire your mathematical ability. Don't forget to read this summer. Smile. Never give up."

"Grades were never a problem," Swolley said of James. "The neighborhood was the problem."

At sixteen, Scurlock's father said, James had rebelled against his father's strictness and run off to Norfolk. Swolley said he and others were concerned about James, but they did not think he was in danger.

They were wrong. James would get locked up, and sentenced to three to five years in a juvenile correctional facility. Two other arrests would follow after his release.

"He had a good, good heart," Marissa Mitchell, a sister, said of James. "But that good heart found itself in some bad places."

On the night of May 30, Scurlock eventually found himself inside the offices of an architecture firm on Harney Street. The windows had been shattered, and Scurlock and a friend, Tucker Randall, were trashing the desks and chairs and computers on the office's ground floor. Just past 10:30, Scurlock and his friend emerged from the office, and darted off down Harney Street.

They were exactly one block from Jake Gardner's club, The Gatsby.

"Fuck the Police"

THE FIRST NIGHT OF PROTEST IN Omaha during the summer of 2020 happened on May 28, outside the Northeast Police Precinct at 30th and Taylor Streets. The crowd, according to news accounts, was small but loud. It had been three days since George Floyd was murdered by Minneapolis police officer Derek Chauvin.

Anthony Baker, one of the leaders of the rally, addressed the crowd early on. Baker could not believe police wanted to arrest Floyd for the crime of forgery—because he might have passed a counterfeit bill in a convenience store.

"Since when does the crime of forgery end with the sentence of death?" Baker asked. "George Floyd was put on trial in the streets of Minneapolis, and so often that is the court of law for Black people. Derek Chauvin was the judge, the jury, and the executioner."

Ernie Chambers was also at the rally. Chambers, eighty-two, was a Black firebrand out of North Omaha, the segregated corner of Omaha that had once been a place bursting with Black businesses and music, newspapers, civil rights marches, and occasionally revolutionary politics. Chambers had been the first Black Nebraskan elected to the state legislature, and he had served North Omaha for close to half a century.

Legend and iconoclast, Chambers had run both for governor and for the U.S. Senate, the first African American in Nebraska to attempt either. His champions revered him; his critics never made the mistake of disrespecting or underestimating him. He had shaken up the city's school system, taken on its business interests, called out its cops for their misconduct, and the Omaha Police Department for often protecting those cops.

"Cops invariably get their jobs back," Chambers told the crowd, "when the victims are Black, brown, or poor white."

The rally on May 28 lasted an hour, and ended without incident.

Omaha's Police Department has just under one thousand sworn officers. Its troubles have never been so grave as to require something like federal oversight, but it has had its share of scandal.

In 2012, local advocates filed a formal complaint with the U.S. Department of Justice alleging wholesale rights violations committed by the OPD. They listed the claims at length:

> *The events that warrant your investigation include:*
>
> *A. A pattern of use of force incidents that include unnecessary use of severe physical force, reckless use of deadly force and violation of department policy, illegal arrest where no criminal conduct is involved, disregard for state law, constitutional principles and official police department policies in a variety of areas, violations of people's First Amendment rights involving observing or recording police officers;*
>
> *B. A disproportionate concentration of abuse against racial and ethnic minorities in violation of federal laws in the U.S. constitution;*
>
> *C. Failure of the Omaha Police Department and the City of Omaha to maintain proper accountability measures for the police department, including the firing of a public safety auditor in October 2006 for his showing a 28-page report on traffic stops that documented many of the problems indicated in this report; since that date, the Omaha Police Department has been without any independent citizen oversight, formal policies, training, and supervision*

that are not consistent with recognized best practices in American law enforcement.

The complaint did not lead to any action by the Justice Department, and that outcome registered for many as yet another dismissal of their legitimate and urgent concerns. The catalogue of problems extended over generations—disputed deadly force incidents; claims of brutality; a record of racial profiling in traffic stops. The city, unlike many in America, has no independent civilian oversight agency to keep check on the police department.

Omaha's last episode of damaging unrest, in fact, had been provoked by the killing of a young Black teen by a white police officer in 1969. It was detailed at the time by news accounts in the *Omaha World-Herald*, and later documented and analyzed by historians.

On June 24, 1969, ten or so youngsters had gathered at an empty apartment in a housing project in North Omaha. They played records and danced. "We did it all the time," one of the youngsters later said. "We even went around to the neighbors to see that it would be all right." But police got a call for a suspected break-in in the neighborhood, and soon Vivian Strong, fourteen, was dead of a single gunshot wound to the back of her head, fired by Officer James Loder.

Strong's nineteen-year-old babysitter, as well as Loder's Black police partner, were said to have asked, "Why did you shoot her?" "He didn't holler or shoot in the air or anything," the babysitter said.

Loder was fired from the force and charged. Loder testified for an hour during the trial, saying he had, after arriving at the scene of the alleged break-in, seen someone hunched outside an apartment window. He shouted a warning, he said, and then shot when the person fled. "If I had known it was a female, I wouldn't have fired the shot," he said. Loder denied claims made by some that he had kicked Strong's body in his attempt to turn the lifeless child over.

Loder was acquitted by an all-white jury, kept his job, and spent two more years on the force.

The killing sparked three days of protest and violence in North

Omaha. Almost ninety people were injured and sixty arrested during the disturbances, and local businesses and buildings suffered $1 million in damages. The local chapter of the Black Panthers protected the neighborhood's Black churches, but the damage done across those three days had left scars in North Omaha. Many of the businesses never reopened, and many of North Omaha's middle-class Black residents moved out.

Now, one night after the emotional but peaceful rally outside the police station at 39th and Taylor, Omaha was increasingly roiled by the maelstrom provoked by George Floyd's killing. That morning, Omaha police got word of a protest planned for 72nd Street and Dodge. The intersection was located in Omaha's acknowledged, if inexact, center. It was the place crowds went to celebrate University of Nebraska football championships, to cheer and get drunk, to celebrate openly and urinate publicly. The police department expected three hundred or so protesters.

A formal police department report laid out what happened next.

At 5:00 p.m., senior Omaha Police Department officials arrived at the northwest corner of the famous intersection and tried to meet with the protest's organizers. But by 6:00 p.m., there were more than six hundred people on the scene. An hour later, the crowd was at one thousand.

"Fuck the police," they chanted.

The protesters began to block traffic—sitting in the street, or walking in the direction of oncoming cars. At 7:45, a protester threw a bottle at the police. Others set upon a Nebraska State Patrol vehicle, with one person climbing atop it with a megaphone. The police started to fire rounds of PepperBall, nonlethal ammunition that sets off an explosion of searing smoke upon impact. Then, at the direction of their Rapid Deployment Force, officers set off smoke grenades. Cops on horses were enlisted as well.

By 9:00 p.m., the scene at Omaha's spiritual heart had grown chaotic. Warnings were being shouted. Tear gas had been fired. Police reported up the chain of command that they were being hit with pipes; bricks; bottles filled with urine. Protesters used wooden pallets to build a blockade across Dodge Street. The crowd filled the streets, sidewalks, and adjacent parking lots.

At 10:30, police got reports that protesters planned to break into the Target store nearby, and a wave of protesters was seen headed that way. Shopping carts were brought from the store's parking lot to the streets. A burning object was tossed into a dumpster. Windows at the Best Buy store in the same area were broken out. Cars were performing "cookies," vehicles spinning wildly in the parking lot of the Sears store. The clerks at a Bucky's gas station convenience store reported that protesters were stealing merchandise. A man with a shotgun was detained by a SWAT team. Amid it all, some protesters were taking selfies.

Eventually, what the police department called arrest buses arrived, and the crowd dispersed. The department's own after-action report acknowledged its officers were undermanned and lacked adequate ways of effectively communicating warnings or commands to the protesters. But the night's unrest was no accident of circumstance, the police concluded. People had come with gas masks, and carrying shields; they had firearms and communicated with two-way radios.

"Although the majority of persons at the protests were average citizens, some clearly came for conflict," the police report read.

Some of those who came saw it another way, and blamed police for provoking and worsening the unrest and violence.

"I watched police intentionally escalate things," said one protester, Robert Fuller. "Tear gas. Batons."

If bad, the night of unrest on May 29 was nothing compared to the next, on May 30. The protests began again at 72nd and Dodge. Eggs were being thrown early; police also noted the delivery of large quantities of milk to protesters gathered in the parking lot of a Petco store. Milk is often used by protesters to counteract chemical agents used by police.

Drones were being flown by protesters; a person using a high-pressure water bottle to spray police with urine was captured and arrested; another person was arrested after a report of a man with a gun. Tear gas was once more in the air.

This time, though, the protests spread, and soon there were hundreds of people in Omaha's downtown. Some three hundred people were reported outside police headquarters on Howard Street. The mounted squad was sent. Then, the Rapid Deployment Force joined them. Dodge and 72nd was effectively abandoned.

Downtown, the police encountered protesters in body armor. An exchange of Molotov cocktails and "chemical munitions," as the police called them, escalated. The police found it hard to move as coordinated units through the streets now teeming with people. At least fifty people were arrested.

Protesters later complained of needless police brutality amid what the Omaha Police Department said were more than 120 "use of force" incidents. A twenty-three-year-old protester was shot by police in the eye with a PepperBall. The department counted nearly two hundred arrests and close to $400,000 worth of damage to more than one hundred businesses, homes, and cars. Civil rights advocates called for an investigation of the police conduct and later successfully sued, challenging the legality of police tactics and requiring reform.

The police called the two nights and the days of additional protests afterward the worst unrest Omaha had seen in fifty years.

"Pretty Crazy"

JAKE GARDNER—WHO WITH HAIR TO his shoulders and a taste for T-shirts that could make him look like a Grateful Dead roadie—lived just blocks from his bar in the Old Market district. He liked to be able to work late, clean and lock up, and then walk to his apartment with the dawn coming. All the better if he'd had a few drinks after closing.

On May 29, the second night of protests, he'd sat outside The Gatsby, armed, but in the end not too concerned. The unrest never got close to the Old Market.

On May 30, he went to the bar in the afternoon. There was work to be done if the place was to reopen amid relaxed COVID restrictions. Given what had happened at 72nd and Dodge the night before, though, Gardner brought more than one gun this time. He sent a picture of his weapons to a Marine pal: his favorite pistol, a Springfield 9mm, and a second sidearm. The bullets in them were designed for maximum damage; if he didn't intend to shoot someone, he was going to make sure he had the desired firepower if and when he had to. He also had a shotgun, but that, he said, was loaded with nonlethal ammunition.

Years earlier, Gardner, as part of the Second Light Armored Reconnaissance Battalion, had driven an LAV-25, an eight-wheel amphibious vehicle, and was among the first to cross into Iraq in 2003—"the tip of the tip of the spear," his fellow Marines liked to say. Gardner and his battalion would make it all the way to Saddam

Hussein's hometown of Tikrit, one of the quickest and deepest incursions behind enemy lines in the history of the Marine Corps.

Drivers of combat vehicles such as the LAV-25 wound up particularly vulnerable to traumatic brain injuries, what would become the signature wounds borne by those who fought in Iraq and Afghanistan as part of America's "Forever Wars." The heads of drivers were more fully exposed to the blast waves caused by the detonation of the improvised explosive devices American forces encountered across Iraq. The turret and driver's hatch tended to direct the blast energy onto the driver's head.

Gardner had emerged from his wartime service with at least one traumatic brain injury, and with profound loss of hearing. Back in the states, Gardner experienced trouble sleeping, and he was often hyper-vigilant in crowds, not wanting to have his back exposed to any potential trouble.

It took years for the Department of Veterans Affairs to fully diagnose and acknowledge Gardner's injuries and resulting disability, and so Gardner himself had acquired a service dog to help with his life after combat. It was part Czech border patrol shepherd, part Belgian Malinois shepherd, and Gardner named him LeBron, after LeBron James, the NBA superstar and Gardner's favorite athlete. Gardner took the dog, complete with a LeBron James jersey, to a handful of Cleveland Cavaliers games. Gardner created an Instagram page for his dog, and LeBron even became something of a celebrity one year in Omaha, when he was named "Bouncer of the Year" for his work at his owner's establishments.

As darkness fell on the evening of May 30, Gardner used his phone to send a meme to his best friend out in Oregon, a former Marine he'd first met in boot camp because their last names both began with the letter G.

The meme invoked President Trump's controversial remark about the unrest that had been set off by George Floyd's killing—"When the looting starts, the shooting starts." The meme Gardner sent came with an attached image of ammunition being misloaded.

"National Guard," Gardner wrote, referencing the image of the botched ammunition loading. Marines loved to mock the Guard as poorly trained, and often incompetent.

Gardner's friend asked how things were in the street outside the bar. Gardner texted back: "It took a while, but I learned my fifth safety rule." The fifth rule of gun safety is: "Be sure of your target and what's beyond."

By 10:00 p.m., things were indeed heating up outside The Gatsby. What had long been a minor annoyance to Gardner—the seemingly endless repair work being done on Harney Street, which could leave it choked with construction materials and wet with water from underground pipes—had turned menacing. The construction debris and equipment in front of his establishment became weapons for angry protesters in what felt increasingly like a militarized zone.

There had been talk in Omaha on the first night of violent protests that business owners should stay away from their properties, let insurance cover any losses, and avoid the possibility of inflaming tensions or being hurt themselves. But Gardner had researched the matter, and found that damages suffered in riots actually were often uncovered by insurance. The notion of sitting back and absorbing recoverable losses was naive. The apartment he lived in, anyway, was literally blocks from his bar.

At 10:28, The Gatsby's security cameras captured a man heaving a construction flagpole against the windows of the bar, smashing them. Rocks were thrown as well, breaking more windows.

Gardner called 911.

Dispatcher: "Nine-one-one; do you need police, fire, or medical?"

Gardner: "I've got some people breaking in all the windows right now. It's Twelve-Oh-Seven Harney Street."

Dispatcher: "Twelve-Oh-Seven Harney. Are you on scene there or are you viewing this from a camera?"

Gardner: "I'm inside the window being broken right now."

Dispatcher: "That The Hive?"
Gardner: "Yeah. Correct."
Dispatcher: "How many people? More than ten?"
Gardner: "Yeah, for sure. There's like a whole mob of them. I have no idea. They're throwing things through windows. I just wanted to call in and make sure that I was on the record."
Dispatcher: "Okay. Anybody inside injured? Need a rescue squad?"
Gardner: "No, we're good. We're kind of pulled back from the windows. I'm pretty sure they used a gun, so we pulled back pretty far so that nobody got injured and then we parked behind a brick wall."
Dispatcher: "Okay."
Gardner: "Pretty crazy."
Dispatcher: "What's your name, please?"
Gardner: "My name is Jacob Gardner. I'm the owner of this place."
Dispatcher: "Okay. Did you see a gun? Just hear it?"
Gardner: "I heard it. Safe to say, if it was a rock being thrown there, I'd be surprised. It was a pop."
Dispatcher: "Okay. Okay. All right. I'll go ahead and get this info out. I'll get a call out. We're going to also see you as soon as they're available; like you said, it's crazy down there."
Gardner: "I get it."
Dispatcher: "Okay. If anything changes, just call back. All right?"
Gardner: "Okay, will do."
Dispatcher: "All right. Bye."
Gardner: "Thank you so much."

"He Was Getting That Reality Check"

JAMES SCURLOCK HAD BECOME A FATHER for the first time in the months before George Floyd's murder. The baby, a girl, had been named Jewels, and Scurlock's family thought the child's arrival had invested James with a source of joy and sense of purpose.

But Scurlock's relationship with his girl's mother, Mari Agosta, was combustible, and one night in February of 2020 it turned violent inside the apartment of one of Scurlock's relatives, Alize Swolley. The official police report of what happened makes plain the ugliness: Scurlock had texted Mari Agosta, 19, asking her to come over to his house. Agosta refused and Scurlock subsequently came over to Alize Swolley's apartment, where Agosta was staying, and busted through the door. He told Agosta, "I told you, you need to leave," and slapped her in the face twice. Swolley tried to stop the assault and Agosta ran out of the apartment and down the stairs. Scurlock caught up to her and kneed and kicked her in the stomach and then punched her in the face. She fell to the ground, bleeding from the nose and lip. Agosta then ran out to her car, whose windshield had been shattered.

Scurlock, nicknamed Juju, was arrested days later, and wound up in the Douglas County Jail.

He wrote to Agosta from jail. He conceded their relationship was "toxic," and he asked her to forgive him for hurting her. If they were finished as a couple, he still was committed to their child.

Mari, look baby mama, I know we have our ups and downs. We have our on and off, but I want to get locked back in. I am sorry I put my hands on you, a hundred percent. Look where it got me. I think we are a hundred percent played, but we most def got a beautiful daughter together. And that is most important to me. . . . No, I have not learned my lessons. I probably never will, but that is me being honest. You probably hate me. And I understand, but I just want to make things right. No, I don't want to be with you. You need something better than I could ever offer, a hundred percent. But I'm the best thing for Jules. She is my world. I'll die behind that beautiful little girl. Lady, please don't keep her away from me, when I get out. I would love to do our family Sundays again and see where it goes. We're toxic baby mama and we both know we love that toxic shit, but it's time for things to change a hundred percent. I'm willing to do anything in my power to give my baby the best life ever. If I can make things right with you, I would, but I can't and don't want to. I love the fuck out of you and I always will, but look, baby girl, you're smart as fuck. You got a bright future. Please stop letting me fuck that up for you. I do want more kids in the future and to possibly be a family too. But right now you got to stay the fuck away from me. . . . I love you a lot, baby mama, but I just want to focus on our baby and get her looking how she's supposed to be. I'm sorry for my time away. I'll make it back up to the both of you. Love, James Scurlock.

Scurlock was released in the third week of May. He stayed with his father some, and with an assortment of siblings, as well. His father, who had spent his life working construction and roofing jobs, said over the years his son often did gigs with him.

"Fridays he's out at the clubs; Mondays he's on the roof with me," James Sr. said.

But Rajeanna Scurlock, a couple of years her brother's junior and one of his two full sisters, said James seemed both humbled and lost. He was delighted to see his baby, and talked excitedly about maybe enrolling in the local community college. But he asked for Rajeanna's aid with rudimentary things.

"It would be simple stuff. Like just filling out an application, he would ask me for help with," Rajeanna said. "And I'm just like, okay. Nobody was showing him nothing. He was figuring everything out as he went."

Scurlock had first been arrested at age eleven; he'd later done close to two years in a juvenile jail. He had obtained his high school degree while behind bars. It was not the best preparation for being a young father.

"Going straight into adulthood," Rajeanna said of her brother's jarring new responsibilities. "He was getting that reality check."

There were few people as close to Scurlock as Rajeanna. They had been together in Denver, then back in Omaha. They'd been in the homeless shelter in Norfolk with their mother. They'd done the tough walks for miles to get food, and they'd done the fun walks to school together. James made her laugh, and he protected her. She saw his talent and his temper, and she tried her best to keep him in line.

After George Floyd's killing, the family had talked about what it meant, what it obligated them to do. Rajeanna said her father encouraged them to protest, that he had sat James down and told him so. The steady drumbeat of Black men being killed—Michael Brown in Ferguson, Missouri, Eric Garner in New York, George Floyd in Minnesota—looked and seemed a lot like James. They were sons and fathers, men with gifts and promise to go along with their police records. They were loved, and by many.

Mari Agosta first met Scurlock on Facebook during her senior year in high school. She'd been born in Lincoln, Nebraska, but had been adopted and moved to Omaha by a white couple when she was seven months old. She'd gone to school in one of the best school districts in the city. Her adoptive parents were a solid couple; her mom, she said, worked as an insurance underwriter, her dad in a job with Budweiser. They'd adopted a Black boy, as well, a couple of years older than Mari.

Mari realized her life—fine schools, a roof over her head, parents daring enough to adopt children of another race—looked kind of perfect to outsiders, but she had struggled in her high school years to figure out who she really was, where she really fit in, what she really wanted to do. Her parents were clear, even insistent: college, a career in law or medicine. She wasn't so sure.

"I was just tired of people expecting so much from me," she said. "And I guess I didn't know how to react to it. I just wanted to do something I loved."

For Mari, petite and possessed of a warm beauty, Scurlock, older at nearly twenty-one, was a mix of the exotic and familiar—a kid with a criminal record out of the tough streets of North Omaha, but a member, too, of a quirky, yet bonded, Black family, one suffused with real challenges and a natural, enduring trust.

Scurlock had always been an undersized kid, and at twenty-one he was close to tiny—not much more than five feet, maybe 120 pounds. He had a quick, wide smile, flashing two prominent front teeth. He loved his head of hair, Agosta said, a big bunch of kinkiness he cherished as his trademark physical quality.

Scurlock, she said, did not hide his record from her. He'd been arrested for the first time at eleven. He'd pleaded guilty for his role in an armed robbery at sixteen. But neither could Scurlock hide what seemed to her to be clear evidence of trauma, the anger and insecurities and suspicions born of poverty, family chaos, and years of his childhood spent behind bars.

Scurlock, she said, was always best trying to explain himself in letters he'd write, usually after he'd made his latest mistake.

"I am bottled up emotionally and I was raised to not show emotions," he wrote to her once from jail. "I just can't fix my lips to express myself to you. I done gave up on love, but you opened a different part of my heart and I feel like I can love again. I really feel confident in loving you. I just hope I'm not making another mistake."

Mari loved being in his presence—his energy, his laughter, his mischief, his hint of menace.

"He would drive me around—'this is where I grew up; this is what I did here,'" she said. "He took me to places in Omaha I didn't even know existed. They're scary. And I think that was cool."

She'd become pregnant months after meeting Scurlock, what she called a planned conception. Scurlock wanted a family of his own, and she wanted to be part of it. Their baby, the girl they named Jewels, was born that November.

Agosta said she shared some blame for how hot their relationship could run. They had their share of fights, some, she said, provoked or driven by her own refusal to be controlled or overly cared for. She was hurt and frightened by what had happened when Scurlock hit her that winter in 2020. But it also felt as much a mystery as a crime.

She couldn't shake the look on his face after he hit her, bloodying her nose.

"I remember looking at him, and it was like, 'I didn't mean to do that; I don't know why I did that; I regret doing it.' I honestly believe he didn't mean to. That sounds weird, but just the look on his face. It's a look I can't explain. A look I couldn't get out of my head."

Agosta had told police she did not want to press charges, but they informed her they were obligated to go forward under the law. When Scurlock was released, Agosta agreed to see him. They met on the back porch of a house belonging to one of Scurlock's sisters. The sister, Marissa, had helped care for Jewels while Scurlock was locked up. Scurlock and Agosta shared a smoke. She told him there was not that much for him to say. What had happened had happened, and only time would tell how lasting the wounds to her body and sense of trust would last. She had a job opportunity in Lincoln, a bit more than an hour away, but she wanted Scurlock to be able to see the baby regularly. They talked about what co-parenting might look like.

"I wanted him not to be away from Jewels," she said.

On the second night of the protests, Rajeanna and her boyfriend were at 72nd and Dodge. On May 30, the third and most unruly night of protests, they saw a repeat of the dustup between protesters and police, the tear gas and bottle throwing. When the crowd set off for downtown, Rajeanna said she'd had enough. She said she had a powerful sense that something awful was going to happen. She thought it could happen to her. She feared more that it could happen to James. She did not want him going anywhere near the intensifying and now-roaming protests.

"I know James," she said, "and he can be a little hotheaded."

Scurlock, it turned out, was with another sister that evening, Qwenyona. He'd spent several nights since his release with her, and another sister, Tammy Johnson. One day, they'd gone to swim at their brother A. D. Swolley's house. On another day, Agosta brought Jewels to see James.

On the evening of May 30, Qwenyona and Tammy and James had gone to a Wendy's near 72nd and Dodge. They'd seen the commotion, and James had said he wanted to check it out. But sirens had gone off—not just emergency vehicle sirens but what sounded like air-raid warnings.

"No, Bro," Qwenyona told James, "we are not about to go to that."

The three returned to the apartment where Qwenyona and Tammy lived. They hung out. A cousin, a teen boy known as P.T., came by. James ate Jolly Ranchers and the four of them swapped stories.

Now with it dark outside and with downtown Omaha in turmoil, P.T. said he wanted to see for himself. Qwenyona said James was reluctant. But he would not let P.T. go alone.

"If he has your back," she said of James, "he's not going to leave you hanging."

Qwenyona said James had to go upstairs to get out of his pajama bottoms. He was soon out the door.

"Lest We Forget"

OMAHA HAS HAD EPISODES OF RACIAL violence seared into its memory, and the details of its painful past can be found inside the Great Plains Black History Museum at 2212 N. 24th Street, across the street from the offices of the *Omaha Star* newspaper and in the first floor of what once was the Dreamland Ballroom.

The building and the ballroom it housed had been built in the 1920s by James Grant Jewell, once regarded as the wealthiest Black man in Omaha. For forty years, the Dreamland hosted performances by Louis Armstrong, Count Basie, Duke Ellington, and others. During World War II, the ballroom was used by the USO to entertain Black soldiers. In the 1950s, Whitney Young, the civil rights activist, spoke to crowds inside Dreamland.

Step inside the building today and there are two rooms crowded with pictures and artifacts, pamphlets, and exhibits. Omaha once had the largest African American population of any city west of the Mississippi other than Los Angeles. Over the years, it had at least four Black newspapers, often founded or run by women. Malcolm X had been born in Omaha; Bob Gibson, the Hall of Fame pitcher, had been, too; and Gale Sayers, the star running back for the Chicago Bears, also spent his boyhood in Omaha.

Eric Ewing is the director of the museum, himself a son of North Omaha. His brother had been the first Black person elected to a countywide office; a family friend would become Omaha's first

Black police chief. Ewing had graduated from Northwest High School, gone off to serve in the Navy, and then gained his advanced degrees believing he'd never return to North Omaha. But the place had a pull, and Ewing now curates all the history that had drawn him back.

Some of it is heartbreaking. Just inside the second of the museum's two rooms, there is an exhibit dedicated to Will Brown. In 1919, a white mob of thousands laid siege to the Douglas County Courthouse in Omaha after Brown had been arrested for the alleged rape of a white girl. The courthouse was lit on fire; guns were fired indiscriminately, and the city's mayor barely escaped being hanged to death.

Will Brown, the supposed rapist, was not so fortunate. He was captured by the mob from inside the courthouse and lynched, his body shot through with bullets as it hung from a telephone pole on the corner of 18th Street. The U.S. military was finally called in to end the chaos and bloodshed.

The exhibit has framed newspaper front pages; Brown's death certificate (the cause of death is listed as "bullet wounds through body (lynched)"; a photograph of Brown's smoking body after he'd been cut down and burned in a makeshift pyre on the street; a picture of Brown's gravestone—he was forty, and the last line on the marker reads: "Lest we forget."

In 2021, the one hundredth anniversary of the massacre of Black citizens in the prosperous Greenwood neighborhood in Tulsa, Oklahoma, became the subject of extraordinary national remembrance. There were marches and memorials. President Joe Biden visited and made a speech. For much of white America, the events of 1921 in Tulsa were a horrifying revelation—a forgotten chapter of hatred in a Great Plains city perhaps not otherwise associated with the country's racial struggles.

Will Brown's corner of the former Dreamland Ballroom is part of another chapter little acknowledged by white America. For Black Omahans, though, it might have happened one hundred years ago, but the memory is alive, and it is embedded into their sense of the city they live and struggle in.

The historian Orville D. Menard pulled together one of the most thorough accounts for the Nebraska State Historical Society.

In 1919, two years before the Tulsa massacre, Omaha was something of a city on edge. Its Black population had doubled from some five thousand in 1910 to ten thousand in 1920. Fights over jobs led white union leaders to accuse Black workers of being little more than strikebreakers; Black veterans from World War I returned only to find their service and sacrifice rewarded with menial jobs and discrimination in everything from schools to housing. At least one local newspaper wrote often about the threat Black men posed to white women.

Menard's meticulous reconstruction unfolds like this:

> *. . . Around midnight on September 25, 1919, Milton Hoffman and Agnes Loeback were assaulted at Bancroft Street and Scenic Avenue as they were walking home after a late movie. They said their assailant robbed them at gunpoint, taking Hoffman's watch, money, and billfold, plus a ruby ring from Agnes. The robber then dragged the 19-year-old Loeback by her hair into a nearby ravine and raped her. . . .*

Loeback and Hoffman identified Will Brown as their attacker, and he was soon found and confronted. A crowd of some 250 men and women had gathered around the house Brown was in, shouting that Brown should be lynched, and they twice succeeded in putting a rope around Brown's neck. Police managed to get Brown to a police jail, then to the newly built Douglas County Courthouse.

> *. . . At about 2:00 p.m. on September 28, Hoffman exhorted about two hundred mostly young people at Bancroft School to follow him to the courthouse and seize Brown. . . .*
>
> *By 4:00 p.m., several hundred people had gathered at the south side of the courthouse . . .*

. . . With the courthouse surrounded and breached, Police Chief Marshall Eberstein climbed to a second-story windowsill to speak to a briefly quieted audience. But after only a few moments the crowd began jeering and shouting and throwing rocks, one of which nearly hit him. . . .

. . . The mob rushed back to the courthouse, and the riot escalated as more gasoline was thrown into the building. Spreading flames forced the police to retreat to the second floor. Firemen brought hoses, which the crowd soon hacked to pieces. Rioters took the firemen's ladders and used them to enter the courthouse's broken second-story windows. While leading a charge up the stairs to reach Brown, 16-year-old Louis Young was shot and killed, one of three people to die that day. Policemen and sheriff's deputies took to the fourth floor with flames and angry men below them. Someone shouted, "Let no one leave," and armed men were stationed at every exit door.

Sheriff Clark led Brown and his 121 fellow prisoners to the roof, but bullets fired from nearby buildings sent them back downstairs. Clark convinced the rioters on the stairs to allow female prisoners to leave. Officers and deputies began telephoning their wives with parting words. . . .

. . . Ten officers in Court House Court Room 1 on the fourth floor were threatened by the flames, but their call for help was refused with calls of "Let 'em burn. Bring the nigger down with you and we'll hand you a ladder." . . .

. . . Anxious to hang him from the traffic tower at Eighteenth and Harney. Several men pulled Brown's body into the air as the crowd cheered. The swaying body became a target for gunfire. Lowered after 20 minutes, Brown's remains were tied to the end of a police car that the mob had seized, and dragged to Seventeenth and Dodge streets. There he was burned on a pyre fueled with oil from the red signal lanterns used for street repair. Brown's charred remains were then dragged behind an automobile through downtown streets. . . .

> *. . . The violence did not evoke any initiatives to assuage racism or improve conditions for Omaha's African American community. Instead, segregation was promoted by covenants that restricted property ownership to neighborhoods where blacks already were in greatest number. Two years after the riot, the Ku Klux Klan formed an Omaha Klavern.*

Today, Greater Omaha is the second-largest city on America's Great Plains, a sprawling suburban and exurban constellation of shopping malls, interstates, expensive housing developments, office campuses, and some 1.5 million people in all. A vast, westward-metastasizing landscape of Target stores and Jimmy John's franchises, maybe handsomer than those in, say, Topeka but lacking, say, Kansas City's volume of enduring, old-school music and drinking haunts.

Omaha's legendary stockyards and reputation as an Irish mob-controlled rough-and-tumble gateway to the West have given way to a place that boasts four Fortune 500 companies, including the insurance giant Mutual of Omaha and the iconic Union Pacific Railroad. The place where Gerald Ford was humbly born and where Henry Fonda began his acting career as an American everyman for a while liked to boast it had more billionaires per capita than any other city in the country. Two of its distinctive landmarks are its zoo and the downtown ballpark where the College World Series is played every year.

Omaha's once polyglot amalgam of early American immigrants and their vibrant enclaves—Irish, German, Jewish, Scandinavian, Greek—has now evolved and hardened into an anodyne city that is nearly 80 percent white. The 12 percent of the population that is African American lives almost exclusively in North Omaha, a part of town whose historic economic and racial isolation was deepened by the construction of a highway that made a section of town already easy to overlook that much easier to bypass altogether.

While Nebraska has been a dependable Republican state in national elections, it for half a century has had a centrist character—sending Democrats such as Bob Kerrey and Ben Nelson to Washington as senators and electing nearly as many Democratic governors as Republican. Along the way, Omaha has been an outpost of modest progressivism, with its own history of Democratic political machines and mayors; its well-financed cultural institutions: an opera and symphony; its openness to new immigrants from Africa; and its vivid episodes of galvanizing injustices like the disputed J. Edgar Hoover–directed prosecution of two Black Panthers for their alleged involvement in the killing by bomb of an Omaha police officer in the 1970s.

In the course of a year in Omaha, then, you can attend the Railroad Days festival, as well as the Freedom Festival inspired by Malcolm X. You can eat fried bull testicles and go to the Junkstock vintage festival or raise a glass at the Nebraska Balloon and Wine Festival, or experience Native Omaha Days, when North Omaha's Black diaspora return for a week of picnics and lectures, gospel music and parades.

And in recent years, Omaha had seen the blossoming of the Old Market district, with its funky and fine dining and slightly bohemian vibe.

But for some Black leaders, Omaha's liberal leanings are more veneer than meaningful. They talk of what they call Omaha's animating sensibility, naming it "nice racism."

White Omaha has plenty of money, they say, and those dollars have often been thrown at North Omaha. But the money, they claim, has chiefly gone to nonprofit organizations dominated by white officials. Those people, several Black leaders said, genuinely want to help but also feel they know what is best for the city's Black community and how to achieve it.

"'We know what's right; we'll take care of you,'" one Black state legislator said in summing up the ethos.

Look at the city's schools, then, and there is enduring underfunding for not surprisingly underperforming schools where kids of color go. Count the Black-owned businesses with more than twenty employees and you can do it on one hand, two at most, they say.

"If Omaha really wanted to solve its race and poverty issues, it could," the legislator said. "We have a lot of money. Money isn't the problem."

"He Owned His Mistakes"

Nearing 11:00 p.m. on May 30, the police had yet to make it to The Gatsby in response to Gardner's 911 call. It wasn't hard to understand why. Officers all but under siege had gathered a block or two away from Gardner's club. Many were in riot gear. And there was an ongoing war of words and weaponry. If the police had a strategy, it seemed to be to survive the chaos, to hope it would run its course without any loss of life. One bar owner's distress call was not going to rate as an urgent matter, even if there was a chance a gun had been used.

At 10:42, those in the streets mounted a second assault on The Gatsby. Two of those involved in obliterating the bar's remaining windows were James Scurlock and Tucker Randall. Randall launched a long pipe or metal beam through the windows. Scurlock fired rocks or other debris from the construction site through the windows of The Gatsby. Then, they both ran off.

At one point, a man from the street jumped up and stuck his head into the broken window. Gardner, inside, racked his shotgun, and the man could be seen leaping from the window over the patio railing and back to the street.

Gardner pulled the fire alarm inside the bar, and the blaring noise from it made it all the way to the street outside.

At last, there seemed to be a lull in the unrest. Gardner, who had been joined during the tumult by one of his regular bartenders and one of his longtime business partners, eventually emerged. The street had calmed some. Gardner also was joined by his father, Dave.

Dave Gardner was sixty-nine. He'd served in the Navy aboard the aircraft carrier USS *Ranger* during the Vietnam War. From its decks in 1970, bombers and fighters were launched for hundreds of strikes inside North Vietnam. The elder Gardner worked on the flight deck, and the pace was often unrelenting, requiring at times shifts of fourteen hours a day, seven days a week.

"No days off at sea," Dave said.

It was on the USS *Ranger* that Gardner's father was involved in an accident while loading bombs onto the planes. He suffered three fractures in his spine and was medically discharged in 1972.

Dave Gardner returned from Vietnam to his hometown of El Paso, Texas, and he went on to help run his father's heating and cooling business. He eventually moved his wife, Sue, Jake, and a second son to Omaha to be closer to Sue's family. Dave then made a career in Omaha managing a number of window-blind establishments. But in recent months, Dave, already a survivor of triple-bypass heart surgery, had been beset by a variety of further medical issues. He'd been receiving chemotherapy for lymphoma, and a port had been installed in his chest to deliver the drugs. He also had been forced to wear a catheter for weeks.

Dave Gardner, though, had still managed to pitch in at his son's bar despite his health struggles, and that night, after he helped rescue his younger son's car from the vandalism downtown, Dave showed up at The Gatsby to check on any damage.

Gardner's first incarnation of The Hive had opened a mile or so from Harney Street. Back from Iraq, Gardner had first tried his hand starting a lawn company, Amerigreen. But the idea of a bar appealed to him, and the initial iteration of The Hive came to be known for live music and a slightly hipster feel on a gritty stretch of town. There would be a jazz night and a reggae night. Someone who worked with him said Gardner had at least once called the police to report trouble at a nearby, much busier bar, thinking maybe he'd pick up business if it was closed down, even briefly.

The first version of The Hive was a start, then, but not a smashing success. Gardner wanted to be in the heart of the Old Market district. When a longtime Italian restaurant folded, he was interested in the property. He knew it was in a spot that his research on foot traffic with the hand clicker had identified as promising. But he was wary of competitors, and because his car was covered in promotional stickers for The Hive, Gardner walked on foot day after day to conduct, unnoticed, his negotiations over the new location. He didn't want any rival establishments to know he was considering moving The Hive to Harney Street.

In the years to come, The Hive would be both a huge hit and a source of controversy. The bar could hold three hundred, and often did, with lines out the door and down the block. There again was reggae night, and salsa night, Sundays when the bar would be full of the city's Latino community. Those nights were the only nights the bar sold beer in bottles, Gardner confident the crowd would be respectful.

Blandon Joiner, a Black man of Panamanian descent, ran the Sunday night salsa program, from 9:00 p.m. to 2:00 a.m. It attracted dancers of every race and age, he said, and was a testament to Gardner's embrace of all of Omaha.

"This is a community," Joiner said of Gardner's approach. "This is a family."

Joiner was born in Omaha and did thirteen years in the U.S. Navy. He, along with his Russian wife, ran versions of salsa night in bars throughout several states. "A straight shooter," he said of Gardner. "No bullshit."

Over twenty-five years of organizing such events, Joiner said, Gardner was the lone bar owner he'd never had a single issue with. Didn't mean they couldn't have their differences.

"We were from different walks of life, but we could agree to disagree," Joiner said. "And do business together."

Gardner was seen as a fiercely competitive, creative entrepreneur, always looking for an edge or a way to extend his brand. But he could drink too much on occasion, and run his mouth. He liked a good argument, sometimes a bit too much. Frank Vance, the owner of the Dubliner Pub, located underneath The Hive, said he complained for years about noise from The Hive bothering his customers. Gardner, he said, blew him off. Vance wasn't alone among Gardner's rival establishment owners.

"He thought he was bigger than life," Vance said of Gardner. "He alienated a lot of people."

Gardner was certainly obsessed and unyielding about dress and security. He had told his mother he wanted to create a bar women could feel safe in, and he developed a manual on nightclub safety that ran to more than seventy pages. There were signs in the women's bathrooms alerting them to steps they could take if they felt harassed or unsafe. Tell the bartender you wanted an "angel drink" and help would be on the way. LeBron, Gardner's service dog, often escorted women to their cars or taxis. Gardner's staff, according to one of his investors, had a healthy mix of men and women and people of color, a diversity that extended to the security staff.

The dress code, his friends and associates said, was the work of a stubborn Marine and a business owner consumed with worries about liability. There would be no flat-billed hats (the bar had a balcony, drinks could fall, and people needed to be able to see something coming); everyone was to wear a belt (there were steep stairs to trip on); there were limits on gold chains (in a fight, they could be used to choke someone); sports jerseys and mixed martial arts attire were a no go (an attempt to limit stupid arguments and even dumber fights). Eventually, Gardner would deny entry to people with facial tattoos, regarding them as evidence of possible gang membership. If it was a sweeping presumption, Gardner was okay with that. He and his business partners did not want to have to sort through the significance of any one person's facial markings.

And Gardner could be less than diplomatic in overseeing the

code. If you'd been denied entrance, he wasn't interested in a discussion; he wanted you gone. A cousin of Gardner's said he was routinely denied entrance because of the code. A former Marine who had known Gardner for two decades said he had been kept out, too.

Joiner, the salsa night coordinator, said none of the people who came to his events on Sunday nights had issues. They dressed up, he said, "as if they were going to the opera." There was no need for security, he said, on salsa night.

"You fight, you don't come back. You come into my place for an event, you pull your pants up off your ass," Joiner said.

But the code came to be seen by some as racially discriminatory and selectively enforced. Reviews surfaced online warning people to avoid The Hive. "Sure they allow a few signature black folks in, but find excuses for those they don't find suitable," read one Yelp review from 2017.

However, Gardner had come under the most intense criticism over the issue of bathrooms for transgender patrons. A woman had been assaulted in the women's bathroom by a transgender person. The person had entered the women's room, and urinated standing up. The woman inside apparently said something, perhaps offensive, and was attacked. She ultimately opted not to pursue criminal charges.

Gardner was alarmed by the assault, and concerned about how to protect his customers. He crudely declared on Facebook that the bar's patrons had to use the bathroom consistent with their genitalia.

It caused an enormous backlash. Advocates were outraged. Politicians took their own positions. Those already upset by alleged incidents of racial discrimination saw the episode as further evidence that Gardner was a bigot.

"I thought I was posting to my friends, and it just went viral," Gardner told a local news outlet. He told the outlet that people should be left alone to live as they see fit, although he stood by his position. "The last thing I would want to do is hurt a member of [the transgender] community," he said. "But people's feelings are going to be hurt when you bring something up that is sensitive. I'm asking transgender folk to use the unisex bathroom. I don't think it's a big ask."

Gardner eventually apologized for his choice of words. He then spent tens of thousands of dollars to build a third, unisex bathroom. He attended a sensitivity conference and donated to a nonprofit, Safe Space Nebraska, that conducted training for bar owners and staff on handling reports of harassment and assault.

In the end, Gardner said he had learned from the episode, including how painful and expensive it could be to get gender reassignment surgery. But he seemed to recognize the upset might be lasting.

"These things have a way to destroy you, or just blow over," he told the news outlet.

Megan Hunt, the first openly LGBTQ person elected to the Nebraska legislature, had worked for Safe Space Nebraska before running for office. She had initially been impressed by Gardner.

"He actually gave us a pretty big donation, and he let us use his bar for trainings and events," Hunt said in a news account.

But Hunt said she remained suspicious of Gardner's character.

"The more I got to know him," Hunt said in the interview, "the more it became kind of clear that what he wanted was to protect white girls from being harassed by Black men."

Joiner, who ran the weekly salsa nights, said Gardner eventually became demoralized by the debacle. He worried for the fate of his club, and for the jobs of the many people who worked there.

"I fucked things up for everybody," he told Joiner at one point.

Some of Gardner's supporters asked what more people wanted from him.

"Jake was human. He misspoke sometimes," said one friend. "He made amends for that. He owned his mistakes."

The costs were lasting, and in certain circles The Hive became the object of wariness and rumor. A Black barback quit and claimed online Gardner had, with a gesture and wisecrack, conceded he "might be" a little bit racist. In interviews, two people who worked for or with Gardner at The Hive said people of color who worked there worried that they were intentionally kept in minor jobs and shorted on tips. There could be coded talk of, say, "how dark it was" on some nights, meaning an abundance of people of color. The two said Gardner presented as an upbeat, generous, long-haired, and laid-back entrepreneur, but it all hid a streak of racism.

One of Gardner's business partners disputed the claims. When the bar closed in the spring because of the pandemic, he said, the weekend staff at The Hive consisted of two Black women, a white man and woman, and a Black security supervisor. The bartenders were paid the same hourly wage, and tips were for them to sort out, he said.

One lifelong friend of Gardner's, someone who had helped him build The Hive into a downtown success, conceded Gardner could be blamed for inviting suspicion.

"Did I ever hear the N-word come out of his mouth? Yes, I did," the friend said. "It was always directed at a single person Jake had concerns about. I never heard it said to anyone but me. But he had bartenders and busboys and waitresses and bouncers who were Black and Latino. So do I think he had a racial problem? I do not."

Two of the people who liked to go to The Hive, it turned out, were James Scurlock and his brother A. D. Swolley.

"That was one of our favorite clubs," Swolley said.

But the two had run up against The Hive's dress code. They'd been denied entrance on occasion. It felt both arbitrary and familiar.

"Jake Gardner," Swolley said, "treated us the way he did a lot of others like us. He targeted people."

In the street outside his suddenly trashed bar on May 30, Jake Gardner stood with his dad and Kevin Moller, a longtime investor in Gardner's nightclub career. Moller was the son of an Army Ranger, raised to be responsible and tough. He'd been a Golden Gloves boxing champ as a kid, and for years he'd help train Omaha's cops and firefighters for an annual charity boxing event. His contacts with the police had made it easy to recruit off-duty officers to work security at The Hive or The Gatsby.

That night, Moller arrived at the Gatsby and came in through the back door during one of the smashings of the windows. He'd quickly gone up to the bar's office to check the security tape and see if in fact a shot had been fired into the establishment. He found no clear evidence anyone had shot at the place.

At 10:57, any idea that relative peace was going to prevail outside The Gatsby dissolved when a man tossed another construction stanchion through the windows of a business next door. There was a young white man with the man who'd thrown the stanchion, and he was recording the assault on the business on his phone. Moller said to the young man, "You know, you are filming a felony." Dave Gardner walked over and shoved the young man recording the scene. The elder Gardner swore, told the man to go, and shoved him again.

Just then, Scurlock's friend Tucker Randall raced half a block and flattened Dave Gardner, the older man's feet lifting off the ground as he crashed backward. Jake Gardner, told that his father was down, began to walk toward where he lay in the street.

Gardner had one of the pistols from the bar in his waistband.

"First One out of the Vehicle"

IN THE LATE WINTER OF 2004, Haiti was in turmoil yet again. Its president, Jean-Bertrand Aristide, was out. The U.S. said he had resigned. Aristide said he'd been the victim of an American coup. There was no question he was leaving the country. It was an embarrassing and dangerous end for Aristide, the former priest who had risen from the troubled country's slums to become its first democratically elected president.

"If it is my resignation that will prevent a bloodbath," Aristide wrote in a letter to the Haitian people, "I agree to go with the hope that there will be life and not death."

U.S. Marines were sent as part of an international force to see to it that any deaths in the country be limited. Tens of thousands of Haitians were in the streets of the capital, Port-au-Prince, some in anger, some in celebration, some in a confused uncertainty.

A U.S. official at the time said the mission of the Marines in Haiti was fivefold: to secure the capital; assist in the delivery of aid; protect U.S. citizens; repatriate migrants who tried to flee to the United States; and prepare the way for a multinational security force.

Secretary of State Colin Powell spelled out what he hoped would be a peaceful effort.

"I suspect our troops and other international troops coming in will help stabilize things," Powell said. "I don't think there will be a great deal of fighting, but they have to be prepared for that."

Sam McAmis was a newly minted U.S. Marine Corps officer sent to help carry out the peacekeeping assignment. McAmis's dad had served in the Army; his granddad had been a paratrooper in World War II and had jumped on D-Day. McAmis opted for the Marines, and it broke his mother's heart. Not because he wasn't following his family's footsteps into the Army, but because he wanted to join the Marines right out of high school. She'd saved her whole life for him to go to college.

His mother proposed a deal: McAmis would go to college, and if he still wanted the Marines afterward she'd support his wishes. McAmis got a business degree at Baylor University in Texas and was all but immediately in officer's school.

McAmis went to what was called platoon leaders school, an accelerated program developed during the Vietnam War, when the Navy was losing young officers at such a rate it could not easily supply replacements. He was commissioned as an officer the day of his graduation and was sent to Quantico, Virginia, "where you learn about every job in the Marine Corps."

McAmis was ultimately assigned to a light armored vehicle unit and introduced to a seasoned Marine named Jake Gardner. Gardner would serve as his vehicle's gunner, seated feet from McAmis in their vehicle and responsible for his safety.

"He's been deployed. So he'll be a good gunner for you," McAmis was told of Gardner and Gardner's earlier combat duty in Iraq. "He knows what's going on."

McAmis, trying to get his legs as a combat leader, was grateful.

"I'm like, okay, cool."

Gardner's unit had been split up after their triumphant tour in Iraq. Half had been sent to Afghanistan for a second combat tour; Gardner and others had been sent to Haiti.

The orders to go to Haiti came quickly and out of the blue for McAmis. He remembers getting a call and writing down what he was told: secure the capital of Haiti; deploy in seventy-two hours. He thought it was a joke, some kind of hazing ritual for a young, inexperienced officer.

It wasn't. Soon, McAmis and Gardner, his gunner, were inside a C-5 Galaxy, the largest military transport plane in the American military's inventory. It held eight light armored vehicles, and in the course of the flight the guns on those vehicles were still being loaded.

"They're actually having to cycle the rounds into the chambers and stuff while we're still in the airplane, which I was like, this is dangerous."

In Haiti, the vehicles were rolled out of the plane and sent to Port-au-Prince. Here's what McAmis remembers as all the instructions he got: "'Hey, you are going to this position and you're going to set up a perimeter, and good luck. Go.' I'm like, this just got real."

Fortunately, McAmis had brought a handheld GPS device, one you might use if you were fishing for bass back in Tennessee. McAmis's vehicle wound up with others parked on the grounds of Haiti's presidential compound. They heard word that Aristide had been taken and escorted off the grounds and out of the country. And they would in the coming days take in a reassuring picture of the state of play in Port-au-Prince.

"There's just a sea of people. You can't even tell where it ends. You know, I'm looking out over this and thinking, man, if they really wanted to, if they really didn't want us to be here, then I don't know what we would do. But luckily everybody's, like, singing songs and happy and holding up signs like, 'Thank you.'"

McAmis said he spent the next five to six months seated next to Gardner. "Much to see," McAmis said of Haiti, its political troubles and desperate poverty. "Much to be sad about."

Gardner had outfitted the vehicle with speakers to better hear his endless loop of songs by his favorite band, his hometown heroes, 311. McAmis came to hate the band but deeply value Gardner.

"Positive, hardworking, the kind of Marine other guys wanted to be around," said McAmis.

McAmis and Gardner slept in the makeshift camp the Marines had made near the country's airport. There were no showers, but a lot of camaraderie. McAmis and Gardner patrolled the streets of Port-au-Prince and helped in the effort to remake and train a new police force for Haiti. There were a few firefights and murky efforts to interdict drug trafficking.

McAmis said that across his career he'd encountered his share of racists in the Corps, men he'd think less of while having to fight alongside.

"Never would I have been able to discern anything remotely racist," he said of his gunner, Gardner.

"Jake was always first one out of the vehicle," McAmis said, "kids on the street immediately on his shoulders."

A commanding officer's interactions with his vehicle's gunner might have been limited and perfunctory, but McAmis enjoyed Gardner's dry wit and respected his combat service in Iraq, a tour of duty that awaited McAmis once he got back from Haiti.

"I knew there was some underlying stuff like, you know, he would mention from time to time about how this is such a cakewalk compared to Iraq, Iraq was terrible. There probably was some PTSD going on. There was baggage there. I got a couple of stories out of him, but not much."

McAmis remembers Gardner being haunted by one moment during the initial campaign in Iraq when, taking enormous fire, commanders had adjusted the rules of engagement: everyone is hostile; shoot anything that moves.

MORE THAN ANYTHING, McAmis said, Gardner struck him as tired. Plain tired. Iraq, Haiti. Death, unrest, heat and long hours, eternal vigilance, little relief.

McAmis and Gardner eventually returned to their base at Camp Lejeune, and Gardner prepared for his eventual discharge. He'd done his time, been in the fight, was ready for home, for Omaha.

Camp Lejeune is an enormous training and staging facility that includes eleven miles of North Carolina beaches. Its 156,000 acres are host to thirty-two gun positions, fifty tactical landing zones, and three state-of-the-art training facilities for Military Operations in Urban Terrain. And Lejeune, like all military bases, is surrounded by supermarkets and bars, smoke shops and strip clubs.

With his discharge pending, Gardner, grateful to be out of the heat and hairiness of Haiti, found himself in one of those bars. McAmis remembers it as a strip club run by an ex-Marine. Another of Gardner's friends thinks it was a place called the Driftwood Bar. The local police department has no available record of what happened, but McAmis, as Gardner's commanding officer, remembers being briefed on the military's investigation.

Gardner was set upon outside the establishment by one or more men, maybe a bouncer from the bar. There might have been an exchange of words. Gardner might have had too much to drink. McAmis said the investigation made no mention of race being an issue. Gardner, anyway, was sent to the ground and his mouth placed up against the curb of the street in front. There's a term for what came next—he was "curb stomped." Gardner lost twelve teeth, and his jaw was broken in two places. He spent days in the hospital, some of them with his fate uncertain.

Gardner, McAmis said, had his mouth wired shut for weeks afterward. He was both in pain and embarrassed by how he looked. But if he had to eat through a straw, he was not going to be denied his favorite food. He once came back to his barracks at Lejeune, scowling and angry at his condition, but determined. He put a Whopper in a blender. Added fries. Then dumped in the strawberry shake. He sucked it all through the straw.

"He was going to have his Burger King," a fellow Marine said.

"Keep the Fuck Away from Me"

NOW, WITH A PISTOL IN HIS waistband, Jake Gardner quickly checked on his father and then moved along Harney Street to seek out protesters in the street in an effort to determine who had leveled his ailing dad.

Gardner's carry permit for the gun had expired, but Nebraska statutes on self-defense grant considerable latitude to someone protecting their home, business, or property.

AS A CIVILIAN, Gardner retained his love of guns, and he was highly trained in their use. He could get on the phone with a former Marine colleague and talk for hours about things such as how to construct your own AR-15 assault rifle.

The issue of former service members and their weapons back home has been the subject of controversy and study and alarm. Former members of the military own guns at greater rates than their civilian counterparts, and two-thirds of those who do say they use them not so much for hunting or recreation, but for protection. Because there are a variety of laws limiting gun ownership among those with mental health concerns, veterans sometimes hide their struggles for fear of losing their right to a weapon. There have been infamous rampage killings involving those who fought for their country and returned damaged or deranged, including an incident in 2013 where a former soldier killed three people and himself inside a California veterans treatment center. The shooter was angry about being kicked out of a program meant to deal with PTSD. But the greatest threat involving former service members and their guns is that they will use the weapons on themselves.

Some people close to Gardner said he was often a man on edge and he wanted and needed his weapons.

"Back home, you can't help but look for your weapon," said Joe Rowland, a childhood friend who joined the Marines the same year as Gardner. "In the military, you are always supposed to be an arm's length distance from your weapon. Not having that weapon is like losing a body part."

Gabe Writer was a Marine from Yakima, Washington, who had fought with Gardner in Iraq and who later did another tour in Afghanistan. He racked up two traumatic brain injuries, and felt most comfortable back home carrying his gun. Writer was charged with a felony after pulling his gun during a verbal altercation with another driver on the road. He lost his right to carry a gun for years as a result.

Matt Brill, who also fought in Iraq with Gardner, came to understand the risks.

"I personally don't carry a gun," he said. "I carried a gun for a long time after I got out of the USMC. But because of my anger and irritability issues, I don't trust myself to carry a gun. Carrying a gun leaves you the ability to use it. If you pull a gun, there's less options at that point."

In fact, Gardner had been arrested for brandishing a gun during a dispute with two employees of a private parking lot in Omaha. A boot had been placed on a wheel of Gardner's car because it might have been parked illegally. Gardner, first charged with attempted assault, was let off with a violation for disorderly conduct and a fine.

On Harney Street, Scurlock, Tucker Randall, and Scurlock's

cousin P.T. were in the street roaming about. P.T. said he and Scurlock had been on parking lot rooftops and had folded into the crowd as it surged through the streets.

"Let everyone hear our voice," P.T. said of the spirit.

Gardner soon had a group of people in front of him, and James Scurlock eventually was one of them. Gardner, his hair in a ponytail, looked nearly ashen, as if the stress of the moment had drained the blood from his face.

The next sixty seconds were captured in bits and pieces in a variety of recordings, including security cameras, news cameras, and the cell phones of witnesses; some of the recordings have audio; others don't; some are grainy; others are clearer.

Gardner is heard in a number of recordings asking who had knocked down his dad. Someone said, "Black Lives Matter." Gardner said, "I totally agree."

Gardner told those in front of him that if they hadn't hit his old man it's "not their fucking problem" and to move on. Dave Gardner, back on his feet, shoved Scurlock. Scurlock shoved another man who was trying to defuse the situation.

Scurlock and others advanced on Gardner, and Gardner began to back up.

Gardner lifted his shirt to show the gun in his waistband.

"I'm telling you, keep the fuck away from me," Gardner said.

Gardner took the gun out of his waistband, and held it at his side.

"Nigga's got a gun," someone in the crowd shouted.

Kevin Moller, Gardner's business partner, inserted himself and told Gardner to put the gun away. "It's not worth it," he said.

Gardner returned the pistol to his waist and backed up once more. He was almost in front of his bar.

Moller said he was certain Scurlock knew who Gardner was. He'd been denied entrance after getting tattoos on his face, something barred by Gardner's door policy. Moller, though, said it was unlikely Gardner recognized Scurlock.

In some ways, the two men were all but identical physical matches—well under six feet and barely more than 140 pounds. They'd both also had experience fighting—Gardner in the Marines, Scurlock in jail, where he more than once had been written up for altercations with others locked up with him.

Scurlock squared up as if to fistfight, feinted, and jabbed a leg toward Gardner.

In the crowd behind Gardner was Rose Melendez, nineteen. She had her sweatshirt's hood up, and as Gardner's confrontation with Scurlock and the others unfolded she tightened it around her head. She was ready to do something.

"I knew soon as I tied my hood that either I was going to go to jail or I was going to get shot," she said.

Melendez had never been to a protest before. She'd grown up bouncing between Lincoln and Omaha and Kansas City, her single mom chasing this new job or that latest promotion with the Coca-Cola Company. Rose had found ways to flourish along the journey—she loved her high school in Kansas City and did well enough to be named an honor student—but she said it had been a childhood marked by trauma and abandonment.

By the night of May 30, she said she'd been the victim of sexual assault more than once and had failed in her try at a technical school where she thought for a second she could be a mechanic. Her father was a ghost, she said, and her brother struggled with personal demons. Her mother had just left her to fend for herself in Omaha when she took her latest job in Sioux City, Iowa. Melendez, in making her way on her own, had worked service jobs at places like Outback Steakhouse.

"I'm a depressed twenty-year-old. I'd just been abandoned by my family. I have been abandoned by my family my whole life. And the only thing that I've ever wanted to do in my life is be known for something, I guess," she said.

Melendez, as a result, went to the second night of angry protests, curious, galvanized about at last taking a stand, prepared maybe to do something dramatic. She'd first thought George Floyd's killing would follow the arc of so many other police killings—headline news for a while, but then a fading national memory. Now, though, there were protests in Omaha, a city she had come to resent for its middle American ordinariness and insularity. She loathed what she called its "contentedness."

Politics was not a feature of her childhood homes. Survival was the order of the day. Melendez had never identified with a social cause or worked on a campaign. Her fair skin and good looks had insulated her from the kind of harsh experience other Hispanics in Lincoln or Kansas City or Omaha experienced.

That second night of protests, she went to 72nd and Dodge with her dog Leo. When tear gas was used, she fled, worried for her pet. She lived off 30th and Leavenworth with her boyfriend, Brian, a photographer. When word spread of another night of protest and when social media lit up later that night with news that the protests were moving downtown, Melendez said she wanted to go. Brian was skeptical but eventually grabbed a camera. Maybe they'd make a TikTok video, they said, laughing.

The two set off in their car and wound up parking it along Harney Street near the courthouse, well west of the major gathering. As they walked east, they were struck by how many white people had shown up to protest. She and Brian witnessed people breaking windows and trashing buildings, but Melendez was untroubled.

"Yeah, it was not what the Black Lives Matter protest movement was supposed to be," she said. "But property damage and glass breaking? That's nothing compared to the four hundred years of the injustices Black people have gone through. So if we break a couple of buildings and that's what catches people's attention, then do it."

When she and her boyfriend got to the intersection of 12th Street and Harney, the mood and scene had intensified. Cops were taunting protesters, she said, and the objects the protesters were throwing were becoming more numerous and more dangerous. Melendez and her boyfriend looked around, but now the large number of white people struck them as unfortunate rather than hopeful. Many, they concluded, were from out of state, certainly not from Omaha. It didn't feel like the scenes she'd seen in Minneapolis. There the protests seemed to involve people of color, people who had suffered and who had a certain right to anger, even violence.

"People were coming from Kansas. People were coming from Iowa. Small-town people. It was almost like they were just unrecognizable to the Omaha I know," she said.

What were they here for? she wondered. Justice or a break from boredom?

"It was like, 'This is my chance to just go buck wild,'" Melendez said of the others. "You could see that there were a lot of people there that were just running around, looking for fights, because nothing happens in Omaha."

Melendez wasn't entirely unsympathetic. She said she'd felt "electrified" by the crowd and the moment, and the rare sense of dangerous excitement and maybe shared purpose. She'd hollered and jumped on a car or two. She gave it back to the protesters who had shown up in support of the police and law and order.

"I'm not afraid to be a part of conflict," she said. "I prefer it."

But increasingly, the night felt like it might be a failure. There would be arrests, for sure. But anything more lasting? She also feared something more regrettable could happen. At 12th and Harney, things felt close to out of control. Tear gas was in the air now. Alarms were being sounded. There were police broadcasts about weapons and calls for assistance.

"People are fighting. People are sprinting. Like that's when things are starting to escalate a little bit more; you hear crashes like left and right from people breaking stuff. And you're like, oh, this is really happening. That's when my body started like vibrating a little bit; I started to get it—that like awareness, that anxiety."

Suddenly, Melendez was in front of Gardner's bar. Brian filmed with his camera. The two of them were struck by the size of Gardner's bartender. And then they heard someone say, "He's got a gun."

That's when Melendez tightened the drawstring on her hood.

"I hear, 'He's got a gun,' and I see him walking back, and that's when I kind of start to come up behind them," she said.

Melendez never saw Gardner put his gun back in his waistband.

"I saw him put his arms back, like getting ready to do something. James, his cousin, and like a big group of people are in front of him. And then there's like a few people behind Jake."

Melendez said she felt some intoxicating mix of daring and duty.

"I want to be able to do something that matters in this world. Even if that means taking a sacrifice. I don't necessarily want to be a martyr. But I would rather be the person that got taken than somebody else.

"I had an opportunity to put my life on the line and save somebody else's. Some people just don't want to do that. And that's selfish and that's okay. But in this moment it felt like this entire protest, this entire thing, was, we're putting ourselves out there for this higher purpose.

"So he puts his arms back," she said of Gardner, "and I said, this is my opportunity. So I take my arms and I grabbed his. And of course I didn't realize he was a Marine and he was a lot stronger than me. I grabbed his arms and he takes me and immediately throws me down to the ground."

Melendez remembers how wet it was when they hit the ground. The water was eight inches deep.

"We, like, fall into a huge puddle. I think he grabs his gun. And I have him down on the ground and I, I don't really know what I was doing—if I was struggling or fighting with him or something."

Tucker Randall, Scurlock's friend, moved in to pile on Gardner and Melendez. Gardner, on his back, fired a shot in the direction of Randall, who was now racing away. He then fired another as he continued to wrestle with Melendez. Melendez said it felt like the bullet passed between her legs.

"Once I realized that he was shooting, I said, like, I gotta go. Like, he's going to shoot me."

Melendez got up and started to run.

Gardner managed to get on all fours before trying to stagger to his feet. He was soaking wet, and looking down Harney Street, away from The Gatsby.

Instantly, Gardner was tackled again, this time by Scurlock. Scurlock came flying off the sidewalk and took Gardner to the ground so violently, Scurlock almost wound up sliding over Gardner and spilling into the gutter himself. Scurlock had Gardner from behind, and they wrestled wildly for fifteen or twenty seconds. Gardner repeatedly beseeched Scurlock to get off him.

Choke holds have been a flash point in police killings over the years. Banned by many departments, they can be lethal, and any number of suspects have died while officers had their arms around their necks. New York police officer Francis Livoti killed twenty-nine-year-old Anthony Baez in the Bronx in 1994 using a choke hold. Baez's football had hit a police car in the street. Twenty years later, a choke hold used by Police Officer Daniel Pantaleo while trying to arrest Eric Garner for selling loose cigarettes on Staten Island contributed to the death of the forty-three-year-old African American man.

Gardner's partner, Kevin Moller, was nearby. He was an accomplished boxer and had dabbled with mixed martial arts. Scurlock, he said, "had established position" over Gardner in what's called a rear naked choke. Scurlock was behind Gardner, upright, his feet set apart, anchoring him to the ground. It's understood that ten seconds in such a hold can render someone unconscious. Fighters, when fearful of that, can "tap out," a signal to their opponent that they have had enough.

"Scurlock didn't let Jake tap out," Moller said.

At one point, Scurlock had Gardner's left arm twisted and pinned behind his back. At another, Scurlock had Gardner's left hand pressed against the watery pavement. Video appears to show Scurlock might have briefly knocked the pistol from Gardner's right hand. Both men's hands seemed to grasp for it on the ground.

Gardner somehow managed to get the gun back in his right hand

and then switch it to his left, which was now free. He reached with the gun halfway over his right shoulder to blindly fire a single shot.

Scurlock was struck on the right side of his neck or clavicle and slumped to the ground. His body twitched in the water and grime. He tried to lift his head before it tumbled back to the ground. Two people came to his aid, trying to get him out of the water and seated upright. Scurlock bent forward at the waist and toppled one final time onto his side.

Gardner, meanwhile, made his way unsteadily to his father in front of the bar. They went inside, and Gardner put the pistol on a towel. He waited next to it for the police to arrive. His father hustled the other guns out of the bar.

Melendez heard the shot that struck Scurlock, and she and her boyfriend turned to see what had happened. Melendez was tempted to go to aid Scurlock, but the police were coming, emergency vehicles as well. People were screaming, and so she and Brian set off running again.

Melendez was quickly approached by someone hosting a Facebook Live called Omaha Live. They asked what had happened.

"I said a white supremacist just killed a Black man," Melendez remembers.

Melendez said she was worried the news of a young Black man being killed in the mayhem of the night might not register as shocking. That a white supremacist had killed him might.

"I just knew. I don't know," she said of her conviction Gardner was a racist. "It's just what came out of me. If some stupid white fucker came to this protest with a gun, that's what he is to me. And I knew that that would grab people's attention."

"Blood for Blood"

JAMES SCURLOCK SR. HEARD THE GUNSHOTS from Harney Street through the Facebook Live feed on his phone. There was no instant alarm.

James Sr., forty-five, had gone to the second night of protests. He'd been hit by the tear gas, and even twenty-four hours later his face and eyes still stung and his body still stunk from the chemicals. He'd been with James the following morning, and his son had asked him, "What's that smell?" James Sr., tiny and tattooed like his son, told James he had no intention of going for Round 2 Saturday night, and he was convinced his son agreed to stay away as well.

It wasn't long after hearing the gunfire before James Sr. heard from P.T., his nephew, who had been with James downtown.

"Juju just got shot by a white boy," P.T. said.

Shot near the right side of his neck, the bullet having torn through his right lung and fractured his spine, James was still alive when the ambulance arrived on Harney Street. He was intubated to help him breathe and placed in the back of the ambulance. But the ambulance, through mistake or bad luck, got caught in the congestion of the chaotic streets and was forced to creep along as protesters both swarmed and fled in the aftermath of the gunfire. The ambulance, sirens blaring, was soon swallowed up by the sea of red taillights of backed-up traffic.

James Sr. instantly set off for the emergency room at Nebraska

Medical Center. He was well-connected, to local leaders and to the city's meaner streets. As he hustled to the ER, his phone started blowing up.

People were sending notes of concern as rumors spread that his son had been shot. Videos of parts of the incident flooded his in-box as people sought to provide him with evidence of what had happened. At the hospital, James Sr. said he had to fight his way to the entrance.

It turned out, he said, he had beaten his son to the ER.

"They told me they didn't have a patient who had been shot," James Sr. said.

James Senior has a solemn bearing; he speaks softly, with the occasional tug on a wispy goatee. In the ER waiting room, he tried to contain himself until the ambulance arrived, and for hospital security and an Omaha Police Department sergeant to eventually come escort him to see his son. He'd posted online word that he was accumulating potentially important footage of the shooting, and in those posts he encouraged the OPD to come retrieve the possible evidence from his phone.

James Sr. was told by hospital staff that his son was alive, but that he was not capable of breathing on his own. His father would have to make a decision about ending life support.

James Sr. was born in Fort Carson, Colorado, an Army brat. His parents, both from Omaha, split when he was a toddler. He stayed first with his dad in Omaha and then moved to be with his mother and her new husband outside Denver.

James Sr. said he and his two sisters had every blessing—a solid household in a good suburban neighborhood. His stepfather ran a janitorial business, and he was required as a boy to help clean buildings on the weekends. His mother was a home health aide, a woman who stayed thirsty for education well into her life, stockpiling this degree or that certification.

"Nothing but work ethic around me," he said. "I felt like I was a millionaire as a kid."

James Sr. had a clear goal—he wanted to finish high school, forgo college, and enter the military like his dad. But James also had an unhealthy taste for trouble. He stole a car as a freshman in high school, and another a couple of years later. He'd earn a high school diploma but do time in jail in Missouri and Colorado, his dream of a military career shot.

"I wasn't a bad kid," he said, "just a kid with bad ideas every once in a while."

He would come to father more than a dozen children, and he grew used to having people deride him as a certain kind of feckless and reckless Black stereotype. But he managed to have real relationships not only with his children but also with their mothers. Despite stints of incarceration and unemployment, he stayed in his children's lives, often deeply, almost always loyally.

"I don't know anybody who has had as many kids as I have who can honestly say no matter what I went through in the struggle, I always found a way to be there for them," he said.

Now James Sr. had to reach one of those mothers to decide whether to remove her wounded son from life support. He could not quickly get to his boy's mother, named Rajeanna like their daughter, and so in the end he made the call to let his son die peacefully. He'd been allowed to see James and it was clear his son was lost.

"You could see the ghost of him in his skin already," James Sr. said.

The autopsy was more grimly specific, detailing everything from the nature of the wound to a "Lion King" tattoo James had on one of his arms:

> *James Scurlock was a 22-year-old man with a [gunshot wound] to the clavicle. Additional information obtained from the medical record indicate that Mr. Scurlock was initially conscious when first responders arrived, lost consciousness, and arrived to hospital with CPR in progress. He was intubated and underwent emergency thoracotomy with evacuation of approximately 1500 ml*

right hemothorax. Examination showed a well-developed, well-nourished man with an intermediate range gunshot wound of the right neck/upper chest area resulting in injuries of the subclavian vasculature, right lung apex, and multiple ribs. A bullet fragment was recovered from the soft tissue of the left upper back just to the left of the spine. The body length is 66 inches and the weight is 143 pounds. The head is normally formed. The scalp hair is long, black, curly, and held back in a ponytail. The irides are brown and the conjunctivae are clear. There are no facial or conjunctival petechiae. The nose and lips are normally formed. The oral hygiene is good. Teeth are natural and in fair repair. There are no upper or lower labial injuries or oral injuries. There is a black mustache and sparse black beard present. Monochromatic tattoos above right eyebrow, monochromatic tattoo above left eyebrow, monochromatic heart with treble clef tattoo on right side of neck, monochromatic tattoo on left side of neck, monochromatic Bugs Bunny smoking tattoo on right lateral upper arm, monochromatic gangster pointing a gun and holding three fingers up tattoo on central chest, monochromatic "Hakuna" tattoo on right volar forearm, monochromatic "Matata" tattoo on left volar forearm.

James Sr. had allowed only his daughter Rajeanna to see her brother at the hospital. He could not deny her that. But he did not tell her James was beyond saving.

Rajeanna remembers getting the call from her father telling her James had been shot. She was almost asleep at home. After she hung up, her hands were shaking so badly she had trouble just getting her slippers on. She ran every red light on the way to the hospital.

The room where she met with her brother was spare and painted white. A nurse stood by quietly. James's face was splattered with blood, and the bandages around his neck were red and still soaked. There was tubing down his throat and a ventilator pumping. The heart monitor appeared to still be capturing a beat.

Rajeanna—her face the same smooth soft cocoa as her brother's—

put a hand on James's chest and felt its gentle rise and fall, and convinced herself he was still breathing on his own.

"It's going to be okay," she whispered. She was not at all sure he could hear her, but she trusted if he could, that her words felt soothing.

A police officer walked her to the elevator when she was done.

"I'm sorry for your loss," he said.

Rajeanna was startled.

"I mean I'm sorry if we might get lost," the officer stammered, aware he had inadvertently broken the news to her.

Outside, she saw her father.

"Your brother's dead," he said.

James Sr. said Jake Gardner's name had already surfaced online and in his circle of informers as the man who had shot his son. James Sr. wanted revenge.

"Blood for blood," he said.

He called his mother in Denver and told her his impulse was to find Gardner and kill him. If Gardner had been jailed, he'd find a way to get arrested himself and choke him out behind bars. If that failed, he knew enough people who could get it done for him.

"He was going to answer for it; he was going to pay for it," James Sr. said. "I just wanted my hands around his neck."

But in the first hours after his son's death, James Sr. was as frustrated as he was enraged, as full of bewilderment as fury. No one from the OPD had contacted him about the endless array of video from the scene that continued to pile up in his in-box. How could they not?

He tried once more.

"This is the last time I will ask OPD to come look at this video of this murder of my son," he wrote online in the early hours of May 31. He then listed his cell phone number.

"This will be the last time I try this," he added. "If I don't get a response, I will fully understand how you guys feel."

James Sr. then had to tell his family what had happened, and word soon spread among the giant tree of siblings and cousins, and at last reached Olivia Scurlock.

Olivia Scurlock was James's youngest sister. She was four or five when her mother, Rajeanna, decided to get them all out of Omaha.

"My mom told us to pack a whole bunch of clothes," Olivia remembered. "When I packed my bag, I put a whole bunch of toys in it. And away I went."

Neither she nor James knew where they were headed. They wound up at the bus station in Omaha.

"And we all just got on a bus, and we went to Norfolk," Olivia said. She had no idea why Norfolk, and neither did her mom. "I think she just got on the bus and wherever it stopped is where we were going to live."

In Norfolk, they made their way to the rescue mission.

"We got off the bus, and my mom went inside. And she was like, 'I have six kids. And I have nowhere to go.'"

James Sr. eventually came years later to collect James and his sister Rajeanna. Olivia, too young to have known her dad well, stayed with her mother in Norfolk. Saying goodbye to James and Rajeanna left everyone in tears. But there were visits in the summer, with trips to the water park and the traveling circus.

Olivia, waif-like and with the high-pitched voice of a toddler, stayed close with James their whole lives. She filled her bedroom with his schoolwork and the lyrics to the rap songs he'd write. She kept his artwork and the letters he'd written when he was behind bars as a teenager.

She and her mother had made a trip to Omaha when Jewels, Olivia's brother's child, was born.

"I think he was nervous to be a dad," she said in recalling the visit. "He said that he didn't really know how to be a dad or if he was going to do it right and stuff. But when I held his daughter, oh my gosh, she was the cutest baby ever."

Still, Olivia teased James about why he needed any women or girls in his life other than her.

"What do you need a girlfriend for? I make your life exciting," she'd joke.

George Floyd's death had hit Olivia and her circle of high school friends hard. One of her friends put it starkly in a Facebook post: "Instead of arguing about dumb stuff, how about you look into George Floyd's death?"

Olivia did. She was horrified by the video of his killing.

"I had a really bad feeling. It's something that you can't explain. It like hurt my stomach. And so then my mom was like, 'Oh, well, maybe food will help.' I'm usually always hungry. I love food."

They set out for Culver's, a burger and ice cream joint. They saw people out in Norfolk protesting, and were briefly heartened.

"We passed the protest people, and they're like, 'Black lives matter.' My mom honks and we cheer."

Olivia was at a friend's house the night James was shot. Her phone was on mute, but she could see her stepsister Hali Myles calling her repeatedly.

"Juju got shot," Hali told her.

Olivia lost her breath; she couldn't speak.

"I was so mad at God. I was so mad. Oh, I broke everything, everything, my door, the chair, the vacuum, all of it. I ran outside. I was cussing God out. I was like, 'Fuck you, man. Why'd you have to take him? Out of all people, why my brother? What the fuck?'"

Memories spun through her mind, and her brain pulsed with regret.

"He was funny. He was annoying. Me and him used to argue about how annoying he was. I was like, 'Juju, you're so annoying, dude. Just go away.' Now I want him back and it is crazy. If he could annoy me one more time, I'd let him."

"This Is Going to Be Pretty Bad for You"

JAKE GARDNER WAS TAKEN INTO CUSTODY on Harney Street 30 minutes after the shooting. Police were everywhere in the neighborhood already. He was brought to the Omaha Police Department station house blocks away on S. 15th Street. Gardner did not know it, but the fourth-floor interview room he was placed in was in the station's Homicide Unit.

At some point, Gardner, still soaked from the puddle in the street outside The Gatsby, was given a new set of dry clothes. He spent the rest of the night in the room, and if he slept, he did it on the floor.

The homicide detectives decided the county prosecutor needed to be brought in early to assess the case. The news of the shooting was already rocketing around an Internet aflame for more than a week about racist cops and the killing of George Floyd. The bare basics of what had happened—a white man had shot dead a young Black man during a protest over police misconduct—were plenty of fuel.

Don Kleine, sixty-six, the county attorney, took the call at his home on the southwestern outskirts of Omaha.

Kleine had grown up and gone to school in Omaha. He went to work for the county attorney's office straight out of law school and then spent some time in private practice that included criminal defense work. He returned to the county attorney's office as its chief deputy and tried a range of high-profile murder cases. After a stint as the chief of the criminal division in the state attorney general's office, he ran for county attorney, and he won. As the top prosecutor, he said he had made it a point to continue to try cases himself, believing it an obligation both to the public and to his staff. He was well regarded by cops, and local reporters considered him a straight shooter.

It was not entirely unusual for Kleine to be called to the scene of a potentially high-profile case. He'd been summoned to come out to Omaha's well-to-do Dundee neighborhood after a gruesome double homicide in 2008, and again when a husband and wife were slain in another part of town in 2013.

"You could tell there was a sense of urgency," Kleine said of the call he got from police headquarters.

Kleine made his way to the station house at 15th Street and Howard Street. On his way, he stopped to stare at what had become of the Douglas County Courthouse, where his offices were located. Windows had been smashed out. Expletives had been scrawled on the outer walls. Kleine took pictures of something he'd never thought he'd see in Omaha.

The homicide floor was abuzz with activity rare for a Sunday morning. Kleine was given what he called a "skeletal" version of the killing, and was told witnesses were being interviewed, including Tucker Randall, Scurlock's friend who had been with him on Harney Street. Kleine was informed Gardner's lawyers were on their way.

Gardner's parents had a friend who served on Omaha's city council, and they called him immediately after the shooting. Their son needed a lawyer. The local representative suggested two of the city's most experienced, one of them a former federal prosecutor, the other a former county attorney.

Tom Monaghan got the call from Gardner's father at 2:00 a.m. May 31. Appointed by President Bill Clinton, Monaghan had served as the top federal prosecutor in Omaha for eight years. He'd worked as a lawyer for the United Nations in Kosovo for several years after his stint as U.S. Attorney and had returned to Omaha to do a mix of private practice and pro bono work. In short, he was respected and connected. He'd hired and helped train many of the lawyers working in Omaha, and had seen some in that cadre of prosecutors go on to become judges and politicians in Nebraska and beyond.

Gardner's other attorney would be Stu Dornan, a New Yorker who had spent years working for the FBI. He'd been named "field agent of the year" during his career with the bureau and had played a role in one of the more notorious cases in Nebraska history, the investigation of a cult leader in the town of Rulo who had tortured and killed two people, including a young boy. The case had become the subject of a book, *Evil Harvest*.

Dornan had also served as county attorney, the office Don Kleine now held, and the one that would be making any decision about charging Gardner. He'd had a celebrated win when he successfully prosecuted a murder case despite the fact that the body of the person killed had never been found.

The two lawyers got to the police station early on the morning of May 31. They found Gardner in the tracksuit he'd been given. Detectives had taken Gardner's phone, so he had little knowledge of the storm that was blowing over the shooting. To the lawyers, though, Gardner seemed to know the person he'd killed had been a young Black man. Gardner was nervous, but he'd been fed, and he'd offered no version of what had happened to police or prosecutors.

Kleine and his top deputy, Brenda Beadle, had convened with top police officials in a conference room on the sixth floor of the station house. Monaghan and Dornan both knew Kleine well. Kleine, a Democrat, had succeeded Dornan, a Republican, as county attorney, beating him at the polls in a countywide race and taking office in 2007.

The lawyers were told video existed of the incident and that prosecutors and police were in the process of reviewing the tape from Gardner's bar's security cameras. Monaghan and Dornan told Gardner to stay quiet and headed for his establishment on Harney Street. If there was video of the killing, they needed to see it.

As it happened, Tyler Reed was at The Gatsby when the lawyers turned up. Reed and others had rushed to the bar after waking to news of what had happened. Reed had the codes to the locks on the doors, but when he got there they were not needed. The doors had been busted out. Reed and others who came made themselves useful by cleaning up the shattered remains of the bar, the broken glass and the variety of debris that had been hurled into it from the street.

Reed had known Gardner for years, and had served as his all-purpose audiovisual tech consultant. He'd installed the sound and lighting in the first incarnation of The Hive and made sure Gardner had dealt with a marketing problem the bar had: a giant billboard atop the building encouraging people to get tested for testicular cancer. Reed figured out how to disable the lights used to showcase the billboard at night.

When The Hive moved to Harney Street, Reed came along with it. For four years, he served as the regular Friday night DJ at the club, and had been the person who had put in place the security cameras.

There were fifteen cameras in all, and they had cost Gardner some $4,000. They recorded action at every door to the place, every bathroom entrance, every stairwell. And there were cameras pointed at the sidewalk and street outside the bar. Over the years, the club had been cited for failing to adequately monitor altercations and other troubling behavior by patrons in the street.

Checking the cameras was the first thing Reed had done upon arriving at The Gatsby. The cameras had worked, and they had captured much of what had taken place the night before. He watched the tape, from every camera and angle. It was hard to take in what he saw—what to him seemed like a long and violent siege of the bar.

"Ruthless, reckless behavior," he said.

And then there was the sequence leading to the killing. Reed was able to manipulate the footage to better see what happened once Scurlock had jumped on Gardner and the two men had crashed into the deep puddle in the street. To Reed, it was clear Scurlock, on Gardner's back, was trying to get the gun.

The lawyers, when they got to the bar, wanted Reed to show them all of it, and the three men spent hours replaying and reviewing the critical thirty to forty minutes from late on May 30. At one point, the lawyers got a call from prosecutors at the police station.

"Are you ever coming back?" they asked.

Monaghan and Dornan did make their way back, but not before they went to their office to do an impromptu bit of legal research on Nebraska's self-defense statutes. What they'd seen on the tape looked to them like an inarguable act of self-defense on Gardner's part. And their improvised legal research that afternoon, to them, supported that conclusion. The law in the state, statute 28-1409, was generous to those who asserted a claim of self-defense: "Use of force in self-protection: Subject to the provisions of this section and of section 28-1414, the use of force upon or toward another person is justifiable when the actor believes that such force is immediately necessary for the purpose of protecting himself against the use of unlawful force by such other person on the present occasion."

That permissible use of force in self-defense could in certain circumstances include deadly force: "The use of deadly force shall not be justifiable under this section unless the actor believes that such force is necessary to protect himself against death, serious bodily harm, kidnapping or sexual intercourse compelled by force or threat."

Once back at the police station, Monaghan and Dornan met with Kleine. They sensed there was little appetite for charging their client. "Do what you want to do," Kleine told the lawyers, "but I want to hear what he has to say."

Gardner's two lawyers were comfortable allowing Gardner to be formally questioned.

For forty-five minutes, Gardner sat with a single female homicide detective. He answered every question. He'd confronted Scurlock and the others, people he didn't know, only after his father had been knocked on his ass in the street. When he was taken to the ground the first time, he'd fired what he called a warning shot. He didn't know who had tackled him the first time, nor did he know who was on his back when he was knocked to the ground the second time, much less the color of his skin. He had yelled multiple times for the person to get off him. He feared for his life.

"Pretty straightforward," Monaghan said of the interview.

Kleine watched the interview with his team, other detectives, and some number of OPD senior brass. Kleine had briefly left the station house and done his own legal research back at the battered Douglas County Courthouse. He and his deputy, Beadle, talked about the challenge of overcoming at trial an affirmative claim of self-defense.

Kleine met again in the station house's sixth-floor conference room to discuss what to do. The chief of the Omaha police was there, as was his top deputy. The city prosecutor was there. The homicide lieutenant leading the investigation was there. Jean Stothert, the city's Republican mayor and the first woman ever elected to the position, had sent her chief of staff.

Everyone was aware of the outcry sweeping Omaha. There'd been comments online asserting Gardner was some kind of racist. The detectives who had interviewed Randall, Scurlock's friend, said Randall denied anything racist had been said in the exchanges between Gardner and Scurlock. The police had opted not to formally book Gardner, a procedural step that would have been typical in a case any prosecutor was going to take forward.

Kleine had also been shown video of Scurlock and Randall vandalizing the architecture firm on Harney Street. Detectives had interviewed people among the protesters who said Scurlock had been threatening others during the course of the night. The detectives asked Kleine if all that would be relevant in considering a case against Gardner.

It was one of the questions Kleine had researched over at his office. The Nebraska Supreme Court, he found out, had held that conduct such as Scurlock's could be deemed relevant to his "state of mind" in the encounter with Gardner, from its start to deadly finish. It could show, the law says, a penchant for violence.

"Everybody said I just don't see how you can charge the guy at this point in time," Kleine said of what was a consensus in the conference room. "I don't see how you can prove beyond a reasonable doubt that he did not act in self-defense," he said in front of the group. "There wasn't anybody that spoke out, 'Oh, my God, you've got to file.' I think everyone realized the seriousness of the decision."

Kleine said he took a call from the mayor. He said she asked, "Can't you just file something, and you could dismiss it down the road?"

Kleine told her no. "I can't ethically do that," he said he told her.

He then met with Gardner's lawyers.

Monaghan, the former U.S. Attorney in Omaha, had been a leader in the state's Democratic Party for years. He recruited candidates, helped raise money, worked on policy platforms with them. Kleine was in his fourth term as the Democratic county attorney, and up until then no one doubted he could keep his office for as long as he wanted.

Monaghan told Kleine the decision not to charge Gardner would be politically unpopular given the national moment. "This is going to be pretty bad for you," Monaghan told Kleine. Kleine conceded he was aware of the rumors circulating about Gardner—that he was a maniac, a Marine looking to shoot somebody, maybe a white supremacist—and was worried about it. But unmoved.

"I'm a big boy," Kleine said.

Detectives used the station's back door to let Gardner go, and it was suggested he might want to leave town for his own welfare. If he chose to fly, he was told, he should fly out of Kansas City, a three-hour drive away, rather than Eppley Airfield in Omaha.

Gardner first went to see his parents. His girlfriend, Cara, was there, as well. The two had dated for close to five years, and had shared Sunday dinners at Gardner's parents' house for all five of those years. It was Gardner's mother who first notified his girlfriend of what had happened. It came in a text: "Jake shot somebody."

The scene inside the house was one of relief and worry. There were guns in the house, and a fear that they might be needed when word got out that Gardner had been released without being charged. Dave Gardner, Jake's father, had gone to the hospital to be evaluated after he'd been sent crashing to the street outside The Gatsby. Reed had come to join the family and told them what he'd seen on the videotape.

Gardner told those inside the house that Scurlock had made clear his aim when he was on Gardner's back, saying, "I'm going to get your gun, nigga."

"Jake said he hadn't meant to kill him," Reed said.

Already, even in the early hours of Gardner's release, there were the most dire calculations being made. It seemed clear Gardner could not stay in town long. Perhaps his family's time there was limited, as well. The club on Harney Street, it was ever more apparent, was a thing of the past.

"It was just breaking my heart," Gardner's girlfriend said. "He'd put his blood, sweat, and tears into that place. That was his dream."

What little he had left to count on, Gardner told his family, included the loyalty of the Marines he'd served with. A small group of them, in the months after their discharge, had come together in Humboldt County in Northern California. There, exhausted, dispirited, even damaged by their wartime experience, they had improvised their own little commune in the redwood forests. Some lived in tents; a couple had enrolled in college, able to use their military service to gain tuition breaks. The locals, a notoriously idiosyncratic bunch famous for their embrace of cannabis and its exploding financial prospects, accepted the Marines without judgment. In return, the Marines had found the use of cannabis a welcome balm for their varying degrees of trauma. At least one saw a business future in it all.

Perhaps Gardner could return there. One of the former Marines had grown up across the state line in Oregon, and lived in Portland. Gardner said he might be safe with him. Within days, Gardner, often moving through Omaha in disguise, had gathered some belongings from his apartment in the Old Market and driven to Kansas City to stay with an aunt, so as not to risk being seen at Omaha's airport. He then set off for the West Coast, with his dog, LeBron. Maybe his parents would join him.

"An alternate life," Reed said.

"A White Piece of Shit Supremacist"

JAKE GARDNER WAS BARELY IN CUSTODY before the Internet exploded with word of the fatal shooting on Harney Street.

At 11:04 the night of May 30, Omaha Police wrote on Twitter that a person had been shot outside The Gatsby. At 11:27 p.m., police tweeted that a suspect was in custody. Eleven minutes later, a person who identified as being associated with the Antifa movement—the often-violent counterforce to the armed white supremacists marching in cities across the country after Trump's election—named Gardner as the likely shooter.

"Victim shot in the neck," the person wrote on Twitter. "Shooter in custody. Unconfirmed if shooter is indeed Jake Gardner, the racist homophobic owner of The Hive."

This was followed by a tweet at 11:45 citing "rumors" that Gardner was responsible and alleging it was premeditated.

"Jake Gardner is a white supremacist and was itching to shoot somebody tonight," one person posted online. "If the rumors are true, this was premeditated."

The initial online claims cited no evidence of any kind that Gardner was a racist, or that the shooting was premeditated.

But a narrative was taking hold, and it gained momentum at extraordinary speed.

At 12:20 a.m., someone tweeted: "Jake Gardner, the owner of the

Hive downtown Omaha, shot a protester tonight. Fuck him and his establishment and I hope he fucking rots."

That same person wasn't done: "A white piece of shit supremacist premeditated all of it. Fuck him. Fuck The Hive. FUCK JAKE GARDNER."

At 1:42 a.m., someone calling themselves "justsomefool" posted a tweet linking to "raw footage" from the scene of the shooting. The tweet shared a screenshot of a post claiming Gardner's family confirmed he was a racist and "Nazi sympathizer who premeditated the killing."

Someone then posted a picture of Gardner and, without any actual support, expanded on the idea that he was an "avowed racist, nazi sympathizer." It included a claim that Gardner had been shouting racial epithets at the protesters.

"Witnesses say he was spouting racist taunts at the protesters as they marched by," the person wrote. "This is premeditated."

The role of the Internet in controversial cases had by 2020 become a known and familiar phenomenon. The proliferation of cell phones had led to bystanders posting often-damning footage of disputed deadly force incidents involving the police, a development that in some cases brought a new degree of accountability for officers in departments across the country. But there had also been frightening episodes of online vigilante justice in the aftermath of high-profile crimes. Self-styled online sleuths, in one terrible example, wrongly identified someone as being behind the deadly bombing at the Boston Marathon in 2013.

At 2:00 a.m., another person took up the increasingly dominant online theme about Gardner, and what had happened outside his nightclub: "JAKE GARDNER OF OMAHA IS A WHITE NATIONALIST AND A MURDERER."

Five minutes later, another voice chimed in: "The man is also a far right white supremacist and is homophobic. Don't glorify Jake Gardner. He's a coward."

Someone posted what seemed to be a reference to Gardner's support for Trump. "Fuck Trump," they wrote. "If you liked or frequented" Gardner's bar, they wrote, you were "undeniably a piece of shit."

A post on Reddit made a new claim. It was Dave Gardner, Jake's father, who had been using racial slurs outside The Gatsby, the person alleged. The person, under the name DickJuggle, said they were at the scene:

> *Hi. Was down there and saw this happen. Young white kids smashed the windows of Hive and Gatsby, I went to take photos and document. An older gentleman was calling a group of us "n***** lovers" and Jake Gardner was there and on phone. People were walking around but nothing was being looted. Walked away for a moment, heard commotion and went back after gunfire. Numerous crowd sources say he was holding up a gun and yelling racist shit and the small group was confronting them for remarks and such, Jake got shoved, some sort of tussle and he shot the kid in the neck. This was not him defending his property. This was him making a snap judgement to murder an unarmed 22 year old because he's a fucking racist and a piece of shit.*

The post found instant support, with another person writing: "He shot a different guy who was trying to disarm him. Jake Gardner is a known bigot and psychopath."

People offered their impromptu analysis and more unsubstantiated claims:

"I'm not a lawyer but I'm pretty sure you shouldn't brandish a weapon at people on the street while saying racial slurs at them."

Another, one that was shared widely shortly after 3:00 a.m., manufactured more detail of something that hadn't actually happened: "Today, in Omaha, NE this white man ran through the protest to 'protect' his club from being 'destroyed' & shot this black man in the neck TWICE. While yelling slurs like 'N*gger Lover' at people. He is now in custody for murder." The post was retweeted over twenty-two thousand times and shared on other platforms including Reddit.

It didn't stop. One woman asserted Gardner had shot Scurlock from behind. Another said they'd heard from "several people" that Gardner had an Iron Cross tattoo.

Another person claiming to be an eyewitness had their post go viral, one insisting Scurlock had played no role in damaging Gardner's bar and made no mention of the assault on his father: "He did not touch any of Gardner's property. I'm the one that took the video of the white kids doing it and I apologized to him in the video for all the broken windows before the shooting even happened. The windows were broken when he arrived. Sooo. He never touched Gardner's property and wasn't in the process of doing it when he was killed."

Another indicated they knew Gardner personally.

"I have five friends in common with Jake Gardner," the person wrote. "I have five friends in common with a murderer. I have five friends in common with a man who lynched a black child in Omaha, Nebraska."

The person then added hashtags: #jamesscurlock #blacklives matter.

Occasionally, there was what amounted to a debate about the actual facts of what had happened.

One person posted calling the killing a lynching: "The definition of a lynching is being murdered for a supposed crime without evidence or trial. The fascist scum is going to claim self defense of his business, he made himself judge jury and executioner. You can take your racist apologist bullshit elsewhere."

In response, someone wrote: "He was not lynched. He was shot after he tackled Jake to the ground. Don't feed the narrative that liberals are more interested in, making sensationalist news to fit a narrative."

As dawn approached, old Yelp reviews of The Hive surfaced and were shared. It was hard to tell if they were old reviews or new ones being posted that night. They painted the establishment as nakedly racist.

"It's clear that Jake's personal bigotry influenced the business practices of his bars," someone wrote as the reviews popped up. "His racism is known around Omaha. He should be charged with a hate crime."

One old review read: "Basically, if you're a fan of racism, homophobia, transphobia and a hint of misogyny then this is the bar you want to go to. Apparently this place turns you away if you're not wearing a belt but only if you're black. If you're white, your pants can be fallen on the floor and nobody cares. Do yourself and everyone else a favor and stay away from this racist establishment. Wish I could give negative stars. Two guys walk up, both dressed nicely. One black, one white. The bouncers refused to let in, you guessed it, the black guy, because he isn't wearing a belt. White guy, no issues that you can't tell if he has a belt on. Laughing my ass off. This bar, it's a group of violent, racist, homophobic, jock wannabes drooling to serve pretty girls alcohol and waiting to attack anyone they feel is threatening to their fragile ego."

Another: "The only reason there isn't a giant 'minority is not allowed' sign outside this bar is probably because of existing anti-discrimination laws. If you're black, don't wear baggy pants or jeans with no belt or a white t-shirt or whatever rules they just decide on the spot to either not let you in or kick you out once you're in. If you're a decent guy of any ethnicity looking to meet or hit up a girl at the bar, be careful. You might just be labeled as a sexual predator and get kicked out. If you're gay, yeah, don't even bother. You might just get punched in the face. Stay away. I've been there twice and seen this place in action. Never came back. Then I kept hearing more and more horror stories. Nope."

The reviews didn't always seem to be firsthand accounts but reflections of what people had heard or what was supposedly known about The Hive. One person encouraged others to post new reviews that night, until Yelp shut down the campaign. True, not true, genuinely felt or cynically manipulated in a volatile moment, the posts served to cement the emergent narrative. People called for boycotts. They highlighted Gardner's Facebook page, and unearthed his claim that the Black Lives Matter movement was a terrorist organization.

"He murdered a man because he valued his business over James Scurlock's life," one person wrote. "Make sure he never makes another dollar."

There were some posts online of people rallying to Gardner's defense. "Praying for you Jake," someone wrote. "Did what you had to do, man," wrote another.

Some friends announced they had created a crowdfunding account for any legal defense Gardner might need. It was instantly set upon by those portraying Gardner as a racist murderer, and a concerted campaign to shut down the crowdfunding site was launched.

The move to report the fundraising page gained traction immediately. The first tweet calling on users to report the fundraiser on GoFundMe was posted at 4:28 a.m. Elijah Daniel, a comedian, retweeted the allegations that Gardner and/or his father had used racial slurs, and urged his followers to report the GoFundMe. Reddit users also called on people to report the page: "Jake Gardner murdered a man in cold blood to 'protect his business.' If you could let gofundme know that, Omaha would appreciate it."

"Some dumbass made him a GoFundMe!" another wrote. "I refuse to link it here, but if you go on FB and search Jake Gardner you'll find it. Everybody needs to report it for fraud. The description claims he was 'forced to defend himself' which is a fucking lie when there's video evidence of him antagonizing people and using racial slurs."

"Tonight we mourn the death of another black American," another wrote. "Know his name: James Scurlock. He was murdered in cold blood by the owner of The Hive. The murderer must be held accountable and charged! Life in prison for being the racist, transphobic and homophobic scum that he is."

The spiral of raw emotion, misinformation, and unverified claims would not let up. Pictures of Gardner with Trump were posted, with people invited to connect the dots—"Trump supporter" means racist killer. News of the shooting also began to appear on a range of news sites, both legitimate and fringe, with one headlining its story: "Trump-loving bar owner shoots Black protester," and claiming Gardner had a lengthy criminal record. One of the stories linking Gardner with Trump was tweeted out by Feminist News, with 1.5 million followers.

At one point, a remarkable post appeared online. A Twitter user named Juniper Fitzgerald, who described herself as a feminist author and former sex worker, claimed Gardner was her cousin and described him as a "white supremacist": "My white supremacist cousin antagonized and then fucking shot and killed a Black man who was protesting in Omaha last night. The murdered man's name was James Scurlock. White people—this shit isn't some fringe white people. It's us and our shitty fucking family members."

The woman did not elaborate on Gardner's alleged supremacist qualities. She didn't cite examples. It wasn't clear if the name she posted under was her true name. She didn't describe anything Gardner had ever done to earn the damning label. She didn't detail how close a relative she was, if she was a relative.

But she did then post this: "For curious minds, my cousin's name is Jake and his phone number is 503-889-8595."

The phone number was quickly rocketing through the Internet. And it didn't take long for Gardner's home address to go online, too. Some people dug it up from state liquor license records. But it was soon everywhere.

Gardner's loyal connection to the 311 band became a topic, and others who loved the band posted regrets that Gardner, a member of their 311 community, could have done something so awful.

"My heart is broken he committed such a horrific act of violence," one wrote. Others called on the band to disavow Gardner and to donate to a GoFundMe site that had been set up for the Scurlock family. The hometown band soon issued a statement: "Our hearts are breaking for a young man named James Scurlock who was killed protesting last night in our hometown of Omaha following the brutal death of George Floyd. James was killed by a longtime fan of 311. We do not stand for bigotry or prejudice of any kind and denounce these senseless killings and those responsible. Peace, love, unity, and respect. Let's keep it that way. This hatred needs to stop, and we need to stand up and work together to end it."

The first mention of Scurlock's name came online at 3:37. One of the earliest tweets mentioning Scurlock's name said that he died while trying to defend himself from Gardner. The early posts naming Scurlock said he was killed by Gardner, and suggested retribution.

In a post accompanying a picture of Scurlock, someone posted: "This is James the young man that was shot and killed tonight by the hive owner Jake Gardner. They better know that the black community is not letting this shit slide. James died trying to protect himself from Jake. Jake taunted these kids and went to the sidewalk to confront them with a gun instigating the situation and murdered this black man during the protests. He was only 22. In videos surfacing you can see Jake pointing the gun at them and James was scared and jumped on his back trying to make him put the gun down. He is a hero and nothing less. My soul is so pissed. An eye for an eye. Prayers to all who love him."

On Twitter, a crowdfunding page for Scurlock had been posted within hours of the shooting. The fundraiser had been shared over one thousand times on Twitter within twenty-four hours, including by high-profile people. On Facebook, the fundraiser was shared by Reptar, a local band, who identified Gardner as a racist. The band Bright Eyes shared the link, helping to amplify it.

Local politicians began to join in. Two-time congressional candidate Kara Eastman shared the fundraiser link within hours of the killing, writing: "Last night a young black man was murdered in Omaha during the protests."

An Omaha activist added his voice, calling Gardner a "Trump-supporting piece of shit."

"There are those who will say white protesters started this violence and are responsible for this death," he wrote. "White, racist Police started this violence, and a known White Supremacist finished it. To call the ensuing riot and property damage anything other than righteous anger is RACIST."

But Scurlock was not spared online, either. A video showing a person thrashing a business was posted to YouTube, titled "James Scurlock." It was Scurlock and Tucker Randall in the architecture firm's office. For some on the Internet, it shifted the portrait of Scurlock from a murdered hero to a wanton criminal. Users posted sarcastically under the video, saying it was evidence of what an upstanding citizen he was.

"He was an innocent angel just out for a jog."

"Wow! What a saint."

"When they say he was 'peacefully' protesting the attorney will be 'I would like to enter this video as evidence.'"

"Seems like a fine upstanding young citizen. A peaceful protestor, if you will."

"Aww look at them peacefully breaking things and going into a building they don't own."

Some of it was downright mean and racist: Scurlock was a thug. He got what he deserved.

"Life's all about decisions. I love happy endings."

"Savage"

"He's such a model citizen. He ate his vegetables and did his homework before it was due. We don't know why he was killed for passing out water to the owners of businesses in downtown Omaha and trying to make a difference!"

"We need shirts for the business owners that say, 'Scurlocked and loaded, try me!'"

"Thank you for your service Mr. Gardner."

"Jake Gardner was the reluctant garbage man that night. Forced into a situation to defend himself against a punk kid who demanded a nomination to the Darwin awards."

"Moral of the story: don't jump on someone who is being attacked and has a gun."

In the chat rooms of the far right, Gardner was hailed as a righteous avenger. There's no indication in any of the posts that anyone writing knew Gardner or could place him in any supremacist group or the like. But celebrating any violence, warranted or not, by white people against people of color had become a trope in white nationalist chat groups.

Within twenty-four hours of his name surfacing online, hundreds of comments praising Gardner for his actions were added to an online thread titled: "A new /pol/ hero was born on this day."

"Jake going Rambo on Sambo."

"Looks like he pulled a gun when the blacks approached him and then they had a nigga moment."

"He stopped an entire riot in two shots. The power of the Golden Gardner."

"God bless this patriot."

"God bless this beautiful bastard."

"Let the Law Take Care of It"

THE MORNING AFTER HIS SON HAD been killed, James Scurlock Sr. met with his family. His desire to kill Gardner had abated. He wanted a lawyer. He had no great taste to sue anyone. He wanted to see Gardner held accountable for Juju's death.

James Sr. got the name of a local lawyer, Justin Wayne. Wayne, forty, was a state senator, and his district included sections of North Omaha, where both he and young James Scurlock had spent parts of their boyhoods. Wayne had a reputation as both a maverick willing to make deals with Republican lawmakers and an insider with connections to prosecutors and judges in town. That summer, he was working on legislation to remove language from the Nebraska state constitution that still said that slavery could be an appropriate punishment for a crime.

Wayne, a former football and basketball player with a bad back and banged-up knees, had been on Harney Street himself the night before when Scurlock was shot. He had seen buildings being defaced and watched as a crowd of protesters set upon a police car. He actually tried to intervene to discourage more of the unrest.

We got to do better, he had said to himself, lamenting the turn the protests had taken.

Wayne had been born to mixed-race parents, a couple who had been run out of his mother's home state of Kansas because she'd been seeing a Black man. In Omaha, his mother was living in a homeless shelter when Wayne was born, and she quickly placed him at the Nebraska Children's Home and offered him up for adoption. He was taken soon after by another mixed-race couple.

He proved to be a precocious kid, his young heart and mind taken up with issues of race and rights and justice. As a schoolboy, he'd noticed that census forms required those filling them out to choose to identify as either Black or white. He wrote to both local and state officials objecting. Why should he or any other mixed-race person have to deny one of their parents?

In eighth grade, he typed out a piece of writing he called "A Dream, My Dream":

> *My dream. In times of suffering and violent acts against each other, we need a dream. Not just any dream, but a dream in which people can make new meanings to the words happiness and salvation. Like Martin Luther King, Jr., I too have a dream. This dream is like no other dream, but a dream of today, which will make a greater tomorrow. My dream. My dream is one day little black boys and girls can close their eyes at night without being scared if they'll see you again, can sleep through the whole night instead of waking up crying out your name because of a flashback or a dream of you being stabbed. When the phone rings, they're not scared to pick it up because they know it's not you calling from jail or someone calling about you. When they hear sirens, they know it's not you because they know where you're at and what you're doing, or not worried about the gunshot they heard because they know it didn't hit you. Can you guarantee this? I can't, but I wish I could. That's my dream. Dream that streets will not be owned by guns, but by people, where little children cry because they fell instead of you or one of your cousins being shot, where your sister or cousin isn't pregnant at the age of 15, but has a happy family at the age of 30. Your sister, God's gift to a man, is not abused or disrespected in any way. A place where you are not stereotyped as a gang member or a thief. You can drive down the street without being harassed by your*

protector. Cops will have no need to have any guns or need to beat you with sticks for the fun of it. A heavenly earth instead of the pile of rubbish we are. This is a dream. My dream. Jails will not be crowded, but have a sign on the window saying vacancy. You can befriend or couple with any race without being labeled as a sellout. One day, every black, white, yellow, red, and even purple girls and boys will join hands and say, "Enough is enough." This is a great dream. My dream.

Wayne had gone to law school at Creighton University in Omaha and worked briefly as a clerk in the office of the county attorney. When the Scurlock family contacted him, Wayne was unsure what, if anything, he could do. He was still on Harney Street when Scurlock had been shot. He'd recorded video from that night on his phone. He thought he might wind up called as a witness in any investigation. But he went to see James Scurlock Sr.

"I met the family at their house," Wayne said. He told them: "I'll be your attorney, but your attorney for what I don't yet know." Still, he reassured them: "However I can help, I will help."

Wayne told James Sr. he had a relationship with Don Kleine, the county attorney. He was sure Kleine would keep the family informed of any investigation or decision about charging a crime.

"I can call Don," he told the family. "I can be a go-between. I can get you answers."

Later that day, James Sr. and Wayne held a news conference at the Malcolm X Memorial Foundation Visitors Center. James Sr. said he'd opted for justice over vengeance. He would not hunt down Gardner or his family.

"Last night, I lost a son," he said. "My kids lost a brother. His daughter lost a father."

Wayne has an easygoing manner and gets a kick out of wearing a rancher's hat around town. But he speaks with the expansive eloquence of a professor delivering a polished lecture. He encouraged Kleine to take a hard look and provide the family with reassurance.

Scurlock said he didn't want people to loot or be violent in his son's name.

"Growing up, my mom always told me she thought I had the voice of a leader," James Sr. said. "I told people, let the courts handle this and be peaceful. Let the law take care of it. All I wanted was Jake Gardner to be taken to court."

"The City's Going to Burn"

ON MONDAY MORNING, JUNE 1, LESS than thirty-six hours after Scurlock's death, Kleine had decided to do two things: tell Scurlock's family he was not going to file charges against Gardner, and then hold a news conference to tell the rest of Omaha and the world.

The National Guard was on its way to Omaha after the third night of protests had descended into mayhem. The online case against Gardner was mushrooming. Omaha's mayor had texted Kleine again. "I'm not sure I can be with you on this one," he said she wrote.

And so Kleine decided he'd do one more thing that morning: he called a number of leaders from the city's Black community to his office.

In a conference room were Cedric Perkins, a prominent pastor from North Omaha, Ben Gray, a Black city councilman, and Chris Rodgers, a veteran county commissioner. There were senior Omaha police officials, and a female detective who was the sister of the department's second-ever Black chief.

Kleine for more than a decade had been comfortable campaigning for votes in North Omaha. He'd made regular appearances at the churches in the neighborhood to talk about crime and alternative solutions for combating it. His office over the years had created a drug court meant to steer more people to treatment rather than jail. He'd recruited more prosecutors of color to his office than any county attorney before him, and three or four of them had wound up as judges.

Kleine played some of the video from the night of Scurlock's killing for those he had gathered. He laid out his rationale for not charging Gardner. Someone asked if it might make sense to wait a couple of days before making the announcement, suggesting more evidence might surface or that tensions might ease. Kleine also showed the group video of Scurlock and his friend Tucker Randall destroying property inside the office on Harney Street. Instantly, everyone told Kleine it would be a mistake to show that video at any news conference. It would be seen as needlessly embarrassing and would further wound Scurlock's family. It likely would inflame the atmosphere in the streets, as well.

Kleine thought the video of Scurlock's behavior was a key part of his legal analysis of the case, but he quickly consented not to show it.

One of the people in the room that morning was Terrell McKinney, a twenty-nine-year-old rising political presence in North Omaha. A onetime state champion wrestler, McKinney was a student at the Creighton University School of Law and making a run for the state senate seat long held by the legendary but now term-limited Ernie Chambers.

McKinney was friends with Justin Wayne, the state senator and the lawyer representing the Scurlock family. When McKinney told Wayne he'd been invited to meet with Kleine, Wayne was confused. And beginning to be angry. Kleine had told Wayne to bring Scurlock's father to his office at ten o'clock that morning. Surely, Wayne thought to himself, Kleine was not going to tell community leaders of his decision before he told Scurlock's family. Before the meeting had begun, McKinney told the others gathered that he thought they should not meet with Kleine until the Scurlock family had. The others wanted to go forward. Some were nervous of being around when the news was delivered to the family, thinking it would be highly personal and emotional.

To McKinney, Kleine's presentation felt slanted.

"I don't know, it just seemed like it was being framed to, in my opinion, demonize James Scurlock," McKinney said.

And McKinney wasn't persuaded Scurlock's killing wasn't a crime.

"I'm looking at the video, and I'm like he cannot be looking at the same video," McKinney said of Kleine. "I felt like, if the shoe was on the other foot and Gardner got shot, James would be in jail right now."

McKinney said he thought Kleine was simply trying to garner political cover for his decision. He said he and Kleine had an uncomfortable back-and-forth.

"The city's going to burn," Kleine remembers McKinney saying.

"It's my city, too," Kleine said. "That's not what I want to see happen."

McKinney texted Wayne when the meeting was over. Wayne, walking with James Scurlock Sr. to their 10:00 a.m. meeting with Kleine, was beside himself. Telling a roomful of community leaders and politicians of the decision not to charge made it inevitable word would get out to the public before Scurlock had met with Kleine.

"In what world is that okay?" Wayne asked.

Once inside Kleine's office, Wayne lost his cool. He'd once worked in the office. He knew the men and women inside. He'd gone to school with some of them.

"Tell Don Kleine we are fucking here," Wayne told the receptionist. "And we've got a fucking problem."

Wayne and Scurlock were led to Kleine's office. He was there with his deputy, Brenda Beadle. They delivered the news. They played the video. They even showed Scurlock and Wayne the video of James and Randall vandalizing the office.

Scurlock took it in.

"He did some dumb shit," the father said of his son.

But they pressed Kleine: How many other videos had he looked at? Did he have all he needed? James Sr. had been sent clips of the scene in the hours after his son was shot.

Kleine indicated he'd seen enough to make a call.

As Kleine prepared for a news conference set for early afternoon, he made a call to Tom Riley, the county public defender. Riley's team had dozens of lawyers and an office close to the courthouse. Riley said Kleine told him he might want his office to clear out in advance of the news conference. Kleine knew what he was going to announce would be explosive.

"That's What the Law Is Here"

HOURS LATER, KLEINE HELD A NEWS conference inside the city's legislative chambers to announce that indeed there would be no charges against Gardner. Kleine said that he and his chief deputy, Beadle, had met with detectives and senior Omaha Police Department officials. They made clear they had watched a number of videos capturing the events outside The Gatsby. Kleine said he had read interviews with a handful of witnesses, including Tucker Randall, Scurlock's friend. Kleine made public that Gardner, with his lawyers present, had given a detailed account after he was taken into custody. He said Omaha police officials, from case detectives to senior officials up the chain of command, agreed with his assessment that no charges could be filed as they stood there that day.

When Kleine and police officials had come to that conclusion the night before, the Omaha Police Department chief, Todd Schmaderer, had promised that he would stand with them at the news conference. He had shared their analysis of the case, and it was standard procedure for senior police officials, and even frontline detectives, to join prosecutors when making major announcements on high-profile cases. Some of the detectives working on the Gardner and Scurlock investigation had told Kleine and Beadle they wanted to be there. They were proud of their work, and realized the value of a united front.

But Kleine and Beadle would now have to go it alone. The chief was a no-show.

Kleine said nothing about having met with community leaders but did say he had taken care to meet earlier that day with Scurlock's father. He had shown Scurlock the video he had reviewed, and walked him through how he regarded what it showed: Gardner had acted in self-defense. His son's death was sadly unfortunate, Kleine concluded, but there was no winnable case to prosecute.

What followed was an extraordinary presentation by a prosecutor about a politically volatile and technically still active case. Kleine took and answered every question. He played the videotape of the incident, and walked through his thinking and his uncertainties. He talked about the details of Nebraska statutes on self-defense, and he made plain his appreciation of the upset generated by George Floyd's murder.

Kleine called the killing of George Floyd "reprehensible" and said, "All of those who are incensed, angry, and frustrated by that event and the treatment of minorities historically by individuals who have stained every aspect of the law enforcement model to serve and protect is understandable."

Kleine, with the ruddy face of the Irish-German stock he came from, had been a good athlete, and he liked to tell the story of his stint as the lone white member of a local softball team. His Black teammates had nicknamed him Petunia. He still had the look of a softball first baseman, one who'd fully enjoyed the beers after the game.

Just weeks before, Kleine had been given grave medical news. He had prostate cancer, and the numbers from his blood work were off the charts. He was set to start chemotherapy within weeks.

In front of the media, Kleine offered a personal opening remark: "Omaha and Douglas County is a community of people I truly love, and I've been very proud, and am very proud, to serve as the county attorney in this great county that we live in. When I say we, I mean my whole office, the people that work there. My chief deputy, Brenda Beadle, and myself, and the sixty-some lawyers that we have in our office and support staff and investigators. We have dedicated our careers to justice for all in our county."

Kleine was the oldest of four children raised in South Omaha, the son of a German dad and Irish mom. His father worked as a carman for the Union Pacific Railroad, and the family considered itself lower middle class. The family were Kennedy Democrats. They saw the Democratic Party as the working people's champion. Republicans were rich folks.

"No one owes you anything," Kleine's father told him. "Be thankful you got a job."

Kleine worked for the railroad during his boyhood summers, went to Jesuit high school at Creighton Prep, and earned a partial baseball scholarship to Kearney State College in Kearney, Nebraska. When the baseball team traveled to Alabama or Mississippi for games against largely African American teams, some players and coaches insisted on staying at local motels. Kleine and a few others had no problem staying at the dorms on campus, alongside their Black rivals.

Kleine had not burned to be a lawyer, and law school was something of an afterthought. But he went to the Creighton law school after all, and into the county attorney's office straightaway. Donald "Pinky" Knowles was the county attorney, a local sports icon who had led Creighton to the quarterfinals of the National Invitational Tournament in the early 1940s.

It was then an office of twenty or so lawyers, none of them Black. Kleine, not a natural public speaker as a kid, actually found himself comfortable in front of juries, and he pushed to try as many cases as possible.

"I'm a newbie; give me a trial," he remembers telling his superiors. "Maybe a dog case. Whatever."

One day, a supervisor gave him a criminal case to tackle. "It's a B on B," he was told. Kleine was confused. He asked someone else in the office: B on B? "Black on Black," they said. "Nobody cares about those cases."

Kleine prosecuted the case, an assault charge out of a knife fight in a bar. He lost when he could not overcome the defendant's claim of self-defense.

At the news conference, Kleine called Scurlock's death senseless, and lamented that it had been provoked at least in part by what he said was the violent perversion of an effort by "very good people who were exercising their First Amendment rights as a peaceful protest."

Kleine then appealed for people to come forward if they had more information about what had happened. He expressed worry about what he called "a lot of misinformation"—put out, he said, over social media and done in some instances by people who were running for public office.

"I'm not aware of them being privy to any of the evidence involved in this case or being involved in the investigation, or having seen anything with regard to what took place in this case and what the evidence consists of. When I see these statements that are made without foundation or knowledge about the case, they are irresponsible, they're reckless, and they're actually dangerous to our community. They emanate from people they think might know something about the case, and it's not accurate, it's not true, and I think that's problematic."

Kleine referenced the video of Scurlock and Randall inside the architecture firm but did not play it. "I don't think that's relevant at this point in time," he said.

And then he had video of the events on Harney Street played for the reporters and others gathered. He identified Gardner as the man with the ponytail and his father as the man in a plaid shirt. He called attention to one video that also had audio.

"So you'll hear the bar owner talking to some people. This is immediately after the man in the plaid shirt, who is his father, had asked some people to leave or pushed one of the young people, and somebody came in and knocked him back about ten feet. You'll see him fly through the air and end up on the ground. So the owner comes up to tell people to move on, and 'who did that, who pushed my dad?'"

What Kleine played had snippets of the talk in the street as the encounter between Gardner and Scurlock escalates. Those captured on the video and audio include Gardner warning people to move on and stay away from him, as well as unidentified folks in the scrum.

"Who hit him?"

"Just fucking keep going."

"You know karate?"

"Get away from me."

"Oh, he got a gun on him."

Kleine then identified Scurlock. "In the black T-shirt, that's James Scurlock."

Next, Kleine wanted to talk about whether racist language had been used by anyone involved in the confrontation. Again, he said he'd seen references to that on social media. There was no audio capturing any slurs, Kleine said. Tucker Randall, Scurlock's friend who was there in the middle of it all, said there were no racist epithets used. A white protester who was in the rolling scrum with Gardner and Scurlock said the same.

Kleine then played the video from The Gatsby's security cameras. He noted the street sign that had been used to smash the club's windows, and pointed out it had been found in the stairwell of the bar next door to The Gatsby. The video shows another angle on Dave Gardner being floored, and his son going to check on him.

Kleine then played a portion of the tape that in his description included Gardner firing three rounds in all.

"Now you see the ponytailed man backing up. He's backing down the street with people coming towards him. He backs right to the edge of that, where the construction equipment is, and that's where he gets tackled and knocked down. There's a shot fired there. Another shot, and that gets the people off of him. Then James Scurlock comes and dives on top of him, kind of maintains a choke hold around his neck. This goes on for seconds, a few seconds, some time period, then he fires a shot, and that's the shot that killed James Scurlock.

"The gun was recovered at the scene. There's also a video that we have that has some audio that comes from across the street. The video's not very good. But in the audio, you can hear the bar owner when he's got Mr. Scurlock on top of him saying, 'Get off me, get off me, please get off me,' many times, and then the shot is fired, which caused James Scurlock's death."

Kleine took a moment, then addressed the reporters again.

"I realize, and I think the whole staff does, the authority and power that we have in charging people with crimes. In particular, right now, we're in a position or a situation because of what's gone on in the community in the last week, and the protest with regard to Mr. Floyd's death, that certainly creates a lot of emotions, frustrations that deal with a lot of other things besides just this case. But we have to look at the evidence that we have in this case, and the law with regard to this case."

Kleine then laid out Nebraska law on the use of self-defense: you can't use deadly force just to defend your property—to prevent someone from stealing your bike or breaking your windows or pilfering a twelve-pack of beer. But he said the use of deadly force can be justified if "somebody's in fear for their own life or serious bodily injury, and that they don't feel like they can retreat safely." Their fear only has to be reasonable, he said, even if it turns out to have been mistaken.

"So, that's what the law is here, and that's what we looked at," Kleine concluded.

"This isn't a law enforcement officer that we're talking about," Kleine added of Gardner in the street. "We're talking about a civilian, who goes outside, is backing up, has told people please just get out of here," and who "really is attacked or jumped on by several people at once."

Kleine was asked whether Gardner had been interviewed.

"The bar owner was interviewed with his lawyers present. He cooperated, told his version of events. He said that the initial shots—again, this is his version—were warning shots to get somebody off of his back. That the other individual then jumped on him or attacked him, that he's doing a choke hold on him, that he begged and pleaded for this person to get off. The person was trying to get at the gun, he thought. He thought he was in danger of losing his life, or some serious bodily injury, and so he fired that shot in self-defense. That's what his versions of events are."

Throughout, Kleine's face radiated unease and a degree of defensiveness. He aimed for a confident certainty, but his pursed and dry lips indicated it was a struggle.

"It's important to me in my office that we're always transparent," Kleine went on. "That's why I wanted the public to see at least the greatest portion of the evidence that we have in regard to videos here. I think that's very important, especially in light of, as I said, some of the misinformation that's out there. We wanted people to see it. We wanted people to know the basis for our decision. We wanted people to understand that that's what the evidence consists of at this point in time. If there's anything further that somebody has or is aware of, we'll be happy to listen to that.

"I certainly wish that none of this would have happened. It's a senseless death. A loss of a young man's life that of course should have never happened. We know that emotions are running very high right now, and maybe this decision may not be popular. It may cause more people to be upset. I would hope that they understand that we're doing our job to the best of our ability in looking at the evidence and the law, and that's all we can do. It can't be based on emotions. It can't be based on anger. It can't be based on any of those things. But I would hope that this great community that we live in will be able to get through this."

Kleine then opened the presentation up to more questions.

A reporter quickly asked if there was any indication that Scurlock or anyone else was trying to wrestle away the gun from Gardner?

"Well, I mean, the bar owner says that he thought they were trying to take it, pull the gun away from him. He said, 'I didn't know if they had a gun. I couldn't believe that they were jumping on me because they knew I had a gun.'"

Another reporter asked about claims on social media that Dave Gardner, the father, had used the N-word.

"We looked for that," Kleine said. "We wanted to see if there was anything out there in that regard. Like I said, there was an individual who was a protester, who honestly said, 'I'm not a fan of the police department, but I was there, and I feel like I need to tell you, I didn't hear anything like that when I was standing there.' Then there's also a friend of James Scurlock who was there who talked about there was a back-and-forth between the parties, but he didn't mention any point in time that there was anything racial. He was specifically asked that question, and did not say that that had taken place."

Then Kleine was asked to expand on what he understood was said between Gardner and the protesters he first approached after his father had been knocked down. Kleine said he believed Gardner asked, "Okay, who pushed him?" and then later said, "Why don't you just move on?"

"That's when people start walking towards him, and he starts backing up, and he's got his hands like this. He's shown them he has a gun. He made it clear to the individuals out there that he was armed."

A reporter asked about whether Gardner's concealed-carry permit had expired, and if it had why Gardner wasn't charged with a gun crime.

"He was showing the gun. I don't know that it was necessarily concealed the whole time, but I know he let them know he was armed. It wasn't like it was in his waistband or covered with a shirt or anything else."

"How did he let them know he had a gun?" a reporter persisted.

"You can see it on the video. He pulls it out like this and holds it on his side. Right like this, then you hear one of the parties say, 'Hey, he's got a gun.'"

Yet another reporter asked Kleine to talk again about what's justifiable in self-defense. Could you bring a gun to a fistfight?

"His version is, 'I felt my life was in jeopardy, or at least I was in jeopardy of getting serious bodily injury, getting pummeled or getting choked out with this guy on top of me. I asked the guy to get off me, and he wouldn't get off me.'"

Reporters then probed how Gardner had fired the fatal shot.

"You can see it in the video if you really break it down," Kleine said. "He has his one hand, but he can't move his arm because he's being held. So he switches it to the other arm, and then kind of puts it around his shoulder."

Kleine was asked about his meeting with Scurlock's father, during which the video was shown.

"He didn't say much, honestly. But he was thankful that we showed it to him."

A reporter said she was struck by how much Kleine had shared with them. She said it was unusual and asked Kleine to elaborate on his decision.

"Well, first of all, what was upsetting to a lot of people that are involved in this case and have worked it is the misinformation that's out there. This wasn't somebody who walked out and was trying to hunt down somebody, as it was called a cold-blooded murder. I think it was important for the public to know that's not what we have here."

Kleine then talked about the burden of proof had Gardner been charged. Gardner, he said, would not have had to prove anything. An affirmative claim of self-defense would have required prosecutors "to prove beyond a reasonable doubt that it's not self-defense."

"We don't think there's any way we can move forward," he said.

A reporter asked what Kleine would have to see in the way of new evidence for him to change his position.

"Well, it'd have to be fairly substantially different. Like I said, we looked at this thing, the Homicide Unit looked at this thing, the individual is in custody until last night, and the Homicide Unit released him, saying, 'We're not going to book him.'"

Kleine was asked about what he thought Scurlock might have been doing. Was it possible he was acting to stop someone with a gun who had already fired it once or twice?

Kleine didn't answer directly, but Beadle, his top deputy, asked to respond. Gardner, she said, could not have known Scurlock's motives. But Gardner was in the middle of a dangerous riot.

"You're looking at the big picture here, the volatile nature of what was going on in the Old Market, all the windows that were broken out. You also have to consider all of that when someone comes out and is looking around and is scared of what's going on. It's not just this on a quiet Sunday night. Or Saturday night."

Was the decision a close call or a slam dunk? Kleine was asked.

"We know there's no such thing as a slam dunk. But I think there was an obvious consensus here between detectives, officers, anybody that had viewed all the evidence in this case at this point in time."

"Has Mr. Gardner shown any remorse or any emotion?" a reporter asked.

"I didn't personally have any conversation with the bar owner," Kleine said. "I have seen his interview, and in talking to the detectives that did the interview he was, I think, remorseful and scared."

"And shocked," Beadle added.

"Pretty much, I think, 'in shock' is a good way to put that," Kleine concurred. "That's how they described him."

The matter of Gardner's posts on social media then came up. Well before the shooting Gardner had posted something similar to what he had texted his friend from inside The Gatsby—his exasperation at having run a popular Omaha business only to have to conduct "48 hours of fire watch" to preserve it. Gardner's talk about having to do fire watch had been shared on Facebook. Online, people had cited it as evidence of Gardner's intent, even desire, to violently take on protesters.

Kleine acknowledged Gardner had used the term "fire watch" but indicated he understood it to be a reference to the simple desire to protect one's property.

"I'm aware of that term from people that I know that own bars," Kleine said, adding that those people indicated it referred to when they might be "staying late" at their establishments "to make sure nothing happens to their property."

Kleine was then asked about the timing of his decision. Had he given thought, a reporter wondered, to delaying his announcement until maybe things had calmed down in Omaha? Kleine made reference to concerns about other cases around the country where prosecutors had waited for months, even more than a year, to make decisions on controversial police-shooting cases involving race. He wasn't interested in repeating such a scenario: "I guess we take the job we have here very seriously, and we think there needs to be decisions that have to be made. Even if they're difficult decisions. Even if they might be unpopular decisions."

A TV reporter again wanted to explore the motives of the people who jumped Gardner, first Rose Melendez, then Scurlock. Couldn't they have been simply looking to disarm Gardner to prevent a shooting? It was the third time Kleine had been asked the question. He attempted an answer.

"Well, I guess I wonder about that when immediately before she gets involved in taking this guy down, he's not confronting them. He's not going towards them. He's backing away from them. He keeps backing up. He's got his hands up. He puts his hands down. He keeps backing away, and that's when they jump him. I don't see how somebody's being threatened when the person who they're saying they're being threatened by is going the other way, or away from them. So it just doesn't fit with the facts as we see them."

A theme that had emerged on social media in the hours after the killing argued that if the races of those involved were reversed—a Black bar owner had shot a white protester—the Black owner would already have been charged and brought before a judge. Kleine was asked to comment.

"There isn't a question in my mind that there is a problem in our great country that we live in with racism. I wish I had the answer, but I think everyone plays a part in this, in answering this question, how do we solve that problem? The color of someone's skin makes no difference to me. We don't look at a set of police reports and usually actually know exactly what race somebody might be, because we don't look for that. So it's a very difficult question. But there are certainly people that we live with in society that are prejudiced or have an issue with someone's race, and that's wrong; it's unfortunate. It's got to be stopped."

He went on to defend the record of his office in the context of race: "Mostly the big cases that I've been involved in involved victims who were people of color. We do everything we can to seek justice for individuals no matter who they are or where they live or what their socioeconomic status is or what their color is."

An hour in, the questions were winding down.

"Did anyone have any criminal background that played a part in your investigation?" a reporter asked.

Kleine said he didn't know if Gardner had a criminal record. He noted Gardner had been able to get a concealed-carry permit, suggesting he'd likely not been convicted of a felony. He said nothing about Scurlock's record.

A TV reporter then asked the final question: Had the courthouse and nearby civic center been evacuated out of fear of unrest with Kleine's announcement? Kleine said he knew of no formal order having been given, and hoped it would not have been required. He did not mention the heads-up he'd given the public defender's office.

"I would hope that people would be sensible, understand what we're doing here, and what our role is, and what our job is, and that level heads will prevail. We'll learn something from this, and we'll move forward from it, not backwards."

"He's Not Going to Have the Same Color"

IN THE DAYS AFTER JAMES SCURLOCK'S death, his sister Chandy Jones agreed to go down to the funeral home to help prepare her brother for his funeral and burial. The Good Shepherd Funeral Home had called and told the Scurlock family they were welcome to pick out an outfit and even come in and dress James themselves. The family business was run by Mike Hoy, an ex–state trooper. He'd told James Scurlock Sr. he'd handle the services for free.

Chandy was two years older than James. They had gone to high school together, shared the same friends. James had loyally come to her volleyball tournaments and track meets. When James had been locked up, she visited him at the county jail and he wrote her letters from inside.

Chandy had earned a partial scholarship to Wiley College, a private school in Marshall, Texas. It is one of the oldest historically Black colleges west of the Mississippi, and its students had led one of the first civil rights sit-ins in Texas when they occupied the Harrison County Courthouse to protest segregation in public facilities. James Farmer, a Wiley graduate, became one of the "Big Four" of the civil rights movement, along with Martin Luther King Jr., Roy Wilkins, and Whitney Young.

Chandy enjoyed the change of scenery but grew frustrated with her diminishing place in the school's athletic program. Wiley heavily recruited student-athletes from Africa, she said, and they seemed to get favored treatment from the school's athletic staff.

She returned to Omaha after two years and got a degree in psychology and nonprofit organization management. She was there at a hearing before a judge weighing whether to release James from jail early. The judge interrogated her, two other siblings, and one of James's best friends: Could James be trusted to stay out of trouble? Did he have the capacity to change?

They said yes, and the James Chandy reunited with in Omaha indeed seemed committed to a new way forward.

James had managed to get his high school degree while in jail, but his greatest energies had gone into writing lyrics for songs. Chandy's boyfriend had his own modest record label, and she had introduced James to him when he got out. Her boyfriend promoted local live shows in Omaha, had spent time in California working with the engineer for many of Tupac Shakur's recordings, and he saw some promise in what James had created. They had worked together to record an initial track.

Early on the morning of Saturday, June 6, a week after James had died, his siblings A.D., Marissa, and Chandy got in Chandy's Jeep and drove to the Good Shepherd home on S. 82nd Street.

"Our Mission is to be a blessing to you at the most emotional, stressful time of your life," the home says in its promotional material. The three were met by an employee, a thoughtful woman who tried to brace them for what was to come.

"He's not going to have the same color," she said of the body.

James had loved to dress in red and blue. They were his signature colors. Chandy and the others had brought a red tracksuit and a beater T-shirt. He'd have liked that, they figured. The Adidas brand was his thing, too, and so they had bought a brand-new pair of sneakers.

Chandy knew it was going to be tough, and she found it hard even to walk the hallways of the funeral home taking the three of them to the room where James lay. They found him on a metal table. He appeared to still be dressed in the paper gown he'd been put in at the hospital.

"I was so scared," Chandy said. "I thought maybe he was just going to jump out at us. But I knew he was not going to get up."

The body was clean and neat, but nothing the funeral home staff could do hid the garish wound at James's neck. The bullet had done extensive damage.

"It was like they had sewed his neck together," Chandy said.

Chandy touched the hand of her brother. Its coldness shocked her. She and the others were no longer sure they could do what they had come to do.

"Just a shell," she said of her brother's body. "Not even him anymore."

They got on with it. They decided to take pictures of James's tattoos, maybe create a kind of before and after record of his life and loves and loyalties. They put new boxer shorts on him, and clean socks on his feet. They had asked a local barber to come with them, and he gave a haircut to their unmoving brother. Chandy in her head was composing the poem she would read at the funeral service two days later.

Across their years together, James had given Chandy endless shit about her favorite necklace. It held an arrowhead she had found as a child, probably when she was out at a park or camping with James.

Despite the teasing from her brother, she never took it off. Until then. She unfastened it from the back of her neck, and placed it around James's neck.

His outfit completed, the three siblings were not sure what to do. They were pleased with their work, but that only deepened the uncertainty.

"We did not," Chandy said, "want to leave him alone."

"I Was Raised in Blackness"

DON KLEINE'S NEWS CONFERENCE ANNOUNCING THERE would be no charges brought against Jake Gardner, and that he had already been released from custody, prompted Omaha to detonate again, online and in the street. Social media users circulated links to pre-written emails demanding Kleine reconsider the case, and they shared Kleine's phone number, as well. Users also spread an online petition to get Kleine removed from office.

The uproar included plans for organized and sustained protests, more erroneous claims about the deadly incident, and menacing calls to hunt Gardner down before he could flee Omaha. Meanwhile, murals honoring Scurlock went up in Omaha and his name was invoked at Black Lives Matter rallies nationwide.

"Jake Gardner walked free today after murdering 22 yr old James Scurlock," one person wrote. "Today he was protected by a system that commends his morals. I am disgusted."

Another said, "James Scurlock was killed by a locally known white supremacist in Omaha, and the county attorney called it 'self-defense.' When you walk up to someone with a loaded gun and shoot them dead, it's not self-defense."

People citing inside information said Gardner had fled to California, and called for him to be caught.

"I have heard from a reliable source that Jake Gardner has left Omaha and is headed to California," one tweet read. "Do not let this man escape what he did. He murdered James Scurlock and Omaha officials set him free."

A tweet posted on June 2 was retweeted over twenty-four thousand times. It read: "I know I only have 163 followers but please get this out to California. Racist club owner Jake Gardner shot and killed 22-year-old James Scurlock during a BLM protest in Omaha, NE. He wasn't charged and appears to be fleeing your way."

At the center of the effort at strategic protests was a young Black man named Ja Keen Fox. Gay, outspoken, fearless, Fox was part of a modest vanguard of younger Black activists in Omaha, people not only tired of living in a segregated and inequitable city but also weary of the Black political establishment that they regarded as overly compliant and not terribly effective. Mayor Jean Stothert had named Fox to her advisory panel on LGBTQ issues.

Fox called for people to protest outside Kleine's home in a gated community in West Omaha. They would stand vigil there for thirty-six straight days, Fox said, one day for every hour Kleine had taken to investigate the case before absolving Gardner.

Fox was the son of an Air Force intelligence officer. He was born in Germany but eventually wound up in the Omaha suburb of Bellevue. He likes to say that his most important schooling happened at home, taught by his mother a version of Black history he was not getting in the classroom.

"I was raised in Blackness," Fox said, "knowing what civil rights was and really cultivating a certain experience of protest and pro Blackness."

With a smile, he said it was not indoctrination, but what he regarded as "supplemental education." "An accurate portrayal of history that doesn't exist in our educational system," he said of his mother's instruction.

His mother said, in fact, she didn't read to Fox so much as he did to her, describing him as a ferocious consumer of books even as a young child. From his earliest years, when asked his favorite color Fox would say "black." While he respected Martin Luther King Jr., he was drawn more to Malcolm X. What he called the "unapologetic nature" of Malcolm's advocacy appealed to him.

"He was passionate and determined," Fox's mother said of her son, "a little bit of what I wished I would have been."

He was, she said, also brave and blunt. He came to her once, she said, and noted that he was the lightest-skinned child in the family. He feared he would experience the world more like a white child than any of his siblings. She said her child was unafraid of saying anything, so long as he believed it.

Fox said he was determined to define his life "outside of what was traditional or conservative."

"Why don't we get taught about the figures that utilize violence or utilize real disruption to achieve those ends?" he liked to ask.

Perhaps not shockingly, Fox's youth had its share of strains—in school, and even within his own family. Fox said he was expelled from Bellevue West High School for looking up gay pornography on a school computer. His father gave him a lecture about his subpar grades, saying he was spending too much time on music and dance. He wound up at Bellevue East, where he felt more comfortable amid greater numbers of kids of color, and where he started a step team.

"Just poor kids with more personality," he said of Bellevue East.

Fox first went off to college at the University of Nebraska in Lincoln. He joined the Afrikan People's Union, a student organization, and was thrilled by the group's emphasis not on protest so much as solidarity and comradeship. It was, he said, an organization that aimed to "acknowledge us and affirm us as opposed to always being in opposition to."

But Fox's sexuality would prove enough of a strain at home that he felt he had to leave. His mother today concedes she disapproved of homosexuality but that she handled it poorly with her son and has since apologized to him for having to keep his true self a secret from his family.

At nineteen, Fox set off for Chicago. He thought he could crash at a friend's place. He had $200 in his pocket. *I have to leave here*, he remembers thinking. *I'm just not doing well.*

Chicago proved a mix of the exciting and terrifying. Fox, describing himself as young and beautiful, met a lot of older men, and eventually moved in with one. But a dispute over sex ended that. There was time in a hostel, a bout of borderline homelessness.

"Homeless, poor, LGBTQ. I really got to live that life for a while," Fox said.

Fox wound up back in Omaha after being robbed at gunpoint in Chicago. He'd been pistol-whipped, and feared being shot, but his assailant stumbled and fell backward. Fox can still see his face. "His eyes were so wild, so scared," he said.

In Omaha, Fox took a stab at working in retail. He got a job at a clothing store in an Omaha mall, and was good at it. He came to see something larger in it than hustling sales. He was remarkably good at connecting with customers, and their conversations often went deep.

"Really have conversations about worth and value and what you deserve and what you feel you have a right to," he said. "We were able to get to the root of that issue around fashion, which I found fascinating. I was able to help them see the truth about themselves."

Fox broadened his search for connection and meaning by posting, randomly online, his desire to work "with the community." He was quickly directed to the Urban League of Nebraska Young Professionals. "A group of Black people just carving out a space for themselves," he said.

And, occasionally, calling out powerful white people. Fox was at a dinner with Nebraska governor Pete Ricketts when Ricketts made a gaffe of a remark. Fox went at him, not just over the insensitive remark, but about his reign as governor of a state with serious inequities.

"There's something to be said about not letting the bad thing go unopposed," Fox said.

The killing of James Scurlock, for Fox, was a bad thing that needed to be opposed. And Don Kleine's release of Gardner was almost worse. Fox had not been among the protesters over those two ugly nights in May 2020. He felt the reasons for the protests were pure; the execution of them, a disaster.

"They're prepared for you," he said to some of the organizers, referring to the police. "When you are ready to think through a different way to do this work, that's when I'll be there."

With Scurlock's death, Fox went online to announce he had a plan.

"I didn't really," he said, "but I wanted to make sure that I had people that were going to be in that kind of ride or die mentality."

Fox ran a pretty efficient protest operation outside Kleine's home. He researched local codes on public and private property, what was allowed, what wasn't. Ditto the use of megaphones. He got a nonprofit organization in North Omaha to serve as a headquarters and staging area. He conducted training, assigned shift leaders, and provided protesters with water and other sustenance. They were outside Kleine's community early in the morning and well into the evening.

Kleine, who lived alone with his wife, was unnerved by the protests. He grew frustrated that the city prosecutor didn't intervene to halt them. Occasionally, Kleine would engage with the protesters. He told them they were misinformed about the laws involving self-defense. On one of the last days of the protests, the marchers walked up to his front door. Fox told Kleine if he couldn't detail some additional evidence for his decision not to charge Gardner, they could not trust the decision he had made.

Fox, it turned out, had been a regular at The Hive. He said he and the friends he came with were treated like royalty. They got to cut the line outside, rarely paid for drinks, and were seen by Gardner as a lively presence.

"I knew he didn't like us," Fox said of Gardner, "but he needed us. Well-dressed, light-skinned, good-looking. We get the party started."

But Fox said he had a friend who worked at Gardner's place, and got wind of disgruntlement about mistreatment of some workers of color. Fox said he had concerns about Gardner's views on race, but he "couldn't really put his finger on it."

Fox's mother began to worry about her son's safety amid the protests. "Oh, my God, yes," she said. Cars lurked out in front of Fox's home. Her son was untroubled, though.

"Ja Keen is not afraid of anything or anybody," she said, and mustered a motto for his stances. "If it's not inclusive, it's not right."

At the tail end of the thirty-six days outside Kleine's home, Fox lost his unpaid position on the mayor's advisory panel after a controversy over a post he'd put online supporting the man who killed five police officers in Dallas in 2016. Micah X. Johnson was a sniper who gunned down the officers during a downtown Dallas rally against police violence. He was a twenty-five-year-old Army reservist who investigators said was upset by recent shootings of Black men by police.

Fox had tweeted a tribute of sorts to Johnson, writing: "Rest in Power Micah X Johnson."

"He valued his life and the life of Black people enough not to wait around and be killed unjustly," Fox said on a radio show when asked about his public support for Johnson.

The mayor, in forcing Fox out as one of her advisers, issued a statement:

Members of our advisory boards are appointed to work with the city to address ways we can improve the quality of life for everyone. Members are of course entitled to their own opinions, but paying tribute to the killer of police officers is an opinion that has no value to the good work and outcomes of our boards. Our Omaha police officers put themselves in harm's way every time they come to work. Their jobs give them the opportunity to change lives and save lives. They understand and accept the risks and rewards of police work. My thanks to every officer for their dedication to our city and the citizens they serve.

Fox did not go quietly. "If it's appropriate to pay tribute to a country that during its formation killed millions upon millions of Indigenous, Black, and Brown peoples, then surely I can pay tribute to Micah X.," he said.

He blasted the mayor for a double standard, citing what he called her failed leadership during the protests over George Floyd's death and in the criminal cases brought against protesters afterward:

> *"Mayor Stothert has no problem utilizing her influence when she deems it necessary. So when asked repeatedly to protect protestors from prosecution, her replying no wasn't a question of if she could, but if she cared enough to do so. When asked how she will hold OPD accountable to the violence they enacted on citizens, during which time police officers were paid over $2 million in overtime, her equivocating wasn't because she wasn't empowered to do something, it was because she wasn't courageous enough to stand up for her constituents. Unless those constituents wear a gun and badge of course. The bias is not new or unexpected, but just made so much more obvious because of this time of social unrest."*

In a later interview, Fox doubled down on his critique of the mayor, crediting her for what he called her transparency about her beliefs.

"One thing I do appreciate about the mayor is she is bold about her racism and her white supremacy and that allows us to interact and engage with her authentically," he said. "I have no problem calling her a white supremacist or a racist because her policies and her actions prove that. And I don't think she'd be bothered with hearing it."

About the circumstances of Scurlock's death, Fox said he had no issue with Scurlock's vandalism that night. Again, he was struck by the notion that Black people were not entitled to be violent given their experiences.

"I think that's really central to race in Nebraska," he said. "The fact that people can celebrate national holidays of genocidal murderers, colonists, mass murderers, but Black people specifically should have no kind of claim to violence, even though our claim would be the most logical. That white people claim violence and disallow it for other people is really interesting."

He said Scurlock himself had been victimized by a bankrupt criminal justice system. His time behind bars as a teenager was seen by white people as evidence of his evil, not as, say, the result of mental health issues caused by a life dented by poverty and racism.

"I don't believe the system to be proper at all," Fox said of the world long ago created by police and prosecutors and politicians. "There's nothing in that system that isn't based on slave catching."

Scurlock's experience with that system entitled him to act, and violently if needed, Fox said.

"We're not blind. We see time after time our faces dead in the street. There's no way around the mental impact and the spiritual and emotional impact that takes on people," Fox said.

He saw Scurlock, in the fatal encounter with Gardner, as shaped by that same background of mistreatment. He rejected the idea Scurlock should have somehow just walked away—from the ugly protests or from Gardner.

"I can't divorce the reason he didn't walk away from the reason he was there in the first place—to advocate and defend the earned place Black people have in this American experience," Fox said. "He had more of a claim to that space than me as an activist. Though I don't think I would have walked away either."

The casting of Scurlock as little more than a career criminal bent on mayhem was predictable, Fox said. Instead, to him, Scurlock was a beloved family member legitimately outraged by Floyd's death, and the many others before.

"He was wrapped up in love," Fox said of Scurlock and his family. "I think a lot of people think we get to the criminal justice system because we lack something in that emotional arena. You can't be well loved as a Black person and do crime because that would upend the story we tell ourselves about Black people and crime. Black people are from broken homes and that's the formula for crime and it can't be mental health. It can't be the stress of Blackness. It has to be poor and dumb and mean and broken. Only white people are allowed to be well loved and misunderstood."

Fox cut Gardner no breaks, for what he understood to be his beliefs or for what he did that night.

"You have a legal obligation to remove yourself from a situation of violence before using bodily force," Fox said. "He left his bar to seek vengeance on whoever he felt harmed his place of business."

When the allegation that Gardner was a white supremacist gained traction online, it made sense enough to Fox. He didn't need to have evidence or examples, he said.

"We're so hyper-vigilant about white supremacy and racism that we can identify the intent without the proof because we're well versed in it," he said. "The same way a doctor can diagnose an issue without running a test."

"The Benefit of the Doubt"

JAMES SCURLOCK SR. HAD WATCHED DON Kleine's June 1 news conference in Justin Wayne's downtown office. Some of his other children were there. Terrell McKinney, who had spoken out in the meeting Kleine held with community leaders, had joined, too.

Of course, those gathered already knew what Kleine had decided to do. But they had hoped Kleine would be emphatic in framing the investigation as open and active, making clear that releasing Gardner the night before had not ended his inquiry. Kleine did invite people to come forward with additional information, but to Scurlock, his family, and their lawyer, the public takeaway from the news conference seemed clear: Gardner had acted in self-defense; he was never going to be charged.

"James took it like a champ," Wayne said of Scurlock's father.

Wayne said Scurlock was more determined than angry. He didn't want payback. He wanted the truth. What had really happened out on Harney Street? Who was Jake Gardner?

"Those people," Wayne said of Kleine and the police, "had disrespected him, and he was like, let's figure this out. We wanted the system to work as it was supposed to."

The criminal justice system in America, certainly in Omaha, Wayne felt, was discriminatory for people of color. Kleine's handling of Scurlock's death, Wayne argued, was the latest painful and telling example: white people in the criminal justice system get the benefit of the doubt; Black people don't.

Wayne did a bit of research on Jake Gardner. James Scurlock was not the only one that night on Harney Street who had a history with law enforcement. Gardner had his own criminal record.

Wayne had discovered the incident involving Gardner, his gun, and the employees of a local private parking lot. Gardner, upset that a boot had been put on his car in the parking lot, attempted to drive off, and wound up displaying a gun in an angry exchange with several attendants. When the police arrived, Gardner failed to properly inform them he had a concealed firearm.

Wayne said the incident didn't prove Gardner was a bad person or a career criminal. Instead, he noted that the charges against Gardner were dismissed or downgraded.

"That does not happen if he is Black, if he is James Scurlock," Wayne said. "A Black man would have been charged with who knows what—destruction of private property, resisting arrest, gun possession, or menacing. Then, he's in the system, and the system can be hard to escape."

Wayne at the time said he had no idea if Gardner was a racist. He couldn't say whether racial hatred of any kind played a role the night of May 30. What angered him was that, having just shot a young Black man to death, Gardner was released twenty-four hours later without even being booked. There was zero chance, Wayne said, that would have been the outcome if the races of the two men had been reversed. "No chance in hell," Wayne said.

"Racism can be blatant, in your face," Wayne said. "But systemic racism can be more subtle. Systemic racism can be the benefit of the doubt. And the fact that white people like Jake Gardner are the only ones who get it."

It wasn't lost on Wayne that the three white men in the room when it was decided Gardner would not be charged—Kleine and defense lawyers Monaghan and Dornan—had all served as prosecutors in Omaha and knew one another intimately. It felt like an inside job.

Wayne's skepticism of the system's fairness was only deepened when Kleine later released the results of Scurlock's autopsy showing he had evidence of cocaine and methamphetamine in his system. Traces of the drugs were found in his urine but not his blood, suggesting he was likely not high on the night of his death. If he had recently ingested the drugs, the evidence of them would have been found in his blood. Kleine had released the information at the request of the media, and was bound by law to provide it. To Wayne, though, it was just another white establishment trope—dehumanize or demonize a Black victim so the world would have even more reason not to care. Gardner had never had his breath or blood checked to see if he was impaired. Why was that? Wayne and others asked.

"Don Kleine has again chosen to victim blame by releasing the toxicology report of Scurlock and not Gardner," Wayne said in a statement. "By not addressing Gardner's toxicology report, Don Kleine is engaging in the exact implicit bias behavior that the country and our community is protesting. Through his actions, Kleine continues to color the public's perception of a Black victim, while protecting the public's perception of a white shooter."

TOMMY RILEY CAME to Omaha in 1975. After graduating from the Creighton law school, Riley went to work for the public defender's office. He tended bar at night to help pay the bills, and he decided for sure Omaha was the place for him when the owner of the bar, Fahey's, went on to be mayor of the city.

The public defender at the time was a Republican former governor of Nebraska, Frank Morrison. Riley figured it might be smart to stick around long term, for as he said, the job of defending the indigent and the city's people of color was at the time "a dead-end job for a Republican."

Riley, short, stocky, and a regular playing traditional music in

Omaha's Irish pubs, was right. He became chief deputy in 1983, and was elected public defender for Douglas County in 1996.

Riley says it's a busy office these days—thirty to forty homicides in a bad year, close to four thousand other felony cases, another fifteen thousand misdemeanor filings.

Riley, casually profane, stubbornly committed, has a dim view of the fairness of the criminal justice system in Omaha.

"Well, the Fourth Amendment's been pretty well eviscerated here," he said, referencing the Constitution's protections against improper police searches.

Riley said he watched the Black Lives Matter protests in Omaha in the summer of 2020 and asked himself: *Do they have a case against the police?* He thought they did. He knew they did.

Riley's lawyers, he said, were best positioned to make that case, and they could put together a powerful opening argument, alleging overly aggressive policing in North Omaha, the city's Black neighborhood; disparities dictated by class and race on matters of charging, sentencing, and the setting of bonds; judges cowed by the police union; a prosecutor's office more interested in pleasing the police than administering justice; jury pools that are overwhelmingly white for a daily churn of criminal cases against defendants who are overwhelmingly Black or Latino.

"A perfect example just today," said one of the collection of Riley's assistants who had gathered in a conference room.

A white man had been charged with sexually assaulting his granddaughter. The defendant had a private attorney, and his lawyer argued he suffered from dementia, and that his condition was a mitigating factor in what had happened with his grandchild. He got probation.

The public defender watched the outcome, looked at a colleague, and they both said it at once: "Doesn't happen if he's Black."

Such a Black defendant, the lawyers said, doesn't get a private attorney; his claim of dementia would be deemed an issue to be settled at a trial; no way does he get sentenced to mere probation without that actual trial.

Another of the office's lawyers said any discussion of justice in Omaha had to begin with the acknowledgment that it is a spectacularly segregated city. She'd gone to its local schools, and been bused to a high school in North Omaha. It felt to her like the right thing, an effort at leveling the playing field for students. But she never once saw a Black child in any of her honors classes. Segregation happened even within desegregation efforts.

"We were talking yesterday about if you're in North Omaha, the police presence is tenfold, probably more than that. If you're driving in North Omaha because you live in North Omaha, you're going to be pulled over at a much higher rate. They're going to be pulled over for very minor traffic infractions that could then lead to searching the car for whatever reason."

She had a recent example: two Black men had been stopped by police because "they didn't use their turn signal one hundred feet before turning into a residential driveway.

"I can't think of a time I have ever used a turn signal in my own neighborhood to go into my driveway. It's outrageous," she said.

The lawyers said African American colleagues or their spouses had found themselves stopped for no good reason by police, episodes that ended only when they'd turned over identification showing they worked for the defender's office or had gone to the Creighton law school.

Once Black defendants are arrested, Riley and his staff argued, prosecutors will routinely file the highest possible charges against them. Murders are almost invariably charged as first-degree, premeditated cases. Lesser felonies, Riley and his staff said, are similarly overcharged.

"Prosecutors have no incentive to file charges as warranted," Riley said. "They think they represent the victims in their cases. They don't. They represent the interests of justice."

The lawyers all but say it in unison: In Omaha, "the tail wags the dog." Prosecutors pursue cases as much to please the cops bringing them as anything else.

Here's one of the lawyers:

"Instead of the prosecutors deciding, when they read the police reports, 'Is this a valid case? What should I charge them with?' the cops argue with them, and they frequently accede to the wishes of the police department, whereas when I first started, the prosecutors would say, 'Fuck you. I'm running this show, not you.'"

Another of the public defenders said prosecutors often felt they had to clear potential plea deals on, say, a gun possession case with the arresting officers before proceeding. It was all backward, the lawyer said. Prosecutors were meant to be checks on cops.

"This is a checks-and-balances system, except that it's not anymore," she said.

And one of the breakdowns in the justice system's intended set of checks is the failure of judges to stand up to the police. The police union, the lawyers said, runs an unabashed and accomplished pressure campaign, posting on social media when they disagree with a judge's ruling in a case or their decision on sentencing.

In a city with a history of gang troubles, one of the lawyers said, "the police union is the biggest gang in town.

"What happens is, you're going to a sentencing hearing, and some of the judges will talk to you about what their sentence is going to be off the record beforehand. Some of them, when they have a weak moment, will admit, 'Jesus, if I give this guy what you're suggesting, I'm going to get crucified in the press, and the police union is going to be on my ass.' That's the reality of the situation. Now, they'll deny that until the cows come home."

The judges can be so intimidated that their behavior defies explanation.

In one case, the lawyers said, the conviction of a Black North Omaha man had been challenged because of a problem with his arrest, the lack of probable cause to have stopped the man in the first place. The prosecutors on appeal themselves conceded the error. The judge still would not revisit the conviction.

The lawyers said the police department's influence over prosecutors extends even to the very programs prosecutors have put in place to address the criminal justice system's shortcomings—drug courts that send defendants to treatment rather than jail; courts for young offenders that exist to figure out solutions other than felony convictions that will haunt youthful defendants for the rest of their lives.

Prosecutors, the lawyers in Riley's office assert, have to get the blessing of the arresting officers if they want to send a defendant to one of the specialized courts.

A case in point, one of the lawyers said, occurred one night when police responded to a report of a domestic dispute at a local motel. When police arrived, the woman who'd been assaulted by her boyfriend was both drunk and distraught. She resisted being restrained and lost her shirt in the course of the struggle. A victim of a prior sexual assault, she wound up causing a minor injury to one of the responding officers. She was charged with three felonies.

The public defender thought she was a perfect candidate for young adult court. She had no prior criminal record. She was struggling with mental health issues after her sexual assault. She consented to getting treatment. Prosecutors actually contacted the public defender to suggest the alternative court.

But the officers involved refused to go along.

"The officers are like, 'Absolutely not. No way,'" the public defender said.

The issues can seem endless. Jury pools have too few Blacks and Latinos, the lawyers for the indigent say. "Every time I pick a jury, the elephant in the room is race," said Riley. The police, meanwhile, have started to wear body cameras, but they often don't use them, or intentionally obscure the recordings when they do wear them, according to Riley's lawyers.

"If you just want to look at the basics to see the inequities, look at bonds. Look at the bond settings on felony cases," said one lawyer.

If you are white, with resources, there seems to be one category of bond. Another if you are Black or poor.

"It doesn't make any sense why they are so drastically different if you just look at the charges that come through every day. It makes more sense when you see the people that appear in front of the judges."

Don Kleine, the county attorney, disputed some of the claims about his office. But he wasn't surprised or offended. He doesn't pretend the system works perfectly, or even well.

For Riley's lawyers, even efforts meant to serve legitimate police aims, such as getting guns off the street, can be twisted into cynical traps for young people of color. A felony conviction would bar someone from legally obtaining a gun. And so cops will go to great, even improper lengths to produce one, the lawyers said.

Once, a lawyer said, police were at the house of a witness in a murder case.

"Keep in mind," she said, "this is not even someone they think is involved in the crime, but they go in and they search the house.

"And in one of the basement bedrooms, they find twelve or fourteen white pills. A cop goes, 'Hey, I think we got enough for a PWID here,' which is possession with intent to deliver, which is a serious felony. This is on a body cam, too. He's excited as hell: 'We're going to get this guy on a PWID.' He grabs one of the pills, and they have some app apparently where you can look at it. It was fucking Tylenol."

Riley said he has served on two committees in recent years ostensibly aimed at addressing Nebraska's prison population and its racial makeup. Nebraska is second in the nation in prison overcrowding. Blacks, who make up roughly 10 percent of Omaha's population, constitute more than 50 percent of those behind bars.

"The math is fucked up," Riley said.

In the fall of 2021, researchers laid out the math, finding in a formal report that Black Nebraskans were incarcerated at nearly nine times the per capita rate of white residents.

The report had a number of recommendations to correct the inequity, including ending arrests and prosecutions for low-level drug offenses.

"The particular drivers of disparity are known to be related to a mix of social policies that stretch beyond crime policies to those related to housing, education, receipt of public benefits, child care and employment," the report said.

The Nebraska American Civil Liberties Union office had done its own study years earlier. Its findings had the same kind of math Riley objected to.

"The ACLU remains deeply concerned that Nebraskans of color continue to be overrepresented in traffic stops and searches and that the trends of this troubling data are moving in the wrong direction year after year," the ACLU wrote.

The office found that Black drivers in Nebraska were nearly two times more likely to be stopped than white drivers. "The percentage of traffic stops conducted on Black drivers has continued to increase since 2013 despite the fact that Black drivers do not commit more crimes than white drivers," the office asserted.

Once stopped, Black drivers and their cars were disproportionately searched. Black drivers were three times more likely to be searched as a result of a traffic stop than a white driver. Native Americans were four times more likely.

Riley said the state committees on reform that he has served on have had these kinds of statistics for years. No meaningful reform has happened.

When James Scurlock was killed and Jake Gardner was not charged, the lawyers in the office were upset but not shocked. Again, to them, if the races were reversed, the outcome would have been different. Indeed, they'd just handled a case that to them proved the point.

The case involved a twenty-four-year-old Black woman who had been assaulted along with a friend by another woman she had already won a protective order against. During the assault on an Omaha street, she fired a gun, and the bullet wound up striking and killing a child seated in a nearby car. The woman who fired the gun had no record. She insisted she'd only fired the gun because she feared for her life. Her public defender claimed self-defense.

They got nowhere with that argument. She was charged with manslaughter and bond was set at half a million dollars.

AFTER KLEINE'S NEWS conference, Justin Wayne said his cell phone was vibrating nonstop. CNN wanted him to go on air; Fox News called, too. He turned down all the requests. He said prominent lawyers from around the country called offering their services, to the family or to any cause the family wanted to get behind. He had no use for them either. Wayne said the Reverend Al Sharpton in New York called.

"Sharpton said, 'I'm flying in,'" Wayne recalled. "I said, 'No, you're not.'

"Our position was, we are about process," Wayne said. "A thorough and complete investigation—that's a cornerstone of our judicial system."

The process Wayne wanted to see take place had to do with a distinctive feature of Nebraska law. Nebraska is one of six states that allow the citizens of the state to petition for a grand jury to investigate a possible crime. If a required number of signatures of registered voters is obtained, the presiding judge in the county can convene a grand jury.

One such citizen drive for a grand jury took place after the 1995 bombing of the federal building in Oklahoma City, when people believed the government had not adequately explored the scale and scope of the conspiracy behind the bombing carried out by Timothy McVeigh; another grand jury was empaneled in 2008 through a citizen drive in Wichita, Kansas, when activists wanted to investigate a prominent local abortion provider, George Tiller. Tiller, who at the time ran one of only three clinics in the nation to provide late-term abortions, was later shot to death in 2009 during a church service in Wichita.

Wayne, in the hours after Kleine's news conference, thought he had an idea about how he could help get enough signatures for a grand jury to be convened in Omaha. If it happened, a special prosecutor would be appointed to reexamine the evidence in the case of Scurlock's death.

Wayne's childhood in Omaha had introduced him to the issues he'd take on across his career as a politician—police misconduct, segregated schools, a Black political establishment that could be as much a hindrance as a help. He'd create a student newspaper in high school and edit it; he'd serve as president of the Black Law Students Association at the Creighton law school; he'd be elected to the Omaha public school board and then be named president. He'd be elected to the state's unicameral legislature and be as apt to make deals with Republicans as stand with Ernie Chambers, the self-styled Black radical out of North Omaha.

It's a proud, pugnacious career that began humbly enough. Wayne's birth mother had spent the last five months of her pregnancy at the Salvation Army Homeless Shelter at 24th and Pratt Street in Omaha, and Wayne soon after being delivered had been put up for adoption. Wayne's adoptive mother already had a young adopted boy when she showed up at the Nebraska Home for Children, and she was eager to add a girl.

The boy who would become Wayne's brother wound up wandering around the facility, and then finally standing by the crib holding Wayne. The boy wouldn't move. It seemed a sign. The plan to adopt a girl was abandoned, and Justin Wayne joined the family.

Wayne grew up in a neighborhood just outside the recognized boundaries of North Omaha; his Black dad cleaned buildings; his white mom was a bookkeeper. As a biracial child, he said, he could have the best and the worst of two worlds. He was accepted into the sports culture in North Omaha, with its legendary neighborhood basketball courts. But when he went with his parents and brother to visit his mother's family in Iowa, they were stigmatized as a mysterious menace.

As a student, Wayne had to navigate a school system long roiled by questions of race and equity. The question of segregated schools in Omaha, in fact, dated at least back to 1867, when an effort in the Nebraska Territorial Legislature to integrate education was soundly defeated.

"The people of Nebraska are not yet ready to send white boys and white girls to school to sit on the same seats with Negroes," the legislature wrote in its formal decision. "They are not yet ready to endorse in this tacit manner the dogma of miscegenation, especially are they far from ready to degrade their offspring to a level with so inferior a race."

A century later, the issue of equal access to education had yet to be resolved. In 1976, the U.S. Department of Justice sued the Omaha school system, and busing was ordered to at last effect the integration of the city's schools.

Wayne thinks busing in the end hurt Black Omaha more than it helped. It's been an emerging school of thought among academics and activists for years. Sending kids from one end of a city to another was a far more costly and complex answer to segregation than was truly required. Just spend equal amounts of money on all schools, Wayne thought.

For Wayne, busing meant Black kids in North Omaha were robbed of the Black teachers who might have best taught them. And it broke up the natural human contacts among people in a section of town such as North Omaha. Every morning of his boyhood in Omaha, Wayne saw kids standing on their own street corner waiting to be bused to some school across town. There were kids who lived down the block from him, Wayne said, who he never became friends with because they were bused to different schools.

"I just think that happened all across America, but for Omaha, it was unique because we bused so many people," Wayne said.

Wayne said when he later served on the school board he learned Omaha spent more money on busing for its schools than it did on public transportation for the entire city.

For Wayne, school as a kid was hit-or-miss. He went to a magnet middle school, only to then have to repeat the science classes he took there when he got to his neighborhood high school. The high school didn't even have the computers the middle school had.

What kind of backwards shit is this? he remembers thinking at the time.

If his school experience was inconsistent, Wayne's dealings with the police were consistently terrible. Two incidents stand out.

Wayne's older brother one year was jumped by some neighborhood toughs, and a gun was accidentally fired. The cops came to the house to arrest Wayne's brother.

"When they came to arrest my brother, they came in with tactical and probably twenty officers surrounding our house. You have all these cops and cruisers like Ted Bundy's in the house or some shit. And they knocked on the door and I answered. They asked if they can come in. And I said, 'My parents aren't here, no.' And I pulled the screen door shut. They ended up coming in. So the search was thrown out because they weren't allowed to come in our house. They didn't have a warrant."

The charge against Wayne's brother went nowhere, but it took time and money to fight what to him was a manufactured crime.

"A middle-class family has to bankrupt itself fighting a bullshit case," Wayne said.

Almost as bad, both Wayne and his brother wound up having their names put in the Omaha Police Department's gang file. Be stopped by the police; be related to someone investigated for a crime; be in a park with someone wearing gang colors. Any or all of it can result in being entered into the department's database. It was, and is, routine in North Omaha, Wayne said. Years later, Wayne, in an appearance in court on behalf of a client, tried to make a point by relating to the judge that he, to that day, was in the department's gang file. The judge didn't believe him. He had a police officer in court confirm it.

"How in the hell is an attorney who is on the school board in the gang file?" the judge asked out loud.

"It just showed how crazy it was," Wayne said.

Wayne over the years tried his best to see that the way the world worked made more sense, that what should happen did happen. Now Wayne wanted a grand jury convened to investigate Scurlock's death. That's the way things should work. When it became public that Wayne was representing the Scurlock family, he was being contacted night and day by people who said they had some relevant information. He created an email account for people to submit their information, and he turned over all of the incoming messages to the Omaha Police Department. Kleine could not have run down every tip or eyewitness account in the thirty-six hours it took him to announce Gardner's freedom, Wayne concluded.

Online, a spontaneous petition to convene a grand jury gained tens of thousands of signatures, including from people overseas. But something a lot more formal would be needed. Wayne would have to have registered Nebraska voters. And a lot of them.

Then the idea struck him: Earlier in 2020, there had been a move to legalize marijuana in Nebraska. It would be done by referendum. But COVID had upended the plans, and the referendum had been postponed. Wayne thought he might be able to use the logistical infrastructure that had been organized for the marijuana referendum to amass the number of signatures he'd need for a grand jury to be convened. He liked his chances.

Over the years, Wayne had grown friendly with a Black federal prosecutor named Frederick Franklin. Franklin was a Creighton Law graduate like he was, and he had been just the second Black prosecutor to work in the U.S. Attorney's Office in Omaha. Franklin, sixty-six, had helped Wayne with a nonprofit sports organization Wayne had founded for kids in North Omaha. Franklin had even helped put up lawn signs during one of Wayne's political campaigns.

Franklin lived not far from Wayne's downtown law office, and so

Wayne took a walk. He made it to Franklin's place, and wanted to talk strategy. Franklin stopped him cold. If a petition drive for a grand jury succeeded, those in charge might want a Black lawyer to serve as the special prosecutor to run the grand jury. There was not a surplus of options in Omaha. Franklin would likely be at the top of the list. He told Wayne he'd have to wait and see before talking further about any strategy.

"It's All You All's Family"

On June 10, roughly ten days after Scurlock's killing, an Omaha lawyer named Ryan Wilkins posted an article online. Wilkins said he had gone to high school with Jake Gardner and until recently had been Facebook friends with him. He assumed he'd see Gardner at their upcoming twentieth class reunion. Now Wilkins was eager to tell the world about Gardner and to call for his arrest for shooting James Scurlock. The piece ran to nearly fifteen hundred words, and drew heavily on a conversation Wilkins had had with someone he described as Gardner's cousin: "We both believe criminal charges against Jake—her cousin and my former classmate—are warranted in this case due to a critical, so-far-under-reported piece of the puzzle: Jake, the killer and instigator, is racist."

The post got basic facts wrong but began from the premise that Gardner and other local businessmen had been warned against going downtown to protect their properties:

> *Gardner nonetheless came, illegally carrying a concealed weapon and declaring on Facebook he was ready "to pull 48 hours of military style firewatch"; Gardner confronted the unarmed Scurlock and others, accusing them of vandalizing his bar—even though he had no evidence that they had vandalized his bar, and in fact they had not vandalized his bar; Gardner's father revved-up the verbal altercation into a physical one, twice shoving a woman near*

Scurlock before another group member pushed him back; and when Gardner showed his gun and began firing shots, Scurlock—at all times unarmed, and until then completely removed from the physical conflict— jumped on his back, at which point Gardner shot and killed him.

Racism aside, this case's potential precedent—that someone could bring a gun he was not authorized to carry to a location he was not supposed to be, start a fight, show and fire a weapon, and then justifiably kill anybody who tries to intervene and disarm him—should be deeply disturbing to anyone.

But more importantly, racism absolutely cannot be set aside here. Because the shooter, Jake Gardner, is racist. And his racism is crucial to understanding his criminal culpability.

Wilkins then laid out the supposed evidence of Gardner's racism, much of which involved Yelp reviews of The Hive, and complaints about discrimination in the dress codes and door policy. He included screen grabs of some of the reviews, many of which dated back years. Wilkins also cited Gardner's online claim that the Black Lives Matter movement was a terrorist organization.

Given his stance, when Jake shoots and kills an unarmed black man during a BLM protest, are we to chalk this up to mere-coincidence?

Wilkins then invoked claims he'd heard from a relative of Gardner's about how their family was a collection of virulent racists. It was the same woman who had posted Gardner's telephone number online in the hours after the killing. She had used the Twitter handle Juniper Fitzgerald and described herself as a cousin to Gardner and a former sex worker.

Her name was actually Jennifer Heineman, and she is a professor at the University of Nebraska Omaha. Her online biography says she "joined UNO as full-time faculty in 2016 after receiving her PhD in Sociology from the University of Las Vegas, Nevada. Her academic and activist work focuses on labor rights, gender, sexuality, and feminist theory more generally."

Days after the shooting, Heineman appeared at an open hearing of the state senate's judiciary committee, which had invited the public to speak out about the days of protests, police action, and Scurlock's death. She spoke for five minutes, with notes and binders in her hands. She again said she was a cousin of Gardner's but did not describe their connection further:

"I am here today to offer my expertise on social movements. I am also here today to talk about my family and I encourage the other white people in this room and on this panel to think about yourselves and your white families as well. I also have a question for the white people on this panel. So first my expertise, we know that social movements like the one we are all bearing witness to don't just come out of thin air. It takes years of being silenced and policed and surveilled. It takes years, decades, generations of violence. Violence, without any accountability to see the kind of organizing and movement that we are seeing today. None of this is an accident. And in the history books that your children's children will read, they will learn that this was a momentous moment and they will want to know where great-grandma and great-grandpa were when all of this was happening. But let me tell you what you don't want. You don't want to be sleepless and disturbed in the ways that I am today. Every time I try to sleep, all I can think about is James Scurlock's little girl, who is close in age to my own child and to whom I am forever indebted. I spend my entire waking life now knowing that my family did this, knowing that all the times my family members used the N-word, which was a lot, all of the times that my family made racist jokes, all of the times that my family ingrained violence into the minds and hearts and souls of their own babies, all of those things were leading up to the death of James. The depth of grief that comes with knowing that your family has the capacity to do this is a kind of grief that I do not wish on any of you. And so I am here to tell you, fellow white people, that this movement is happening in response to us, in response to our families.

I have no doubt that many of the white people in this room consider themselves to be not a racist. And that's great, but none of this is about one person. None of this is about whether you personally are racist or not. When we say that racism is systemic, this is what we mean. It is so ingrained in our culture that literally any one of your family members, if you are white, could have done this. If you don't want to end up in my situation, which is to say incredibly troubled, you have got to start listening. And not just to the voices of protesters, but to the things your own family says behind closed doors . . . I think that in this conversation that is inherently about accountability, I am here because my family did this. I want to be accountable and I want my family to be accountable. And I want you to be accountable. And I want you to tell me what you're going to do, because it's not just my family. It's all you all's white family."

Heineman never named any of her family members other than Gardner. She did not detail how exactly she was related to him. It was unclear whether she was talking about her own parents, or uncles or aunts or grandparents. Or his. Or what exactly it meant to ingrain violence in the family's babies. She did not allege anything specific to Gardner—how close she was to him, if at all, what she might have ever heard him say or do, what the alleged assault charges were he was supposedly guilty of.

Wilkins, having just met a woman who said she was Gardner's cousin, clearly had adopted her take on the family's racism. In his post he called it "Ever-present, always-understood, and frankly so obvious that the issue never needed to be analyzed or discussed."

Wilkins in his post also suggested that he'd made a concerted effort to talk to people who were at the scene of the shooting—a bartender who said Dave Gardner had called protesters "N lovers," a Hispanic person who said Jake Gardner had told him to "kiss his white ass."

Wilkins then referenced his legal training:

> *I have limited but impactful criminal-law experience: In law school I studied advanced criminal procedure, interned in the St. Louis*

County Public Defender's Office, and clerked for a federal judge. In private practice I represented a handful of inmates and criminal defendants, pro bono. I once hoped to be a federal prosecutor.

Thus armed, he laid out his legal analysis, citing Nebraska self-defense laws:

Under Nebraska law, deadly force "shall not be justified" except as necessary to protect oneself from death or serious bodily harm; I'm not convinced the evidence shows James Scurlock ever posed such a threat to Jake Gardner. Moreover, self-defense is unavailable where the shooter, with the purpose of seriously harming another, "provoked the use of force against himself in the same encounter." I believe substantial evidence suggests Gardner purposely started the very fight that he ended with his gun, again negating his self-defense claim. I do not doubt that our public prosecutors face legitimate obstacles in convicting Gardner. But I believe it's absolutely vital that they charge him and try.

Wilkins offered an explanation for why he had decided to get involved in the case. He'd watched the recent news of a Black man's killing in Georgia, and had "made a promise I would work to be better at calling out racism wherever I found it."

He then finished up the post:

So here it is, my former classmate, in my own backyard: Jake Gardner is racist, his racism is highly relevant in assessing his motive, intent, and the legitimacy of his self-defense claim in the killing of an unarmed black man at a BLM protest, and he deserves criminal prosecution.

Wilkins was only just beginning what amounted to a single citizen's case against Jake Gardner. Days later, Wilkins posted again, an article twice as long, with pictures and graphics, all of which he said added up to "a damning, evidence-based account of deeply entrenched family racism, unabashed white-supremacy allegiances embedded in the shooter's business enterprises, and the haphazard initial investigation that cleared the shooter of any criminal charges."

Wilkins revealed that he had been contacted via text by a second Gardner family member, someone he would not name. He printed the text:

> *This has been tearing me apart ever since James Scurlock was murdered by Jake, and I use that term because I have no doubt that both Jake and his father went downtown looking for trouble. From my experience with the family, they would love nothing more than to have an excuse to use their guns against any minority. They've been looking for this chance.*

Wilkins said he had spoken over several days with the second supposed Gardner relative, calling the person Taylor, and what he'd heard, he said, "was credible, specific, and stunning." He began with Dave Gardner, Jake's father:

> *In the early-80s, Dave got busted and did time in a Texas prison. Among the family, it became common knowledge that his racist views were reinforced behind bars, where he rubbed shoulders with white supremacists. At family events like holidays, conversations were common about how "those n-words" would have killed Dave without those white brothers.*
>
> *Dave Gardner, Jake's father, is a former drug-trafficker. He sold large quantities of marijuana from El Paso, Texas for years, sending some to Omaha for distribution—even by family members. It was a full-scale operation that Taylor regularly witnessed: "Weed, scales, bags, deseeding trays—it was just a fact of life." According to open family conversation, by the early-80s Dave had inherited a job trucking large loads of marijuana into Omaha along the I-80 corridor from Humboldt County, California—the crown jewel of*

the "Emerald Triangle," the largest cannabis-producing region in the United States, and a known bastion of white supremacy.

When Jake was still in high school, he sometimes joined his father on I-80 drug runs between Humboldt and Omaha. "I remember this was big gossip in the family," Taylor said. "Not if it was wrong to be a drug dealer, but if Jake wasn't too young to be involved." Dave was "always a really intense father," and he pushed Jake to join the Marines. "He wanted Jake to be cut from the same mold as himself—and he really wanted him to have that weapons training," Taylor recalled. After leaving the Marines, Jake moved to Humboldt County—where Dave continued to pick up drug hauls— and attended school at Humboldt State University. "Coincidence?," Taylor asked, rhetorically. . . .

". . . I have heard horrendous things from family members about what should happen to minorities, or what they would do during a race riot. Maybe for some it was drunk, angry talk. But for Dave, it wasn't just talk. It was deep hatred." When Taylor saw the video of Jake's shooting of James Scurlock, she "knew in an instant" that he and Dave had inserted themselves into the Black Lives Matter protest "to antagonize people and push a fight." "He was there to do all the things he had long threatened to do," Taylor said. "It was horrifying, but no surprise to me after watching and listening to him for years."

Wilkins had more. He said he had talked with the Black barback who had accused Gardner of racism after he'd been fired from his job at The Hive. Before he'd left, though, the man told Wilkins he'd been clued in to "something more sinister." The bar had created some promotional material in which the logo for The Hive contained Nazi codes. The man told Wilkins two white co-workers had let him in on the secret.

The logo in the materials allegedly discreetly contained the numbers 1488, the 14 referencing the 14 bedrock words for white supremacists: "We must secure the existence of our people and a future for white children," the 88 referencing the "88 Precepts," for securing an all-white state.

"Once identified, it cannot be unseen," Wilkins wrote as he broke down his analysis. "The harsh, industrial, serifed numerals '1' and '4' embedded in the 'H'—at odds with the curvy, playful, sans-serif font completing the word. The overlapping '8s' vertically honeycombed to complete the white supremacist's rally cry."

There was more. Gardner, Wilkins wrote, had a swastika tattoo. Jews weren't allowed in the family home. Three former friends of Gardner had told Wilkins so. Wilkins said he'd been reliably told Gardner got an armed escort to Omaha's airport after he was released by the cops and fled the city. He repeated once more the claims of the witnesses to the shooting he'd spoken with: Gardner had picked the fight; there was no need for him to shoot Scurlock; Scurlock was a hero for trying to disarm an active shooter.

Wilkins's original post on June 10 about Gardner received over seventy-five hundred shares. However, the second article Wilkins published on June 19 gained more traction. People shared it widely online, and thus well beyond Omaha.

"Required reading for today. Learn how a racist is getting away with murder in my hometown of Omaha, NE," someone posted.

"This is long but it's definitely worth the read," said another, linking to the article.

"Fucking racist had kkk shit embedded into his logo," said one more, subscribing to the allegations made by Wilkins.

The article was shared by some activists as evidence of Gardner's guilt.

"Omaha, do not forget a young, black father was killed on our streets downtown for trying to disarm a known white supremacist," wrote one. "Have you called your officials? Have you donated to black orgs? Have you protested in ways you are able?"

The depiction of Gardner posted online by Wilkins would become a dominant narrative of who Jake Gardner was, and what was behind his killing of James Scurlock. The Scurlock family accepted it.

The echo chamber of the Internet amplified it. Local politicians even got on board.

Megan Hunt, the state senator who had tangled with Gardner over the transgender bathroom issue, lamented that the decision not to charge Gardner meant his freedom would only embolden other white supremacists like him, she said.

"White supremacist groups, including ones Jake Gardner was in communication with, rely on you thinking none of this is a big deal so they can organize their support," she wrote on Twitter. "They have been successful: white supremacist violence now makes up the majority of domestic terror in the US."

"The Times Today Are Very Different"

IN THE END, IT DID NOT take Don Kleine long to realize his decision not to charge Jake Gardner would not be the last word on the case. There were protesters outside his house. He'd successfully run for four terms as Douglas County Attorney, and he could count votes. A public petition to convene a grand jury would likely succeed, he figured. Some of those who had shared his analysis of the evidence were backtracking.

At a meeting convened by Gov. Pete Ricketts with Black community leaders and some of the Omaha Police Department brass, the city's police chief, who had endorsed Kleine's choice not to prosecute Gardner, threw Kleine under the bus. A recording of the meeting was made public, and on it the chief, Todd Schmaderer, could be heard telling the governor and the Black leaders that he actually had tried to get Kleine to pursue charges.

Kleine and his deputy, Brenda Beadle, were taken aback. Beadle heard the recording played on a local radio broadcast while she was in her car. Kleine and Beadle had worked closely day in and day out with the OPD, and its boss. That Schmaderer had decided not to show up at the news conference announcing Kleine's decision not to charge was disappointing, but maybe understandable. His officers might have been targeted in any protests or violence after the announcement if they had stood with the prosecutors.

But now he was rewriting history.

Beadle had been Kleine's deputy for the entirety of his time in office. She had worked every corner of the office, including time spent working on civil commitments for the mentally ill. She was considered a pro's pro, and a fearless champion of Kleine. When Kleine and Beadle later met with the police chief, Beadle let him have it. What he'd done in the meeting with Ricketts and others was dirty pool, and the act of a coward.

"Pretty chickenshit," she told Schmaderer.

The chief stormed off, not keen on being dressed down by a woman.

Kleine decided he needed to get in front of any movement to convene a grand jury and appoint a special prosecutor. Kleine asked for a meeting with Omaha's presiding judge, Shelly Stratman. In her chambers, he told her he was consenting to a grand jury.

"She looked at me, and said, okay, who's going to be special prosecutor," Kleine said of Stratman.

They both acknowledged it might be helpful to the process for the special prosecutor to be Black. Fred Franklin's name was all but instantly raised. Franklin was the former federal prosecutor Justin Wayne had gone to seeking advice on strategy in representing the Scurlock family. Kleine knew Franklin, and liked him. Franklin had only recently retired from the federal prosecutor's office in town, and would likely be available.

"Fred Franklin is a good man," Kleine said. "Do whatever you need to do, Judge."

After the meeting, Kleine consulted with the current U.S. Attorney in Omaha. Kleine said the man who had most recently been Franklin's boss openly wondered if Franklin was built for the job. "Fred's not a ball of fire," he said to Kleine. "And he doesn't have a lot of experience doing cases like this."

But Stratman, the presiding judge, had made her decision.

Soon, Kleine was once again in front of the local media to announce the decision to convene a grand jury.

"I've always worked hard to do the right thing and I don't believe this office should be political nor should it ever bend to pressure of any kind," he said. "We make decisions solely and only based on the evidence and what the law is. I've never been somebody to pass the buck. I've always felt the responsibility to make these kinds of decisions no matter how difficult the case might be. One thing, though, that I've learned about this job and life generally is that I listen. And I do listen."

He told the reporters he had asked for a grand jury.

"The times today are very different than I've ever seen in the tenure that I've been here at this office, both locally and nationally. I believe in our system of justice. And I realize it's not perfect, but I realize also that many others do not have the same faith in the system that I do. I was elected to make these difficult decisions. And I'm not wavering in any way in the decision that we've made on this case or the findings. However, I am not afraid of having a decision that I've made reviewed by others. Therefore, I welcome and support the calling of a grand jury to review the evidence in this rare instance."

He said the decision carried some risk, that it might be seen as a precedent for other cases whose outcomes might disappoint some segment of the public.

"One of the fears about this part of the process is that we make decisions every day on very difficult cases. And so it's not a situation where just because somebody is unhappy with a decision I've made that we're going to call a grand jury, but it's more about a systems question. I think that people generally have a question about the criminal justice system. And I would like to do everything I can to assure people that the system works the way it should work."

For all the generous words, it was a bitter pill for Kleine to swallow.

Don Kleine could not believe how he had been portrayed—a racist, a tool in an unfair criminal justice system, an abetter of a white supremacist. Whether it was warranted or not, Kleine was nonetheless dumbstruck by the blowback.

He had long befriended the Black pastors in North Omaha, and listened to them when they came to his office to ask for leniency for a good kid who had done something regrettable. He'd overseen nearly four hundred cases involving felony convictions where his office agreed to a sentence that did not involve incarceration. His office ran what is called an "open-file" policy with defense lawyers—granting them access to investigative material on cases early in the process. As a defense lawyer earlier in his career, he had won acquittals for two Black defendants who had killed someone and claimed self-defense. He'd even won an acquittal in the kind of case that had too often been poisoned by racism. A Black man had been accused of serially abusing white children. Kleine not only took the case but prevailed.

Kleine said he'd rejected the ugly dismissiveness with which other politicians in town regarded North Omaha, people he said who had suggested the city "just build a fence around North Omaha and let them do whatever they are going to do to each other."

Kleine had his office run some numbers, and he presented them at the news conference. There had been twenty-seven Omaha cases over the last decade, he said, in which people had been found to have acted in self-defense after killing someone; eighteen of those found to have legally defended themselves were Black.

Kleine liked to note that his office had more Black prosecutors than ever in its history. He was godfather to a child of one of those former Black prosecutors—Darryl Lowe, who had gone on to serve as a judge in Omaha. Lowe had been a mentor to Justin Wayne, the Scurlock family's lawyer.

Lowe had grown up in Montgomery, Alabama, and Atlanta. He'd waited on line at Spelman College to pay his respect to Martin Luther King Jr. after his assassination. When Lowe first came to Omaha to go to the Creighton law school, he considered the experience a real-life version of the TV series *Mayberry R.F.D.* As a young Black prosecutor in the county attorney's office, he'd seen and felt the snide racism of the white prosecutors he worked alongside and the judges he appeared before.

He was an aggressive prosecutor but was not blind to the overrepresentation of Black people in the cases that were brought to him by Omaha police. Lowe said that after he left the office and got word of a promising Black law student at Creighton, Kleine would take his call and make the effort to recruit some of them he similarly determined to be talented.

"Don Kleine doesn't have a racist bone in his body," Lowe said.

Brenda Beadle stood with Kleine at his latest news conference. She, like her boss, was offended and confounded by the attacks against Kleine, the calls for his resignation, the suggestion he was just another cynical white prosecutor comfortable with the system's flaws and prejudices.

Over her years of prosecuting major felony cases, Beadle had used the back of her office door to post pictures of the murdered men and women, boys and girls, she had sought justice for. The panels of pictures are almost all of Black victims. There was Amber Harris, a twelve-year-old girl whose murderer she and Kleine had helped get convicted and sentenced to death. Brittany Williams was there, too. She'd been shot dead while getting food at a Kentucky Fried Chicken restaurant by a white man who had sat in wait, rifle and scope in hand. He'd been enraged by a call made by a Black referee in a Green Bay Packers football game he'd been watching on television. He was going to shoot the first Black he could find.

Beadle had heard over the years the criticism that the police arrested, and prosecutors convicted, a disproportionate number of Black people. She conceded there are problems with fairness and competence in the criminal justice system. But, as she liked to say, the answer was not to stop incarcerating people who commit real and often-violent crimes. The majority of such crimes happen in Omaha's poorer neighborhoods of color. Black residents there are the victims. She won't stop seeking justice for them or apologize for it.

Kleine agreed to take questions. A reporter asked whether the case ought to be moved out of Omaha.

"I'd like to think that the community and the people in this community want justice, whatever that justice might be, just like we do. And I certainly think that when jurors or grand jurors take an oath, that that's what they're supposed to do, that they'll follow the law."

Kleine was asked if any new evidence had surfaced. He said not much and the additional evidence had tended to support his decision not to charge.

A reporter wanted to know if he had felt pressured to make the move he had.

"I don't think it's ever succumbing to pressure when you just try and do the best thing, the right thing, and, more than anything, have people be assured that justice is going to be done here, no matter what that might be. You know, sometimes it's not what people like. They have this thought process in their head as to what they think should be the result here, but the result is based on what the evidence is and what the law is. And we don't have a problem with anybody, whether it's the Department of Justice doing a review of this case or a grand jury or whoever it might be; we'll be transparent about it. That's part of the process."

In short order, Fred Franklin was announced as the man to run the grand jury inquiry. Franklin, tall, with a tiny gray goatee, had the bearing of a onetime athlete, and the deliberate demeanor of a preacher.

At a news conference, Franklin said he was impressed by the amount of work the police department had done in investigating the case. He called it voluminous.

Franklin said he wasn't concerned by all the volatile stuff about the case that had been appearing online. He said he wasn't on either Facebook or Twitter. He said he was both outraged by George Floyd's killing and sympathetic with Omaha's business owners who had seen their establishments vandalized and trashed. He lived in downtown Omaha, and had seen what had happened.

"To those who use protests, peaceful protests, to hide and get into riotous behavior, I would suggest that you are doing harm to the cause," Franklin said.

Wayne, Franklin's friend and the Scurlock family's lawyer, issued a statement approving Franklin's appointment, calling him "an attorney and litigator that I greatly respect.

"Justice requires time and resources," Wayne said, adding that he hoped Franklin would be given all the assistance and expert help Kleine had been afforded.

"Uniquely Suited"

FRED FRANKLIN GREW UP ON THE South Side of Chicago, the only boy and the oldest of four children. His mother and father had come up from Mississippi during the Great Migration, and while neither had a high school degree, they had built a solid working-class life. His father, a Navy veteran from World War II, worked as a machinist, and his mother cared for the children. She had help from Franklin's paternal grandmother.

Franklin said he often had long conversations with his grandmother and by the time he was thirteen those conversations had turned to what he was going to do with his life. She wanted him to be either a doctor or a preacher. He told her he wasn't cut out to be a doctor.

"As for being a preacher, I told her you have to be called by God, and that as far as I knew, I hadn't been called by anybody," Franklin said.

"She laughed," Franklin recalled, "and said, well, I best be a lawyer."

Franklin got the call he had told Justin Wayne he calculated he would get. The presiding judge in Omaha contacted him asking if he'd be interested in being the special prosecutor to oversee the grand jury investigation of James Scurlock's death.

"I felt I was not only competent, but uniquely suited," Franklin said.

One, he said, he was a former federal prosecutor who had made many presentations to grand juries. Two, he was Black. Still, he thought it best to run the idea by his family one night over dinner.

"My kids were actually surprised to learn their dad was a big deal," he said, laughing.

The family signed off.

Franklin had gone to the Creighton law school. Creighton, for him, still had the shine of being known as the "Harvard of the Midwest." Franklin sold real estate to make ends meet in law school, and entertained the idea of going into real estate development.

Greg Rhodes, a law school student ahead of Franklin, was delighted at Franklin's arrival. There was not an overabundance of Black students, and Rhodes was from Chicago's South Side as well.

"I did a little jig," Rhodes said upon Franklin's coming to Omaha.

Out of law school, though, Franklin wound up doing a mix of private practice work— some criminal defense, some personal injury. But the U.S. Attorney's Office recruited him to join the Department of Justice, and he soon became just the second African American to work in the Omaha office. Rhodes, it happened, had been the first.

Franklin's appointment as special prosecutor, then, was well received by many, including by one of Gardner's defense lawyers, Tom Monaghan. Monaghan, it turned out, was the U.S. Attorney who had recruited and hired Franklin.

"We thought Fred was a pretty good lawyer, and he came from a different background than many prosecutors," Monaghan said. "Our office needed it." He said the office was mostly filled with white former county prosecutors. "I wanted to change the culture a bit," Monaghan said.

Franklin did two decades working both criminal and civil cases— white-collar crime; drug cases; employment discrimination; immigration; serial bank fraud; identity theft. He had a couple of big wins against top local defense lawyers, including a very successful, endlessly self-promoting lawyer named James Martin Davis.

"Fred kicked his ass," Monaghan said.

Franklin said taking the federal job amounted to taking a pay cut. But he liked the formidable resources the office could bring to bear on investigations and cases, and he knew he'd learn how to litigate.

"I probably had the most varied workload of anyone in that office," Franklin said. "Money has never been a motivating factor. I'm not a person of extravagant needs."

Franklin figured he could always return to private practice if he wanted, likely with sharpened skills and a reputation before the federal bench.

One federal judge said he considered Franklin a more than competent lawyer. He said Franklin had his own style, that he didn't wear his ambition on his sleeve the way some other hard-charging Assistant U.S. Attorneys did. He was not the kind of prosecutor to buck the system, which his superiors must have appreciated. And juries liked him, even if his manner of speaking could sometimes seem discombobulated.

"Fred sometimes started his sentences at the end and then worked them back around to the beginning," the judge said.

Darryl Lowe, the Creighton graduate and former prosecutor who rose to be a judge in Omaha, agreed.

"Smart, hardworking, always gave measured answers," Lowe said of Franklin. "He was always thinking."

The federal judge said anyone alleging Franklin was a subpar lawyer was guilty of racist stereotyping.

"Omaha's a racist city, simple as that," the judge, who is white, said. "And the local bar is no different."

The judge said Franklin often would choose compassion over submitting to the wishes of superiors who might have wanted more aggressive and punitive outcomes.

Franklin, though, was not universally admired by his colleagues. One government lawyer who worked alongside Franklin for six years questioned Franklin's work ethic and his commitment to seeking true justice in every case. Those in the FBI, he said, often didn't like working with Franklin as a result.

"Many agents did not like working with Fred because he never worked prosecutions very diligently and he never liked going to trial, particularly on tough cases," the lawyer, Christian Martinez, said. "Fred would give very favorable plea agreements on the eve of trial. The federal agents who presented the case wanted those cases prosecuted to the fullest extent of the law."

One longtime member of the U.S. Attorney's Office said Franklin was on no one's list to do something as significant and detailed as running the training seminars the feds conducted with local law enforcement agencies.

"Fred was a likable guy," the person said. "But Fred was out for Fred." The person said Franklin saw the special prosecutor's job in the Scurlock case as a "payday" more than anything else.

Without question, though, Franklin had become a respected, even revered figure in Black Omaha. Rhodes, his friend and colleague, said Franklin single-handedly revived Omaha's Black bar association. He hosted meet-and-greet receptions at his home for Black incoming Creighton Law students. He ran a book club. Rhodes said Franklin, while in private practice, routinely took on clients he knew could not pay his fee. Franklin lived in North Omaha, the city's Black neighborhood, and his daughters went to public schools.

"I've met a lot of people who say things but don't mean them," Rhodes said. "They don't stand for them. They don't take up unpopular causes. They do what's politic, what's popular, what will help them. Some people talk a lot and do little. Fred talked a lot and did a lot. Fred took no bows." When it came to receiving or needing credit, Rhodes said, Franklin didn't carry "a sign with his name on it."

Franklin, indeed, loved Omaha. Or he certainly fit in comfortably. Franklin was a Harley guy, and a member of an Omaha motorcycle club. He was, too, likely the only Black member of one of the city's prominent car clubs. He considered Omaha emblematic of many midsized American cities. Race was an issue, but not one as raw or explosive as it was in his native Chicago.

Franklin was confident in taking on the job of special prosecutor.

He said the presiding judge told him he had been at the top of her list, and that there had been a big gap between him and any second choice. Franklin said he recognized it had the potential to be a no-win assignment, but he felt a sense of duty. If he encountered racism in his efforts—from the police, the public, Gardner's supporters—he would confront it head-on.

"God watches over me and protects me from the nonsense," he said of his life in Omaha to date. "If I'm confronted with nonsense, I'll deal with it. I understand injustice, and believe in trying to force the country to live out the principles on which it was founded."

Brenda Council, who had been the first Black woman elected to the city council, said her respect for Franklin was only deepened by his decision to take on the case. It was, she said, evidence of his integrity.

"He didn't have to do it, didn't have to subject himself to all that scrutiny," she said. "He did it because he believes in justice."

Not everyone was sanguine about Franklin's prospects for success. Monaghan, Gardner's attorney and Franklin's former mentor, said Omaha was a divided city to begin with and its chasms had only widened with the Scurlock killing. Producing an outcome that would please all felt like a long shot.

"Omaha has come a long, long way," Monaghan said. "It has a long, long way to go. There's white Omaha; there's Black Omaha. You can't meld them."

Franklin was assigned two retired Omaha Police Department detectives to be his investigators. He was promised the full support of the police department.

Don Kleine, for one, wasn't sure Franklin understood the nature and obligations of his assignment. He said Franklin called him after being named and suggested the two men hold a joint news conference. Kleine told him that was unwise. Franklin's existence as special prosecutor was premised on independence from Kleine.

Does he get it? Kleine said to himself.

Kleine came to suspect Franklin was not aware of all he might have to do.

"Look, Fred," he told Franklin, "you indict this case, you understand you're going to be the one trying this case?"

Franklin, Kleine said, responded cryptically, saying, "Well, I don't know about that."

"This Is Not a Time for Celebration"

On the afternoon of September 15, 2020, Fred Franklin appeared in the same city legislative chambers where Don Kleine had earlier announced there would be no charges filed against Jake Gardner. Franklin's investigation and presentation to the grand jury had lasted more than three months, hampered in part by continuing restrictions involving the COVID-19 pandemic.

Justin Wayne, the lawyer for the Scurlock family, had called Franklin earlier when he got wind that an announcement was forthcoming. Wayne told Franklin he thought the family needed to know the outcome first. Franklin told Wayne he would not prematurely divulge the results he was about to declare to the public.

Inside the chambers, Franklin took off his jacket, saying nothing. He walked and waited and checked his phone. He exited, then returned. He was now ready to go.

"I got the phone call," he said.

Whatever the grand jury had decided, it was now official.

"I've been given strict instructions not to make any comments until after that event had occurred," Franklin said of the call. "But the grand jurors did reach a decision this afternoon, and I'm here to generally outline what they did decide. But before I do that, what I want to do is to give you guys a little bit of an understanding of what the grand jurors, the evidence that they received, and generally what the process was."

Franklin first recounted his version of the case history. He said Don Kleine had decided there would be no charges against Jake Gardner "because there was a determination that the action by Jake Gardner was self-defense." Franklin made a point of saying Kleine had been open to that determination changing, and that the Omaha Police Department had kept the investigation going.

Franklin said the police had interviewed sixty people "in conjunction with this homicide investigation." He said he had worked with two "very experienced retired Omaha police officers." He added that they had looked at some number of "video clips from members of the public.

"I can tell you that the grand jury, at the point in time that they made their decision, it's almost a slam dunk that they had much more information available to them than what was had at the time that the initial decision was made," Franklin said.

"The grand jury returned an indictment today against Jake Gardner, and that indictment charges the following counts. The first-count charge is manslaughter in connection with the death of James Scurlock. The second charge, or the second-count charge, is the use of a firearm in the commission of a felony. The third count that they decided to charge was attempted first-degree assault. And the fourth charge, or count, is terroristic threats."

Franklin said he could not discuss the evidence but that he wanted the reporters and the public "to have some understanding of what those particular counts connect with as it relates to what's understood out there about what ended up happening on May 30 of 2020 down in the Old Market."

Franklin said the terroristic threat count "essentially addresses the conduct of Jake Gardner in the verbal confrontation with James Scurlock at a point where a firearm was brandished and, ultimately, displayed. It includes the commentary, the back-and-forth between the two of them."

Franklin said he of course did not participate in any deliberations with the jury but said the jury came "to understand that Jake Gardner was threatening the use of deadly force in the absence of being threatened with a concomitant deadly force by James Scurlock or anyone who was associated with him."

The attempted first-degree assault count, Franklin said, was "tied to the shot that has been characterized as a warning shot." He was referencing the shot fired in the direction of the fleeing Tucker Randall.

He then turned to the top count, for manslaughter.

"What I can tell you is that particular count does not rest solely on an analysis of the video that has been played in the media already. There was evidence that was gathered and presented to the grand jury about activity that Jake Gardner was engaged in prior to even coming in contact with James Scurlock. And that evidence can reasonably be construed as an intent to use a firearm for purposes of killing someone."

Franklin, acknowledging the reporters, went on about the additional evidence.

"You all want to know what it is, and I can't tell you about it," he said. "But what I can tell you is that that evidence comes primarily from Jake Gardner himself."

Franklin then detailed what that might be.

"The grand jury was able to have information from his cell phone, from his Facebook Messenger account. They were able to review video from inside Mr. Gardner's business, and they were able to get evidence relative to Mr. Gardner's state of mind as a part of what was presented to them from this investigation."

Franklin offered that, when he'd accepted his assignment as special prosecutor, he had not expected this outcome.

"I told those grand jurors when I first was appointed to work this case that I expected to ultimately end up at the conclusion of their decision-making to stand in front of the press and say the same thing that Don Kleine said, which was that the shooting was justifiable self-defense. That was my initial reaction. But I can tell you that there is evidence that undermines that. And, again, that evidence comes primarily from Jake Gardner himself."

Franklin thanked the Omaha Police Department for its help, and then took care to talk about Don Kleine and his team, including his top deputy, Brenda Beadle.

"Those are two people who I have known for probably twenty-five years, and I know those two people to be people of the highest integrity, the highest integrity. There is nothing about what this grand jury has done that should be taken as some sort of a knock or an indictment against Don Kleine or Brenda Beadle or the Douglas County Attorney's office. They're excellent people, they're lawyers and prosecutors of integrity, and they were also of tremendous assistance to me and my team in terms of bringing this matter to the grand jury."

Franklin said that, in indicting Gardner, the grand jury had a lower bar to clear than a jury at trial would—probable cause that a crime had been committed rather than a belief a crime had been committed beyond a reasonable doubt. Franklin quickly added, though, that he believed there was "confident, credible evidence to support the decision that they in fact did make."

Franklin then said he wanted to address the people of Omaha.

"I've been alerted to the fact that there were folks just waiting for an outcome that would reignite a bunch of riotous behavior and vandalism. And as a person who spends a significant amount of time in the downtown and in the Old Market area, it saddens me to see people have to walk around with those kinds of concerns, with businesses having to be boarded up. For the people who are supportive of James Scurlock, his father stated right after he was killed that he did not condone and did not want that type of behavior."

He was not done.

"I just want to echo that engaging in vandalism and the destruction of property, when people engage in that sort of behavior, you are dishonoring the memory of the people who have died," he said. "You are playing right into the hands of the people who are against what it is you are protesting for.

"Folks, you're all getting played when you engage in that behavior and I'm going to respectfully state to folks that are allies to justice movements that protests and demonstrations absolutely have a place. They should be part of the toolbox, but they shouldn't be the only tool in the toolbox. There are other things like economic boycotts, like registering and voting, like uniting behind a particular business, or other things that people can do in the name of generating the justice that they want to see happen, rather than just simply destroying stuff. I'm suggesting to you folks that now is not the time for that.

"The Scurlock family and their attorney Justin Wayne wanted to have this grand jury take place as a process, and that process has taken place, and we'll go on to the next step."

Franklin said he would reach out to Gardner's lawyer and see if Gardner wanted to surrender or be arrested after a warrant was issued.

Franklin then agreed to take questions. The first involved how long the grand jury had deliberated. Franklin said he couldn't or wouldn't disclose that, "but I can tell you that they spent more time deliberating on it than what I anticipated."

He was asked about the racial makeup of the grand jury.

"I'm not at liberty to disclose that," he said.

"You will continue as the special prosecutor in the case, correct?" Franklin was asked.

"That's my expectation," he responded.

Another reporter wanted to know more about the evidence that might have come from Gardner himself.

"Some might read between the lines there that the grand jury thought that Jake Gardner was a racist. Can you shed any light on that?"

"Being a racist is not against the law," Franklin said. "He's not indicted because he may or may not be a racist. I'm confident that the grand jury looked at evidence relative to the homicide statute, the terroristic threats statute, and the first-degree assault statute, and determined that that is the evidence that they had that implicated those particular statutes."

Franklin, unprompted, opted to then open up about himself.

"I just want to make folks very, very clear about who I am and how I operate. I accepted this responsibility not to advance any organization's agenda, not to advance the agenda of Black people because I'm African American, not to rubber-stamp what Don Kleine's office had decided to do. When I accepted the responsibility, it was with the understanding that I took an oath to be impartial in terms of gathering the evidence and then presenting it to the grand jury in a manner that allowed them to make decisions as to whether or not those facts implicated certain sections of the Nebraska Criminal Code. And if I were to do anything other than that, then I don't know that I could look at myself in the mirror.

"There's been discussion about whether Jake Gardner is a racist, and I'm not commenting on whether or not that evidence was presented to the grand jury, but I can assure you that, to the extent that they received any such information, they would have completely understood from me that it would have been improper to indict someone because they are perceived by the grand jury to be a racist."

Asked, Franklin would not say if Gardner had testified before the grand jury. He said he had not informed Kleine or his office of the outcome before announcing it.

A reporter asked if there would be a preliminary hearing, during which Gardner might seek to have the charges dismissed. Franklin said the indictment effectively served as the preliminary hearing.

"This is not a time for celebration or exuberance," Franklin said. "These are simply charges. Jake Gardner is a man presumed innocent as I stand before you right now."

Justice for James
NOTICE

PART TWO

"Stay Humble"

My very first job in journalism was as the lone white reporter at a Black weekly start-up in Brooklyn, New York. The father of the only Black family on my childhood block in Brooklyn, a man named Andy Cooper, thought New York was sadly lacking in an aggressive, principled Black press. He wasn't wrong.

Cities across the country had rich histories of Black newspapers—Chicago and St. Louis, Pittsburgh and Baltimore. Omaha, it turns out, as well. But not so much in New York. And so in 1984, with Ed Koch as mayor and race relations at a nadir, Cooper felt the moment could not be more right to try.

I wound up as one of the half-dozen people who conceived and built the paper, the *City Sun*, from scratch. Hustled for funding. Scouted for talent. Identified sources. Wrote news stories and editorials both. Our motto ran right at the top of the front page: "Speaking truth to power." It was a little self-regarding. But it felt needed and heady, too.

A decade earlier, New York had been given up for dead. The city was all but bankrupt. The Bronx was burning. Brooklyn looked in places like Dresden, the German town bombed into rubble in World War II. Whites were fleeing. The growing numbers of Black and Latino residents were often met with suspicion and worse.

When I was a kid, my dad used to take me with him on Saturday mornings to help him with a long-shot but telling project. We'd drive through Brooklyn and take pictures of the bombed-out blocks. I'd record the locations on a handheld tape recorder. My dad's aim was to have Brooklyn declared a federal disaster area. Maybe it could get a vast infusion of government money. As we drove through the devastation every weekend, it appeared he had a point.

Race was certainly a ready and raw issue in the neighborhood I grew up in, a middle-class enclave of Irish and Italians divided up chiefly by Catholic parishes—St. Thomas Aquinas, St. Augustine, St. Francis Xavier, St. Saviour, Holy Name of Jesus. Fifth Avenue on the neighborhood's western edge was a combat zone, the whites warring to keep the Puerto Ricans out.

I myself was an unimpressive mess of contradictions and inadequacies. My mom was a radical Catholic feminist. My dad—well, he was the guy taking me around Brooklyn in search of a case for federal aid and relief for the communities of color living in Brooklyn's 1970s disaster zones. We marched as a family against the Vietnam War. I rooted for Muhammad Ali in his epic fights against Joe Frazier, a set of fights that were a kind of racial litmus test. Frazier, the hardworking heavyweight out of Philly, was the white man's fighter. Ali was the fighter of the radical left. My parents, in a move not exactly met with wholesale support in the neighborhood, or even our Catholic parish, adopted an infant Black child.

At the same time, I had racist toughs among my inner circle of friends. We scored reefer in Brooklyn's Black neighborhoods, but we didn't hang out there. Whether I felt the racism among my friends was outrageous or harmless, I didn't protest or challenge it. Stay quiet, feel guilty, hope for the best. Not a profile in courage in the face of pretty unvarnished racism. Maybe it made me a racist, as well.

But out of college, almost on a whim, I was a founding member of a trailblazing Black weekly newspaper.

I was assigned to cover sports, and I smiled at the inadvertent irony of the reverse token experience. Black reporters at newspapers across the country for years had rightly complained they'd been relegated to less important departments inside newspapers, taken on not so much to chase consequential stories as to check a human resources box on diversity. They got to cover the National Football League, not the White House. Now a bold start-up Black paper in New York thought its only white reporter would be best used writing sports.

Serving as the one and only sportswriter for the *City Sun*, then, was revelatory and thrilling. The Rikers Island Olympics, held at the city's largest jail complex; one of the city's enduring Black chess clubs; the rise of a young baseball prospect in Brooklyn, Shawon Dunston; the promise of a Brooklyn schoolgirl sprinter, Diane Dixon. Mercifully, the stories seemed endless, and that many of them had never been covered by the city's half-dozen or so daily papers invested them with a sense of purpose to go along with the fun.

The founding members of the *City Sun*, like many participants in daring acts of idealism, eventually splintered over issues of ethics and ambition and, well, money. A number of us quit when we'd grown weary of not being paid, and then uncomfortable with some deals Cooper was cutting to sustain the paper's finances.

I stayed with sports, scoring jobs with United Press International and the *Syracuse Post-Standard*, but ultimately could not stay in Syracuse for very long. I wasn't built for the snow or the isolation or the morale-crushing routine of covering the scandal-plagued or incompetent sports teams of Syracuse University, what struck me as a smug, white, monied school without much soul. And so I fled and returned to Brooklyn, lacking both a job to take and a place to sleep. As I was on the way out the door, though, one of the paper's editors threw me a lifeline—a tip on a potential apartment coming available.

I took down the address, 271 Warren Street, and turned up there to meet the landlady. She was lovely and the studio on the third floor was indeed in need of a new tenant. She also turned out to be something of a miracle—for her day job was as deputy sports editor of the *New York Times*. She gave me a stern lecture about how few illusions I should entertain: I was a tenant, not a job candidate; she would not so much as read my clips, so I shouldn't bother showing them to her.

Fair enough, I said. But I knew the newspaper game by then. The

City Sun or the *New York Times*—they'd never have enough copy or enough reporters to bang it out. There would be a moment when the *Times* would be desperate, too, and the third-floor tenant at 271 Warren Street would suddenly be seen as an option for answering that sudden need.

It took a couple of months. Then there was a knock. My landlady was there. If she was chagrined, she didn't show it. She cut to the chase: Could I possibly cover the national cross-country championships that weekend in Van Cortlandt Park in the Bronx? Of course I did, and of course the requests kept coming—a Rutgers women's volleyball match; a Fordham University basketball game; even, in time, the odd Yankees game or Jets practice.

I enjoyed the assignments and the sense of comeuppance for the lady with the fancy title at the world's best newspaper. I was out of my depth, but I'm nothing if not a good faker, and I ad-libbed my way to filing on time and getting the names and scores right. And then, in the fall of 1987, the *New York Times*, with a staff of hundreds, an unparalleled reputation, pockets deeper than those of any other paper in the country, somehow did not have someone to cover a decisive weekend series between the Detroit Tigers and the Toronto Blue Jays, teams locked in a late-autumn fight for the American League East pennant.

I flew to Toronto; every game was decided late, and narrowly, but I didn't choke. Not choking is a bigger deal than one might think. It earned me, at age twenty-seven, a staff job with the Old Gray Lady, perhaps the least pedigreed hire she'd ever made.

I'd spend six years as a sportswriter, covering some of the worst and more degenerate Mets teams ever. Seeing your sports heroes up close will kill the fan in you. It's not that you just discover that they're all human. It's that you discover so many of them are limited humans.

But covering sports builds some good muscles and instills a certain amount of personal accountability. You learn to write fast, get the scores right, become familiar with the basic arts and arcs of storytelling. And you are forced to own what you write; you rip a right fielder in the morning's paper, you are in front of him in the locker room that afternoon. Man up, stand your ground, concede mistakes when appropriate, or get out.

In 1993, a family tragedy left me a single dad of two young girls. My sportswriting days were over. Hard to make a West Coast swing with the Mets when you are fully responsible for a five-year-old and her two-year-old sister. Max Frankel was then the executive editor of the *Times*, and he took the care and time to send me a handwritten note: "Joe, you are a star. Go be a reporter on the Metro Desk. Be a star there. Take care of your girls."

And so I jumped to the Metro desk, and made my bones as a more fully legit reporter. It was as if the world was born anew. You got to talk with people who actually wanted to talk to you. You got to talk to people who actually had something to say—about education or crime or health care or politics. It was eye-opening and invigorating. And scary as hell.

And it meant if you were going to be a city reporter in New York, competing with the *Daily News* and the *New York Post*, you were going to cover cops.

I'd grown up with cops. They'd break our balls for drinking on street corners but also be there when a neighborhood lunatic would be firing off rounds in the street. Tom Gleason across the street was a senior detective, and when cops were needed on our block they came fast. Pat Timlin, one of the neighborhood's best athletes and toughest brawlers, would rise to become top brass within the New York Police Department.

As people in their own universe, cops never struck me as anything much different from New York's uncountable other human galaxies—heroes and devils, driven by good intentions and bad judgments, machismo and fear, compassion and racism.

My upbringing was part of the reason I got called on to cover the city's dark and wide variety of crime stories. Serial killers, race riots, child deaths, mob justice. I was Irish and Catholic, a product of Brooklyn, a former sportswriter, and an accomplished beer drinker. Who better to talk to cops, and maybe keep the *Times* competitive with the half-dozen or so other papers in town on the big crime story of the day?

The 1990s were a fascinating time to be covering cops. There were twenty-two hundred murders in New York in 1990 alone. Rudy Giuliani rode to the mayor's office promising to actually fight crime rather than simply be overrun by it. Corruption among cops would produce a handful of enormous scandals. Computer analysis of crime statistics would be brought to bear, and murder rates would plunge. Young Black and Latino men would be the targets of what became known as a stop-and-frisk policy, a routine interrogation of often-innocent citizens that a federal judge would eventually find unconstitutional.

I was in the middle of the storms of success and controversy. I broke the story of widespread perjury by police officers in criminal cases. I became good friends with one of the police department's chief architects of its policy to lock people up for minor offenses in the belief doing so would both stabilize troubled neighborhoods and sweep up more serious offenders. I'd investigate cronyism at the Brooklyn District Attorney's Office and favoritism in the cases he chose to prosecute. I'd try my best to slug it out for scoops on the latest competitive story—the Zodiac killer in Queens, the child tortured to death by her parents under the child welfare agency's nose, the dirty cops in the 48th Precinct in the Bronx. I was both valued and viewed with suspicion by some at the *Times*. The paper liked winning some crime stories it was used to losing. But its appetite for stories where cops were the stars could be limited.

Anyway, if you were going to cover cops, you were going to cover cop shootings. They happened regularly. The cops tended to be white, but not always. Those killed tended to be men or women of color, but not always. Each shooting, then, held the potential to become a scandal or a cause.

The experience of covering those killings over close to four decades steeled in me a commitment to be aggressive, but fair, to recognize the systemic racism of much of America's policing policies and tactics, yet afford all parties in such fatal encounters, the cops and those killed by them, my best effort to examine the specific and distinctive particulars of what happened. To do so, I found over time, one had to set aside assumptions, about a white cop, if that was the case, or a Black victim. I'd learn to mistrust initial accounts, which almost always proved incomplete, sometimes badly flawed. I'd need to insulate myself not only from the upset in the community that often attended such encounters but also from the passions of my own newsroom. The *New York Times*—awesome, noble, enraging, brave, imperfect—was and is an indisputably liberal organization. There's nothing wrong with that. But there's no point in pretending otherwise.

In 1994, having just moved from the Sports department to the Metro desk, I was the lead reporter on the police killing of thirteen-year-old Nicholas Heyward Jr. in a Brooklyn public housing project. It was a brutally sad story to tell, and I can almost recall from memory the start to the first account I wrote.

> *The rules of the game Tuesday night at the Gowanus Houses in Brooklyn were these: there would be two teams, one cops, the other robbers; each team member would have three lives; get shot by one of the plastic guns everybody had and you would lose a life.*
>
> *Shortly after 7 P.M., Nicholas Heyward Jr. stood on the roof of 423 Baltic Street with three other team members, all 12 to 14 years old. Several of the children had been called to their apartments by their mothers. Darkness was descending.*
>
> *"Nick said he wanted to go down," recalled Ronald Herron, and playfully pushed one of them so that he could be the first down the stairway.*
>
> *"I heard Nick say, 'We're playing,' and then I heard a boom," recalled Katrell Fowler, a friend.*
>
> *Nicholas Heyward, his 18-inch toy rifle held up by his right ear, got to the final step and then his life was ended, by a real gunshot from the revolver of a real police officer, Brian George, a 23-year-old on routine patrol for the Housing Authority.*

Not as often, but just as surely, I wound up covering police shootings where it was the cop who paid with his life. Didn't justify bad police shootings but offered some fairly important context: for police, the idea that you might have to kill or be killed was real and unforgiving.

In 1995, a year after the young Heyward's death, Officer Raymond Cannon, a twenty-six-year-old newlywed, was shot in the face and killed during the robbery of a bicycle store in Brooklyn. Those involved included a teen boy with a toy gun.

There were even cases of cops shooting cops, by mistake, and with the question of race always front and center. In 1994, Peter Del-Debbio, a white cop on his way home after his shift, mistakenly shot a Black undercover officer who had drawn his weapon during a chaotic couple of moments inside a New York subway station. The Black cop, Desmond Robinson, survived; Del-Debbio was later convicted of second-degree assault.

"In a job where a decision must come faster than thought itself," I wrote at the time, "the instinctual judgments about race and crime built into an urban culture are often more important than all the sensitivity training a police department can offer."

One of the most notorious police shootings across my career covering them was the killing of Amadou Diallo, an African immigrant shot to death in a hail of forty-one bullets in the Bronx in 1999.

Four officers with the police department's aggressive undercover Street Crime Unit confronted Diallo as he stood in the vestibule of his Bronx apartment building on the night of February 4. The four officers were later said to have been concerned about a series of rapes and/or robberies in the neighborhood. The officers said Diallo had not responded to their commands and that they opened fire when he appeared to have drawn a gun.

The gun turned out to be Diallo's wallet. He turned out not to have been responsible for any crime spree. The killing sparked protests. Bruce Springsteen wrote a song: "American Skin (41 Shots)."

For me, though, even this sensational case warranted scrutiny.

Prosecutors in the Bronx had sought and gained murder charges against the four officers. Was that appropriate, or an overreach produced by the inflamed emotions and politics the case had generated? The forty-one shots seemed an outrageous number, and made for a powerful popular song by a rock superstar. But to me, the first shot was the one that most mattered. The officers had perhaps needlessly suspected Diallo was a criminal and fired a gun without adequate cause. They should have lost their jobs, and that first shot might have constituted a crime. The forty that came after, to me and any number of experts, were evidence less of murderous intent than panic on the part of poorly trained officers with automatic weapons capable of firing sixteen shots in mere seconds. Did such distinctions matter?

They did, apparently, to the judge who oversaw the trial of the four officers and who found them not guilty of murder. The verdict upset many but surprised few.

The killings kept happening and the questions about reporting on them, for me, only grew. How to measure a cop's sense of personal risk? How much could one's personal beliefs, vile or virtuous, color behavior in moments of chaos, even panic? How valuable was eyewitness testimony, how dispositive was the increasingly common element of video recordings? Did such recordings, explosive but limited, settle matters or twist the full truth?

I had risen to metropolitan editor of the *Times*, overseeing a staff of close to one hundred reporters, when a shooting happened that haunts me to this day.

In 2009, Omar Edwards, an emerging star in the police department's detective ranks, was knocking off one night in Harlem. He texted with his wife of three weeks back in Brooklyn, said he'd be home soon and was looking forward to some days off.

Edwards was something of a rarity—a Black cop from a family of cops. Such a narrative, the multigenerational lure of police work, was a staple of cop lore, but one usually restricted to the Irish and Italian families that dominated the department. Edwards's uncle had been a cop in Brooklyn's 69th Precinct, and Omar had followed in his rather trailblazing steps. He'd become a celebrated running back on the NYPD's football team, and at twenty-five he was on the rise in the department.

Upon stepping out of the precinct house, Edwards saw someone trying to break into his car in the parking lot. He raced to the car, confronted the thief, and wound up in a struggle. Edwards managed to pull his off-duty revolver, and when the thief raced off he gave chase, gun in hand.

Andrew Dunton was a lot like Edwards. He'd grown up on Long Island and he'd played soccer at Siena College upstate, and had made a quick ascent in the department to its anti-crime squad. He worked in plainclothes and his chief mission was to get guns off the street. He was white.

That night, as Edwards pursued the thief, Dunton was among three officers in an unmarked car just about to turn onto the street Edwards was sprinting along. The cops in the car saw Edwards with his gun and quickly pulled over. Dunton was in the front passenger seat, and he stumbled briefly as he quickly got out.

"Drop the gun," he ordered. "Drop the gun."

Edwards turned to Dunton. It's possible he tried to say something. He did not drop the gun. And Dunton shot him through the chest. It was the first time Dunton had ever fired his gun in the line of duty.

An ambulance was called. Emergency Services cops arrived. Edwards, per protocol, had been handcuffed as he lay shot on the ground. Now there were people trying to save his life. He was turned over and his outer shirt cut open. He was wearing a Police Athletic League T-shirt, the cop charity involving youth sports. The cops and medical personnel could now access his wallet. It held his detective's shield.

It was a devastating story, and I ordered up reams of coverage. Profiles of the two cops. A history of cop-on-cop shootings. A look at the grand jury inquiry that was ordered by the legendary Manhattan District Attorney, Robert Morgenthau.

Was there fault to be found? How did the families feel? Were the roars of protest and upset justified, or a reflexive response to familiar story outlines?

The grand jury did not indict Dunton, who had testified before it. Prosecutors, in making the announcement, released an account of what happened, saying the panel had heard from nineteen others—police officers, medical personnel, and witnesses on the street.

Three officers in an unmarked car, one of them Officer Dunton, saw the thief and Edwards running, the prosecutor's narrative said. They, too, saw Officer Edwards's gun. Officer Dunton got out of the car while it was still moving and crouched behind the front passenger door, yelling, "Police, don't move; drop the gun, drop the gun."

The fleeing thief stopped for a moment, the account said, then ran past the officers. Officer Edwards was about fifteen feet from the unmarked police car. "He slowed," the account said, "but did not come to a complete stop.

"In response to Officer Dunton's commands," the account continued, Officer Edwards "turned his body toward the anti-crime officers, making eye contact with Officer Dunton and pointing his gun at him." Officer Dunton fired six shots "in very rapid succession."

One of my reporters covered the reaction.

The Black Law Enforcement Alliance called the grand jury's finding "disturbingly predictable." The alliance's political affairs director, Marquez Claxton, a retired detective, said investigations of police shootings needed to be independent of the police department and the district attorney's office. "The relationship between the police and the local prosecutors is incestuous and threatens public confidence in the integrity of the process," he said.

Stuart London, Dunton's lawyer, said that Officer Dunton was "gratified his actions were deemed to be justified" but remained "shaken up." "His reaction is the case has always been a tragedy," Mr. London said, "and his heartfelt prayers go out to the Edwards family."

Officer Edwards's father, Ricardo P. Edwards, expressed anguish but resolve as well when a reporter told him about the grand jury's decision.

"If they feel they're not supposed to indict him, what am I going to say?" Ricardo Edwards said. "There's nothing I say or do that can stop the situation. That was my son's job; he knew his life was always on the line when he was on the street."

The case stayed with me all these years because of that outcome—a conclusion shared by those representing the two cops, one white, one Black, one still on the force, one dead, that what happened was tragic but not criminal. The Edwards family never sued; Dunton for a time worked as a community liaison officer, meaning he was charged with assisting efforts to see police and residents come together, have open lines of dialogue.

The memorable case came near the end of my twenty-five years with the *New York Times*. By the time I left in 2013, I'd had the privilege of running two major departments at the world's best paper—five years as metropolitan editor, two as sports editor. Oddly, the big stories never scared me much—9/11, citywide blackouts, the Penn State sex scandal, or a miracle plane landing in the Hudson River. What frightened the hell out of me was not having enough stories for the next day's paper. Embarrassing, but true.

The strange, real, but often-irrational fear had been captured best for me in a poem published improbably enough by one of my very first bosses in the news racket—the sports editor of United Press International, the legendary news wire service. He smoked cigars, talked shit, barked orders, pleaded for poetry through the use of his own profanity. I fell for him. Hard.

He'd go on to be a published and respected poet, and write a collection of poems on the life of a newsroom, including "City Editor Looking for News."

The poem's a tribute to an enduring, inarguable truth about daily journalism: news organizations, large or small, local or legendary, are, day in, day out, driven by a considerable degree of desperation. For the next exclusive development, for the next day's lead story, for anything—anything!—to fill a hole in the paper's Sports or Metro section. It's as true for the *New York Times* as the *Clarion-Ledger* in Jackson, Mississippi. It's how I got hired by the *Times*, the knock on my third-floor studio apartment by an editor in need of a body.

It was, then, a familiar bit of desperation that brought the story of James Scurlock's death in Omaha to me. I had left the *Times* to become a senior editor at ProPublica, the nonprofit investigative news organization. Now it was a Thursday in early July 2020 and I got a call from ProPublica's editor-in-chief. Our publishing schedule showed we had nothing to post on our website the following Tuesday. The boss wondered if I could quickly turn around a story about a racial killing in Omaha.

He sent me an email ProPublica had received from Ryan Wilkins, the lawyer in Omaha who had called for Jake Gardner's arrest after the shooting. Wilkins said in his note that he had pleaded with other major news organizations to look into the case but had become frustrated when none did. He beseeched ProPublica to step up.

"I'm an attorney, not a journalist, but I've poured considerable time into my own reporting on this out of sheer disbelief that local law enforcement and media could ignore such clear evidence of the shooter's racism when reporting on this," Wilkins had written.

Another senior editor at ProPublica had first read the email and indeed thought there could be an exposé to be done, especially with George Floyd's death still turning the country upside down.

"Compelling argument that the Omaha DA gave a white supremacist a free pass to kill a black protester," the editor wrote.

I said I'd take a look.

I found plenty of local stories about the case. A number of national news organizations had parachuted into Omaha and delivered more takes on the killing. And I read and reread the online post by the lawyer in Omaha alleging the Gardner family had white supremacist roots and connections.

I'd been one of the editors on a project at ProPublica called "Documenting Hate," an ambitious effort to explore racial hatred in America in the aftermath of Trump's stunning election. We dived into the legal history of hate crimes, investigated how well local and federal law enforcement had prosecuted such offenses, built a database of both recorded reports of racial violence and tips from everyday Americans at a charged and dangerous national moment.

The rise, or in truth reascendance, of organized white supremacists was undeniable. They were many, and they were unafraid about declaring their ideology and intentions. The deadly rally in Charlottesville, Virginia, was but one coming-out party, for both the hardcore extremists and their younger, theoretically more politically clever counterparts of the alt-right.

Reporting done by one of my reporters, A. C. Thompson, led to the arrests of at least eight white supremacists on federal charges, including four members of a violent outfit called the Rise Above Movement. They'd assaulted men and women at a variety of rallies, including the bloody marches in Charlottesville. But until Thompson's reporting, they'd eluded prosecution. The headline on Thompson's initial article summed it up succinctly: "Racist, Violent, Unpunished: A White Hate Group's Campaign of Menace."

Thompson's work would grow to include an exposé on a neo-Nazi group called Atomwaffen, responsible for half a dozen killings in 2018, as well as a plot to carry out acts of terror aimed at destabilizing American democracy. He penetrated their secret chat logs and established their connection to the murder of a gay Jewish college student in California. His work once again prompted federal authorities to act.

The reporting, much of it captured in two documentaries for PBS's *Frontline*, would both win Thompson an Emmy Award and imperil his personal safety. The FBI learned of a plot against his life by white supremacists, and he and his family barely escaped harm when an Atomwaffen associate phoned in a fake 911 call, leading police in Thompson's hometown in California to descend on his house, guns drawn, and march him in handcuffs down his driveway until the dangerous prank became obvious.

I sent Thompson the post by the Omaha lawyer, including the claim that Gardner's father had been indoctrinated into white supremacy while behind bars in Texas. He called me shortly afterward. He'd done a pretty good check on Texas prison records and there was no evidence Gardner's father had ever been locked up in the state. Thompson over his years of reporting on white extremists had also become pretty adept at scouring social media for both obvious and hidden online activity. He could find no online extremist footprint for Gardner.

If I was going to report out what ProPublica's editors had taken to be a racial killing by a white supremacist in Omaha, I should be careful, he said. It just might not be true.

I took his caution seriously. By then, I'd developed a career's worth of concerns about going slow, taking care, tuning out the noise of upset, justified or not, and focusing on both what was knowable and what was not.

Videotape of the incident in front of Gardner's bar that night was easily available on the Internet. I watched it repeatedly. I recognized that such video evidence is limited, sometimes misleading—capturing some things vividly, but leaving out who knows how much other information, interactions, or context. What I could see of what happened in Omaha struck me as heartbreaking and regrettable, one more casualty in a country awash in guns. It didn't seem like murder.

Over time, it became clear to me that Gardner and Scurlock had been reduced to grotesques—Gardner a bloodthirsty white supremacist, Scurlock a hoodlum who provoked his own death, both of their histories cherry-picked to push one narrative or another.

It wasn't hard to find evidence that both Scurlock and Gardner were more than the caricatures the Internet had created.

My very earliest conversations with Scurlock's father and siblings revealed a young man not just with a criminal record, but with an adoring and forgiving family, one Scurlock was fiercely proud and protective of.

"Why is he being ripped apart?" one of Scurlock's sisters, Marissa, asked me about his portrayal.

A. D. Swolley, one of Scurlock's older brothers, posted a tribute after his death.

> *It's easy to lose sight of the question that really matters after all the videos, press conferences, rallies and media commentary—that question being, 'Who was, James Scurlock?' A father, a brother and a son. My little brother. He strived to be successful and family oriented after graduating high school. James would spend the majority of his time hanging out with his siblings when he wasn't working, until November 1 2019, when his daughter and only child was born into the world. From that point forward James' goal was to ensure that he was the greatest father and a better man to provide for his daughter as best as possible. Going as far as setting up a trust and savings account for her, then 6 month old, and collecting information to start college in the fall of 2020. James was a very enthralling, intelligent and productive 22- year-old with loyalty and a heart astonishingly larger than his personality, who was quick to jump at the call for any help no matter how far out of his way.*

As for Gardner, a video had surfaced of a TV news segment that ran in early 2017. Gardner was in Washington during the women's march to protest Trump's inauguration, and in an interview Gardner, his dog, LeBron, at his side, sounded diplomatic and self-aware, even funny.

"These people just want to be heard," he said of the women protesters. "It's a very appropriate venue and very appropriate weekend.

"It's kind of crazy being in the belly of the beast," he added with a smile. "Here with my Trump gear and my Make America Great vest on my dog. Everyone loves the dog until they read the vest."

Whatever happened in Omaha, it wasn't going to be written up to fill the hole in the next week's publishing schedule. But I was not letting go either. I found myself drawn to it with both genuine interest and a degree of dread, for it already appeared to have come to involve many of the country's toxic ills: racial mistrust, misinformation, a suspect criminal justice system, irreparable political divisions, the abandonment of so many of the country's wounded warriors suffering back home in plain sight, and the power, and perhaps menace, of the Internet.

I would hire a brilliant woman who had become expert at searching and analyzing social media activity in the aftermath of major news events. For her, what happened online after Gardner shot Scurlock fit a familiar script. Social media had set an early narrative that would both seep into mainstream media coverage and prove hard to alter or correct. Social media would be used to pressure public officials, and to target, with personal information and a taste for vengeance, both Gardner and Scurlock.

She recalled for me the old adage that a lie can travel halfway around the world while the truth is still putting on its shoes, and how it had been proven out in various studies in the aftermath of the 2016 U.S. presidential election, which spurred a wave of research and reports about the reach of misinformation and divisive news.

She cited an MIT study that found that, on Twitter, falsehoods diffused "significantly farther, faster, deeper, and more broadly than the truth."

For instance, false news stories are 70 percent more likely to be retweeted than true stories are, the study found. It also takes true stories about six times as long to reach fifteen hundred people as it does for false stories to reach the same number of people. When it comes to Twitter's "cascades," or unbroken retweet chains, falsehoods reach a cascade depth of 10 about twenty times faster than facts. And falsehoods are retweeted by unique users more broadly than true statements at every depth of cascade.

Another study from Harvard found that for both right-leaning and left-leaning media, negative news spreads farther through Twitter than positive news. Social media algorithms are designed to push divisive content because it keeps us using and engaging with the platform.

Over weeks, then months, I wound up spending time with both the Scurlock and Gardner families, as well as with Gardner's business partners, fellow soldiers, and friends; I got access to multiple video recordings of the deadly events outside The Hive; I read police records and cell phone texts involving Gardner and others on the night of May 30; I spoke with witnesses who were there that night, and the local lawyer who had campaigned for Gardner's prosecution.

Reporting was never meant to be neat or easy, even in the best of times or the healthiest of democracies. It could be messy and dangerous, whether in Syria or in Cincinnati. But reporting this story made me consider the truth of a piece published not long before in the *New York Times*, one that proposed American democracy was falling victim to political sectarianism—that its opposing factions didn't just disagree but saw each other as alien and immoral and a threat.

One witness to the killing of James Scurlock I interviewed accused me of trying to "gaslight" him when I simply checked and rechecked his account of what happened that night. When I contacted Jennifer Heineman, the relative of Gardner's, to ask about her claims that their family was full of ugly racists, she said she not only would not speak with me but would only consider talking at all if she was interviewed by a Black, female reporter. When I first contacted the woman who had jumped on Gardner that deadly night, she would have nothing to do with me unless I stipulated at the outset that Gardner was a racist. Again and again, I was told by people close to the Scurlock family that they had heard I was involved in some conspiracy—that I was secretly working on behalf of the Gardner family.

I also engaged at length with many of Gardner's friends and associates, including former Marines. They told me Gardner had received more than sixteen hundred death threats and they wanted no part of that. They would talk, but they would not be named. Seasoned, decorated combat veterans scared of using their names. To some, the Black Lives Matter movement was a dangerous threat. One friend said his family's business in Omaha had been targeted for retribution after he'd publicly tried to raise money for Gardner should he need a lawyer. The family of a close friend of Gardner, a Marine named Ron Payne who had fought with him in Iraq and was later killed in Afghanistan, made clear they held dear their son's relationship with Gardner but indicated to me that saying so might taint the public's perception of their child and his service. He'd been saluted as a war hero; Gardner and a handful of the other Marines who served with Payne had got memorial tattoos paying tribute to him. Yet Payne's family would not be interviewed or quoted.

One of the former Marines who would not be named was the recruiter in Omaha who had worked with Gardner to identify men and women interested in joining the Corps. A big man whose business was security, he said he could not be named for fear his children would be harmed. He was a bit embarrassed and absolutely adamant. And he was profoundly demoralized that he felt that way in a country he'd served in uniform to defend.

"Nobody can make mistakes anymore," he said in assessing the country at that moment. Sides must be taken, he said, and never be rethought.

"It's like religion," he said. "You can't argue with religion. People believe in their faith. You can't argue them out of their faith."

The local National Public Radio station dialed back its coverage of the case once it got complicated and ever-more heated, confusing and disappointing its reporter. The legal director of the Nebraska chapter of the American Civil Liberties Union faced a backlash from his staff for having had the temerity to suggest Don Kleine's legal analysis of the case was right.

I would come to have a long, substantive back-and-forth with Justin Wayne, the Black state senator and lawyer for the Scurlock family. He remained angry at Don Kleine, the white county attorney, and insisted to me that the entire set of events had to be seen in the larger sweep of Omaha's racist history. He said it was not the Scurlock family who had pushed the idea that Gardner was a white supremacist with neo-Nazi leanings. That narrative, he said, had been promoted chiefly by whites in Nebraska, elected officials and overzealous activists. "The white savior complex," Wayne said.

Wayne said he shared my concern about how polarized the country was, and how basic facts and an openness to them had become endangered traits.

"America is tough; America is hard," Wayne said. "Getting at the truth takes work. And it's work America's not always interested in doing."

It made me wonder if the very idea of tragedy was dead in that America. It's as if, as Gardner's Marine buddy said, there can't be flawed characters caught up in disastrous circumstances. There have to be villains. Agendas must be pushed. Facts become casualties. But was it possible what happened in Omaha was a story involving two imperfect young men, a story of bad luck, bad timing, of human beings making choices in moments of confusion and fear?

Maybe Jake Gardner shouldn't have been out there with a gun that night. But maybe he had, in several critical seconds, legitimately feared for his life while under repeated assault from unknown people he had no reason to know were white, Black, or brown. Maybe James Scurlock should not have been out vandalizing businesses that night, but maybe he, in the same critical seconds, legitimately wanted to prevent more gunfire and had jumped on the man with the weapon.

Could Omaha accept that? Could America?

I hoped maybe but feared not. I had several long, emotional, painful conversations with a Black former Marine who had served with Gardner. They were both from Omaha. They met early in their Marine Corps careers, and became fast friends. When Gardner was discharged, he called the Marine to come get him in North Carolina, and the two drove across the country together, a Black man escorting a white man back into civilian life, trading stories and laughs and regrets along the way. When Gardner opened his bar and the day regarded as the birthday of the Marine Corps rolled around, the two men would drink together at Gardner's establishment. They even appeared together in a local TV news segment honoring the men and women who had fought in Iraq and Afghanistan.

I asked him, more than once, if he felt Gardner was a racist. "All the time I knew Jake," he told me, "nothing about him triggered a response where I didn't believe he loved me like a brother."

A not dissimilar worry percolated in my own heart. Across my career, I could be all manner of things—hardworking but vain, outwardly curious but deep down too self-certain. At the *Times*, I bucked authority and spoke my mind. It earned me steadfast colleagues and wary detractors both. People who saw me as their champion, others who saw me as a bully.

As I've got older, I've tried to embrace humility a little more. I'd worked long enough to have made a bushelful of mistakes, from the venial to the mortal. While at the *Times*, I'd once received an email from the executive editor's secretary. She was passing along an inquiry from a young man in New Jersey who said his dad as a soldier in Iraq had been troubled by some of what he'd seen Americans do. He wanted to talk to someone. I was an editor on the Metro desk, not someone running war coverage. I blithely forwarded the email to a Pentagon reporter and never thought about it again. The young man's father had photographs of horrific abuse by Americans against Iraqis inside the Abu Ghraib prison in Baghdad. It was an immense scandal. Another news organization got the scoop. I'd blown it, out of laziness. Yikes.

Stay humble, then, I'd tell myself more and more after that. Mistrust my own certainty more often. Listen better. I failed in the effort, for sure, but liked to think I kept making it.

And so I asked myself questions about the story in Omaha. Could a white man with his own failings in racial matters richly report out the life of James Scurlock? Could that same reporter, who had never entered the military or fired a weapon in his country's name, adequately appreciate the life of someone who had? Would anyone trust that account? Was that the wrong question to ask?

Newsrooms across America were themselves gripped by questions of race and equity and were grappling with the issue of who got to tell whose stories. And there was the legitimate question: in a country with such manifest and inarguable harm being done to people of color, in our schools and in our streets, in our health care systems and in our prisons, was a nuanced story that might upend the narrative America had already settled on be worthy of precious journalistic resources? People I talked to about the story told me to be prepared to be "canceled" if I ever wrote it.

There were, then, reasons enough to stand down. That empty Tuesday on the publishing schedule had come and gone. The national media didn't seem too interested in digging any more deeply into Omaha's tragedy. There were a million other stories to chase. I was sixty-two, and had a wonderful career and solid reputation. By early 2021, I'd left ProPublica and hooked up with an old *New York Times* colleague running a daring nonprofit news organization dedicated to covering the world's oceans, the planet's last untamed frontier.

I didn't, then, have to inquire further into the case of Jake Gardner and James Scurlock. But in the end it felt cowardly not to try.

"Juju"

SHORTLY AFTER 9:00 A.M. ON SEPTEMBER 22, 2015, James Scurlock appeared before Judge Mark Johnson in Madison County District Court. The courthouse is a single-story structure bordered by cornfields on one side and the Calvary Community Church on another.

"Your Honor, I've been in jail for a long time," Scurlock began. "I have learned a lot of things; I have matured and come a long way. I'll do very good with my mom. I would do good and go to school. I won't get in trouble again."

Scurlock was sixteen when he was arrested in nearby Norfolk, Nebraska, for his role in an armed home invasion. Now seventeen, he had been in the local juvenile detention facility for close to ten months. Scurlock's lawyer had earlier tried to have Scurlock charged as a juvenile. The break-in and robbery, Scurlock's lawyer had argued, had been Scurlock's older brother's idea. Scurlock had gone along to earn his brother's respect, a bid to seem tougher than he was. Scurlock had carried no weapon and had no prior criminal record of violence. If he was treated as a juvenile, Scurlock would face probation instead of incarceration.

But the judge had rejected the idea, and Scurlock ultimately had pleaded guilty. Now, on this morning, he was facing sentencing for one count of burglary—a crime with a potential prison term of three to five years. His mother, Rajeanna, was in the courtroom, along with two of his sisters.

Scurlock's lawyer, Jason Doele, told the judge Scurlock had barely had any high school credits when he was taken into custody. But he'd done well in classes while in detention, and his instructors had been impressed by his diligence.

"I know I made a lot of bad choices in the past, but I changed a whole lot," Scurlock told the judge. "I didn't think I was going to do school at all, but I got a lot of credits; I got a lot of things done and a lot of things accomplished."

Scurlock's criminal record had been an issue of confusion, and a tool for partisan combat, in the days and weeks after his death. To some, his record was evidence he was a serial offender, not just a troubled kid but a violent threat. To others, his experience bore all the hallmarks of a broken criminal justice system, one that favored punishment over treatment, that used the mistakes of a child to close the door on an achievable, brighter future.

I had to appear in court in Madison County to get the transcripts of Scurlock's sentencing hearing. The local court official had told me I'd have to make a formal request to the judge. In a brief hearing, I told the judge I was interested in telling the full story of James Scurlock, the good and bad. What had happened in Madison County, in its streets and its courthouse, had done much to determine the nature and arc of Scurlock's life. The Madison County prosecutor, Joe Smith, raised no objection, and the judge granted my request. I'd soon obtain an additional fat file of records involving Scurlock's criminal history—a complete narrative of the December 2014 home invasion, the full details of his first arrest at age eleven, the arguments in court about his chances at rehabilitation.

In those files, in the typed-up record of police and court proceedings a decade old, I got to, in effect, hear Scurlock in his own voice. I could listen to the scared eleven-year-old, living at the time in a homeless shelter with his mother and other siblings, try to explain away how he had taken a PlayStation game from a house in the neighborhood in Norfolk. I could get a sense of his teenage bravado when, questioned by police about the home invasion five years later, Scurlock refused to rat out the others involved.

And in his appearance that September day in 2015, I could sense his desperation not to spend additional months or years locked up.

"I really want to be with my mom," he said.

There were in the files hard, ugly facts to be alarmed by. The home invasion had involved at least one gun, and threats of harm. The files made clear Scurlock and his brother James Harden, known as J.T., had been involved in selling drugs. But in poring over those records, one could also watch unfold in almost slow motion the experience of so many poor Black families in America's criminal justice system.

When he was arrested for stealing the video game at eleven, there's no evidence Scurlock was offered support services that might have helped keep him out of future trouble. Instead, he was ordered to submit to a 6:00 p.m. curfew and told not to associate with anyone over the age of fourteen other than family members.

In a hearing on the home invasion case, the judge took note that Scurlock's mother had failed to appear in person early on and wound up having to be subpoenaed. The judge seemed to wonder if incarceration might give Scurlock the structured supervision his absent or unconcerned mother seemingly couldn't. He had questioned Scurlock's mother when she appeared before him asking for her child to be treated by the courts as a juvenile.

"Just curious, there have been I think at least two previous hearings to have this juvenile transfer hearing; we have not been able to have a parent attend either one," the judge said to Scurlock's mother. "Is there a reason that you have not been in attendance previously?"

The answer was she had a job she couldn't afford to lose and there were other children to look after.

"The only reason is that I work and that sometimes," she told the judge, "it's hard to get back over here with, you know, trying to make it over here, being responsible for my other children as well, to have them supervised."

The judge later made clear he didn't think Scurlock, by law, was a candidate to be spared imprisonment. The option of a formal diversion program—a period of probation during which Scurlock might enroll in school and mental health programs—was reserved for first-time offenders. Scurlock's lawyer didn't object, noting Scurlock had the prior burglary conviction. It is unclear whether either had fully read the details of the case involving the theft of a video game. At one point, the records show, the judge referred to the offense as a robbery, which it was not. There was no one home when Scurlock walked through an unlocked neighbor's door and took the games—a console and a couple of dozen games or movies such as *Star Wars: Battlefront* and *The Lord of the Rings*.

"I'm somewhat at a loss for what type of treatment would be appropriate for Mr. Scurlock," the judge said in evaluating Scurlock's role in the home invasion. "I do know that this type and level of behavior is not generally rewarded with a sentence of probation. He has received at least one term of probation previously. That was in the juvenile case I referred to earlier. Unfortunately, that term of probation has not deterred or scared him enough to prevent future criminal activity on his part."

WHEN I FIRST contacted members of Scurlock's family, it was late summer, 2020. The COVID pandemic limited air travel, and so I did some initial interviews over the phone. The family's loss just a couple of months earlier was still raw, but Scurlock's father and several of his siblings were willing to talk.

In my first conversation with Scurlock's father, he acknowledged his son's mistakes but was still hurt by how his son had by some been reduced to little more than the crimes he'd committed.

"His record does not say who he was," the father said. "It describes what he was going through."

He first said James had gone to prior protests over police killings, and that his purpose on the night of May 30 was just that: to stand up for justice. But he later tacitly conceded he wasn't sure how James had wound up downtown, and that he could not explain why he had done what he'd done—participated in the vandalism that swept the streets that night.

I talked with Marissa, known as Riss, one of Scurlock's older sisters, who was then working as a paraprofessional in the Omaha public school system. She said she'd been more of a mother to James than a sister, that he had lived with her during some of his time in middle school. She insisted her brother had been distraught over George Floyd's killing, left, like many African American young men who'd had dealings with the police, furious and afraid. She'd seen her brother referred to as a thug, and it cut her to the quick.

When I finally made it to Omaha, Scurlock's father agreed to meet me. I encouraged him to bring some of his other children, and we met one morning at a Denny's restaurant in South Omaha, off Interstate 80. The elder Scurlock had worked at the restaurant, as had a handful of other family members over the years. He was treated like royalty by the staff, who got him what he always had: a limitless pot of black coffee.

One by one, the women arrived, biological daughters, stepchildren, informally adopted members of the wider Scurlock clan. A couple brought grandkids, and the moms fought playfully over the chance to talk about their lost brother. The affection among them all—Rajeanna, Qwenyona, Heather, and Hali—was obvious, and abundant. They rattled off the names of other sisters I should talk to—Chandy, Tammy, each one smilingly described as her brother's closest sibling. And they all referred to James Scurlock Sr. as Dad—naturally, respectfully.

Rajeanna, who shared a mom with James, described to me from memory the exact layout of the house she and her brother had lived in with their grandmother in Denver. The long staircase, the dining room set on what felt like a platform, the piano, the picket fence outside. She and James and the three other half-siblings there with them went to charter schools, and she can still remember the impressive names—Denver Arts and Sciences, the Pinnacle school. They went to church, she said, and they wanted for nothing. Rajeanna was a natural poet and James was a whiz at math, and so they became useful partners in homework. They told each other everything, and they conspired together to enrage and exasperate their grandmother by staying up late and trying to hide the light in their room.

Qwenyona Evans is a member of North Omaha's Revolutionary Action Party, an upstart organization in North Omaha that has worked to clothe and feed the needy in the neighborhood and that has taken on local lawmakers, Black and white, as well as their favorite target—the Omaha Police Department.

"Why do we have clothing programs? It's because of the negligence and irresponsibility of our government, and we're going to highlight that," Bear Alexander, one of the group's leaders, said in an interview with a local TV station. "But we're also going to take care of our community members and remind them that we're family."

"Our love for our community can be misconstrued as hatred for the system," he added.

Qwenyona is determined to get her master's degree in nonprofit administration, but that hasn't kept her from starting her own enterprise already—the James Scurlock Sports Academy. It runs volleyball and wrestling programs, and she'd love to see it be a platform for her to push for social justice.

"I want to be a voice," she told me.

The siblings who had come together, then and in the months ahead, forgave me for my struggle to keep the family straight—who was the child of whom, who had lived with whom, and when. There had been households in Omaha and Denver, Junction City, Kansas, and Warren, Ohio. There were a surplus of nicknames and abbreviations for the kids—Fat Boy and Dre, J.T. and A.D.

All along, the shifting network of children seemed to appreciate my openness to seeing the collection of people and family connections, biological and/or improvised, not as something curious and dysfunctional, but as something distinctive and remarkable.

I asked Qwenyona to describe her brother James, a trickier question to answer than one might guess. James had always come to her volleyball games; he'd run in a marathon for a fundraising event she was involved with. He stood by her, supported her. But he'd also been a brother, a jokester and an arguer, a loyalist and a ball-breaker. Where, then, to begin? They'd been children together for the vast majority of their lives. Could a short, silly answer be a betrayal? Was it enough to say she loved his madcap energy?

"He was strong and compassionate," she said of James. "And he didn't bow down to anyone or anything."

I asked her, with interest and earnestness, to tell me what held the small universe of a family together.

"Dad," she said.

He had help. James Sr. had four children with April Whiteman, and when these were added to the five children James Sr. already had, including James, April for years wound up overseeing nine children.

"It was a busy household," she said with a smile.

April had grown up in Warren, Ohio. Her mom was a maid at the local Best Western, her dad a dispatcher for an ambulance company. She didn't much like school or her long-term prospects in the smallish city between Youngstown and Cleveland. She dropped out of high school, had a child early, and eventually busted out of Warren, joining up with a friend headed to Omaha.

In the overflowing household she'd help run in Omaha with James Sr., April created chores charts, not that they worked all that well. On grocery runs, each child old enough would be assigned to carry two bags. April would cook dinner in the morning, rally the children for daycare or school, and go off to her job with a telemarketing firm. For her, James, Rajeanna, and the three others who had been out with their grandmother in Denver for their early years were every ounce her own.

"My babies," she said.

Even after James Sr. and she split up years later, April took young James and the others to doctor appointments and for haircuts. Talk to anyone in the family and there is little doubt James considered April the closest thing to a fully reliable mom he ever had.

"We weren't always faithful and loyal to each other," James Sr. said of April and himself, "but we were always faithful and loyal to the kids."

Over months, I met with James Scurlock Sr. again and again, at length and briefly, at his house in North Omaha and over meals with his children and their mothers. His demeanor never changed—quietly, stubbornly proud, capable of introspection and apology. He never once refused a question, however personal or potentially insulting. He regularly talked about how he, using learning kits at home, in prison, and later online, had developed a facility with both French and Arabic. He spoke, too, of the skills in reading construction blueprints he'd acquired while locked up. He made no secret of his propensity for trouble and the months or years behind bars that could result.

He was the son of an Army dad, and had always wanted to join the military. His youthful joyrides in stolen cars ended that dream. He'd spent almost two years in a Job Corps program learning trade skills that could serve him a lifetime, like concrete masonry.

"People always need a place to live," he told me, "and every building is built on a concrete foundation."

But he was denied graduation and certification from the Job Corps after he and others enrolled broke into the program's commissary.

"I always had the wrong idea when something was going good for me in life," he said.

I did not hold back. Was having all those children wise? If he was aware of his knack for undermining his best opportunities, was it fair—to the mothers he was involved with or the children they produced?

He didn't ever flinch, and yet he never could really take on the question. His life choices might strike others as random or irresponsible, he'd say, but then he'd insist he tried his best to hold together all that he had helped bring into the world.

James Sr. had been sent away for two years when his son was young. It had been one of the great ruptures in the boy's life. It hardened his mother against his father. It was an embarrassment and a hardship, too. The older Scurlock's prison term became a talking point for the warring detractors who, in the aftermath of his son's death, liked to draw a line between the criminal records of the father and his boy. "See, no surprise," was the idea.

I asked James Sr. to walk me through what had happened. He managed a deep breath, and laid it out, every understandable and inexplicable bit of it.

The elder Scurlock's children were in Denver with his mother. He'd been trying to make a go of it living in a house that belonged to his mother's family. But in a matter of days, he'd lost both his job at Taco Bell and a line of construction work he'd been able to sustain with a local contractor. One of the checks he'd received for his construction work—for $6,500, he said—bounced. He didn't face eviction, he said, for it was a family house. But he could not even pay the electricity bill.

"I felt the world was closing in on me," he said. But he would not ask for help. "I'm a prideful person. So, I was, like, I will not explain my situation. I will figure it out. That's just me. That's James."

He decided to rob a video game store in Omaha. It was one he frequented, named Gamers. He resented the owners, and the financial security they radiated. He did not use a gun, but he was brazen.

"I wanted it all," he said. "I wanted the safe. I wanted it all."

James Sr. was arrested not long after. Shockingly, he'd gone back to Gamers to drop a friend off who wanted to buy some games. Workers inside recognized him as he sat outside in a car.

"I do not regret the action," he told me, "because at that moment I believed it was necessary for survival. Learned from it? Yes. Regret it? No."

Behind bars, James Sr. said he resolved not to waste a minute of his sentence. Nebraska, he said, had an impressive array of training programs for its inmates. He brushed up on his math skills, and dived into carpentry.

"All I did when I was in the pen was go to college," he told me.

When it came time to apply for parole, he opted not to. He did not want his freedom if he was vulnerable to being returned to prison for any of a wide variety of infractions. "That's a revolving door designed for you to come back," he said of parole. He chose work release, something that felt both safer and more productive.

"I'd made an intentional mistake, and I knew I was going to have to pay for it," he said. "What I wasn't going to do was become a statistic. I was not about to become institutionalized."

THE STORY OF young James Scurlock could not be reported without a fuller appreciation of North Omaha, the place of his birth and where he lived when he was killed. I bought books and watched documentaries. I drove its streets, learned of the museum dedicated to the ugly history of redlining in North Omaha. I attended its Native Omaha Days parade, an event held every two years that brings North Omaha's former Black residents back to their roots.

Churches were well represented—Mount Moriah, Zion Baptist. The Revolutionary Action Party had a float. There were women on motorcycles and elderly men in Shriner hats driving tiny motorcars. There was a Save the Youth marching team and the Pryme Time Steppers.

"Look presentable," the woman leading the Steppers told them. "Who knows how many cameras are out there. You look lazy, I'm going to pull you out my line."

Four generations of a single family could be seen lining one block of the parade.

Over my weeks and months in Omaha, I met with North Omaha legislators and activists, young and old. Some had lived the glory days of North Omaha, when it was a neighborhood of Black accomplishment and enterprise, electric with music clubs and the gospel choirs of its many churches. Others had worked to recover that glory after the damaging unrest of the 1960s, and the decades and years of governmental neglect since.

One was Preston Love Jr., whose legendary father had played with Count Basie and Duke Ellington. Love had worked in senior roles on both Jesse Jackson's unsuccessful presidential bid and the successful campaign of Harold Washington to become Chicago's first Black mayor.

"I was happy in segregated North Omaha," Love told me of his childhood. "We felt the trauma of racism. But we felt it together."

But Love, still in North Omaha, said he today was saddened by the fate of his community. It had suffered both the further betrayal of Omaha's white establishment and the surrender of its own people to political apathy. The number of people who voted in North Omaha was embarrassing.

"I'm shocked and dismayed," he said, "at the state of my beloved North Omaha."

I met with Brenda Council, too, the first Black female city council member and a two-time candidate for mayor of Omaha, and Ben Gray, who did years of gang intervention work before being elected to the city council, as well.

Council said she'd gone to a school with no gym, no cafeteria, and not a single white student. The shared bond within North Omaha, though, was strong enough to ward off any sense of inferiority or grievance.

"We didn't know how poor we were," she said.

Among the more fascinating characters I met in my makeshift research was Adam Fletcher Sasse, a white man who easily convinced me, through his published work and excited phone calls, that he was the unparalleled expert on North Omaha.

Sasse had lived homeless in Canada in his early years, and wound up in Omaha, at age ten, after his family car broke down three times on the city's outskirts as they tried to make their way to Kansas City. He grew up among the poor whites who lived in the trailer park north of Dodge Street, but he became charmed and then consumed by researching the history of North Omaha. Those efforts now run to more than five hundred articles online, many of them collected in four volumes he self-published. Detailed and sweeping, his work gets at it all, from the neighborhood's fur-trading days, to its polyglot collection of ethnic neighborhoods, to the impact of the Trans-Mississippi Exposition. He has captured North Omaha's economic trajectory, and he's created elaborate timelines of its racial history—including, by his count, one hundred riots. He writes candidly of the crack wars and, with as much alarm, the Black exodus from the city quietly taking place in recent years—down from 20 percent of Omaha's population to 12.

North Omaha is a kind of invigorating, illuminating obsession he, with a smile, still can't fully make sense of. But his scholarship and crusading have a clear and convincing declaration: you underappreciate North Omaha at your peril. It is not, he argues, what many of the white people in Omaha have often reduced it to—an irredeemable ghetto.

In one of our conversations, I asked him about a documentary I had seen called *Out of Omaha*. Sasse worried the film, however well-intentioned, risked reinforcing the hopelessness that can dominate discussions of North Omaha today, but he acknowledged its power, and did not question whether it had an appropriateness for anyone trying to understand James Scurlock's world.

The 2018 film, directed by Clay Tweel, is a ninety-minute feature that traces the tale of the twin Trotter brothers, Darcell and Darnell, as they do daily struggle against what one character, Wayne Brown, called North Omaha's "gravitational pull." Brown had grown up in North Omaha but gone on to become a successful lawyer. He said North Omaha's pull—of affection and danger, of family and history, of hard racial realities and easy street money—can be so great that it makes it near impossible to "fly out of."

Of life in North Omaha, one of the twins, Darcell, says, "I'm dying the same time I'm living."

The documentary unfolds over seven years, from 2010 to 2017, and it, like all stories about today's North Omaha, tries to capture the systemic challenges of the neighborhood without reducing it to a place of fatal pathologies.

The father of the boys is an addict and drug merchant, but he also takes both of them in when they manage the modest flight out of North Omaha to Grand Island, Nebraska, a rural, virtually all-white town where they find work and ultimately a future. When Darcell is implicated in a violent break-in and decides to turn himself in to the authorities, his father gets to him before he heads to jail.

"He showed me the ropes, how to survive inside," Darcell says with gratitude.

It's not perhaps an ideal episode of fatherly advice, but it is a conscious act born of care and loyalty all the same.

Segment by segment, I watched the film, and could feel the echoes of it all in the story of James Scurlock. The broken-up parents; the dad capable of love and disappointment, a victim of his own demons; the experience outside Omaha and how trouble could find one there, too. But the sense of community and durability, as well. How music was both a soundtrack to daily life and a career goal that might launch them from North Omaha's loving but sometimes lethal grip. And how children searching for identity and joy can find it in having children, perhaps too early.

Guns are a fact of life in North Omaha and a character in the film. Picking up a gun, Wayne Brown says, is "expected by the community, by family, by police." But Darcell makes clear, having one is as often as not an act of self-defense, not criminal intent.

Brown grew up in North Omaha, the son of a man, he says, "in the heroin business." He got out, got a law degree, married a doctor, and returned. He made it out long enough, then, to become a supposed example of what the academy likes to call Black exceptionalism.

A kid who faced down danger, refused to be defeated, made something extraordinary of himself against all odds.

He's not having it. He did the thug thing, the dope dealing and gun carrying and gang activity. To the extent he became exceptional is as much as anything else a matter of luck.

"I didn't get caught," he says.

The webs for young Black men, in North Omaha or Grand Island, are many—traps of their own making and those spun by the cynical systems of failed schools and predatory police.

Darcell always denied playing a role in the home invasion he was charged with, and after he spent four months in jail the authorities conceded they didn't have a case, and he was released. In Grand Island, both twins, along with a friend, were falsely charged with sexual assault by a woman who later recanted and was herself prosecuted for filing a false report. The news of the arrests makes the local papers; the news of their innocence doesn't.

In one scene, Darcell calls a local reporter and asks why. The reporter says he'll look into clarifying the issue. Darcell hangs up, and shakes his head.

"I'm proud of my composure," he says with a sad smile.

Both Darcell and Darnell work jobs in Grand Island. The mother of a friend gives them a basement room to live in after their father relapses and then runs. The two become concerned for a stepbrother back in Omaha, and try to persuade his mother to let him join them.

She doesn't, and her son is later charged with murder. He insists he didn't kill anyone, but the local prosecutor, Don Kleine, then in his third term as Douglas County Attorney, rejects the claims and charges the boy as an adult. He is convicted, sent away for decades.

Darcell feels the regret and anger of a failed parent: "I tried to save him."

It is a child who saves Darcell, his child. He is twenty-one when she is born, and he makes the most of a shared-custody arrangement.

He provides for her and plays with her. He delights her with french fries and instructs her in how to safely cross the street.

"She's my best friend," he says of his daughter, then two.

The twins are twenty-five when the film ends. Darcell and Darnell are about to open their own salvage shop in Grand Island. They are optimistic but not cocky. They make no promises, but neither do they set limits.

"No way am I done," says Darnell.

Darcell had always wanted a future in music. He wrote and recorded rap songs as a teen. He briefly got into a program run by a local nonprofit, and wanted to pursue musical engineering. As the documentary closes, Darcell goes back to writing lyrics and recording them into his phone.

"I'm rusty," he says.

He's also nostalgic for North Omaha. He returns there with the filmmakers, drives the streets, points out former hangouts. It is full of danger and deep bonds. It is home, and he aches for it.

In July 2021, Darcell recorded and released a single, along with a video, called "North Tales."

"I'm ecstatic to be revealing the cover art for my new debut single 'North Tales' dropping next Friday!!" he wrote on Twitter. "This song is my truth and it highlights challenges that my people face every day in North Omaha."

In the video, he is surrounded by the people of North Omaha, proud and grateful.

"We just glad to be here," Darcell raps in one of the song's refrains.

North Omaha, Wayne Brown says in the film, is a "black box," one created by humans and that to this day isolates and ensnares humans.

"It's a black box created by educational policies, housing policies, law enforcement, a criminal justice system. It keeps people in one area in poverty.

"But because it is man-made," Brown said, "I believe it can be unmade. But it's a hard road."

CRIMINAL CASE JV09-140 in Madison County, Nebraska, involved, its paperwork shows, "a child under the age of 18 years." The child was James Scurlock, and he was eleven. The police report on the case ran to twenty-seven pages. The single-spaced, typed-out narrative of the case prepared by detectives was eight pages long. The case involved the theft of a video game console and a number of videos and games.

While the language of the court records says that Scurlock, in carrying out the theft of the games, "did willfully, maliciously and forcibly break and enter" the house in Norfolk, Nebraska, that held the goods, the pages of detective notes suggest something a bit less sinister.

The games belonged to a twenty-five-year-old Norfolk man, and he reported on July 20, 2009, that the games were missing along with a cell phone and charger. The police notes indicate they suspected the man's house had been ransacked, for there was stuff thrown everywhere. The man, for his part, said he suspected kids had stolen the games, for there were things of value left around the house. He said the place had not been turned upside down by anyone; the house, he said, was a mess of his making.

As for the break-in, the police talked with a girl who lived next door. She told them two boys had simply opened the door to the house and gone in and out. She said they told her not to tell anyone. She was eight years old, and she told the cops the names of the boys.

Scurlock was living in Norfolk at the time with his mother and five brothers and sisters. They had arrived on a bus from Omaha and been taken in at the rescue mission homeless shelter. The children described their stay at the shelter as safe and stable. J.T., one of Scurlock's older brothers, said being seen as shelter children at school could be humiliating and the rules governing the shelter included a curfew of 6:00 p.m. Sometimes, J.T. said, he and James would stay out all night, sleeping in someone's car. J.T. said he and his siblings would find a way to trick their mom and make it out into the neighborhood for fresh air and a whiff of childhood freedom.

"We just wanted to play," J.T. told me.

The police first interviewed the boy who had gone into the house with Scurlock. He was twelve, and already under what the police paperwork says was "house arrest" for striking the principal at school. The boy told his mother and then the police a variety of versions—that James had borrowed his bike and later appeared with the games, saying a friend had loaned them to him. He later admitted going to the house but said his role was limited and his ignorance of what James was up to was considerable.

Scurlock was with his mother when police next interviewed him. He'd had no other brushes with the law. He was well-liked by his teachers at school. His younger sister Olivia has kept a bunch of artifacts of her brother's school years in Norfolk, stashed away in her bedroom along with rap lyrics he wrote and letters written to him from girls who had crushes on him.

Olivia, seventeen when I sat with her in Norfolk, held several boxes of the material on her lap as we talked. She smiled at each item she pulled out. One of them was a red-covered album, titled *James Scurlock 4th Grade Memories*. Scurlock had graduated from fourth grade—"Mrs. Wittgow's class"—a month before he and his mother met with police about the video games.

Inside the album, there was a chalk drawing of a "great horn owl." "First, the great horn owl is not a mammal," an attached note scribbled in pencil says. "Next, it sleeps during the day, hunts at night. It has a special bone in its neck that makes it turn." There are paintings of the planets, posed dancers in a line; dinosaurs constructed out of colored paper. There is, too, a modest one-page research project on Norfolk's most famous resident—the *Tonight Show* host Johnny Carson. "First, he came to Norfolk when he was eight. Also he started to entertain people. Every night he listened to the radio. Also, he donated a lot of money to Norfolk." It is signed, in printed letters, "James."

On one of its last pages, there's a personal profile: James S. "Careful, helpful, joyful, runner."

Lover of: "running track."

Who feels: "excited when doing something the first time."

Who fears: "tripping on the track when running."

Who would like to see: "track stars."

Who needs: "gifts and love."

Who gives: "toys and happiness."

Talking with police, Scurlock told a shifting set of stories about how he'd come by the console and games. He said a friend used to live in the house he went to. He walked in as he had many times before. He said a lady was there and told him his friend was moving. She had asked if James wanted a going-away present, he said. Challenged, Scurlock said that, no, that wasn't true. He'd just borrowed the games from his friend. Eventually, J.T., Scurlock's brother, showed up and admitted he might have had a role in the caper. The boys produced the console and games. It would take another day, but Scurlock's mother would find the stolen cell phone and give it to the pastor at the rescue shelter.

The detectives, according to the records, contacted their superiors. They wanted to know if the eleven-year-old Scurlock should be brought to the station house. They were told to issue a citation, and Scurlock's mother was told her son would have to appear in court or a warrant for his arrest would be issued.

Scurlock did appear, and the records recount the disposition: he pleaded guilty to one count of burglary; he was sentenced to six months of probation; he would do community service and abide by a 6:00 p.m. curfew. The stolen games and videos were itemized in court documents: *Grand Theft Auto*, *Richard Pryor*, *NCAA Final Four*, *NASCAR 2001*, *Fight Club*, *Boondock Saints*. Scurlock signed the formal court papers by printing his full name: James Reginald Scurlock. The available records make no mention of any services being offered to the family aimed at limiting the chances there would be future problems with James. In May of the following year, at the recommendation of the authorities, he was released from the terms of his probation.

It was not a shock Scurlock and his brother J.T., five years older, might have been partners in the burglary in Norfolk. They'd been the tightest of siblings, and Scurlock had worshiped the ground J.T. walked on.

"People think I'm exaggerating when I say he was literally with me twenty-four-seven," J.T. said of James. "But that's literally how it was."

I met with J.T. in Omaha, and we spent several days sketching out his life story, and his connection to his younger brother. Over the years, the two would be together in Denver, Omaha, then Norfolk, and back again in Omaha. They'd survive separations along the way, caught up in the sometimes-competing claims of custody by their parents.

J.T. joked that they both had ADHD and fed off each other's compulsive restlessness and energy. They'd partnered up early on when they were with their grandmother in Denver to do combat with their rival team of brothers, Nick and Antwan. And they both liked to stare together at a picture of their mom, a woman who had been out of their lives as much as in. The image left them both aching with hurt and angry with confusion.

J.T. was in seventh grade when everyone returned from Denver to Omaha. Omaha did not come with the charter schools and handsome house they'd enjoyed in Denver, but he and James were for a while reunited with James Sr., and introduced to an array of half-siblings they'd never met. J.T. and James fished and camped; it was in Omaha that he first got to formally celebrate his birthday; J.T. intervened at school if James was being picked on—he could be targeted for his small size or tattered shoes. The two endured their stint with their mother in the homeless shelter in Norfolk, including the burglary fiasco, and both were brokenhearted when James Sr. came to claim James and Rajeanna and return them to Omaha. "Worst day ever," J.T. said.

Ultimately, it would be J.T. who introduced James to life in the streets. In his late teens, and living back in Omaha, J.T. began to run with North Omaha's rougher crowd. He got into dealing marijuana. He came to carry a gun. Today, he sometimes tries to play off his and his brother's street life as a kind of lower-level threat—they weren't in formal gangs, he said, and they liked to come off as tougher characters than they were, to make money, maybe, or to attract girls. He said he felt "trapped" as a kid and the street life felt like an exciting kind of liberation.

"I thought it was okay," J.T. said. "I thought it was normal. I didn't know there was more to life than what I was seeing."

James Sr. saw what was happening. He sensed he was losing James along with J.T. He'd heard word of what the two were up to. When James Sr. was briefly jailed for driving with a suspended license, he heard from others in the lockup that James was in the street life. He confronted James, and James pushed back.

As I was seated with James Sr. in Omaha, he hung his head in front of me and pulled at his goatee as he remembered the night he felt James's future was foretold. He'd been after James to at least attend school. His sister Rajeanna had pleaded with him as well. James Sr. told James he was getting regular work; there was money in the house for what James might need.

"So, I sit down. I think I ask him one day. I was like, 'Dude, I'm hearing rumors that you're out here, you're robbing, you're stealing.' I was like, 'But you don't have to. Not at this moment of life, you don't have to. You don't have to do nothing that I did to survive.'"

James Sr. stared down as his thin, tattooed arms, their muscles rippling as he wrung his hands. His downcast eyes unblinking, he went on.

"He just looked at me. He didn't really say too much. I knew what he wanted to say. He wanted to tell me he's just like me. I could see it in his eyes. I'd seen that same look. I gave it to my mom."

Here's what James was saying: *Look, I'm no longer that person you know. This is who I am right now.*

NOT LONG AFTER, J.T. and James lit out for Norfolk. James Sr. was told the boys had run away. J.T. told me they had gone to help out their brothers Nick and Antwan, who were behind in their rent. The idea was to hustle weed in Norfolk, scare up the rent money, and head back to Omaha. Rajeanna was in Norfolk, as well.

It was barely twenty degrees on December 2, 2014. The plans for what would take place that night were hatched on the back patio of 108 S. 9th Street. James was there, and J.T. would soon arrive. Two Chicago men who had wound up in Norfolk, Pierre Evans and Rochester Pruitt, were there too.

James, then sixteen, would later tell police it was his idea to stick up the inhabitants of a nearby house, 108 W. Madison. One of the people who lived there was a drug dealer whom he'd got into a beef with. Word was drugs and money were in the house. Rajeanna, however, said the entire gambit was J.T.'s idea, and before the four of them left she pleaded with them not to go through with it. She thought it was wrong and reckless for J.T. to take his younger brother along. She knew James could not resist—he'd want to look big and unafraid to the brother he'd been side by side with their whole lives.

"It was split second; there wasn't a debate," Rajeanna said. "They didn't care what I had to say. I was younger and needed to stay in my place."

J.T. told Rajeanna to go stay with a friend for the night. Rajeanna can still see her two brothers and the men from Chicago walk out the door. Some had masks on; others didn't. It seemed destined for disaster.

The break-in at 108 W. Madison lasted five minutes, eight at most. The house had at least two floors, with three bedrooms on the second floor. The dining room, the police records show, was unused. What happened to the four people inside—one person was confronted on the first floor, the other three in bedrooms upstairs—had to have been scary, maybe terrifying for a while. There was a gun and it was sometimes pointed at the heads of the four people inside the house.

As a criminal enterprise, it was, when one reads the entire case file, a darkly comic bust. It netted the four robbers thirty-five dollars and less than an ounce of marijuana. J.T. had carried a black BB gun and the two men from next door might have had guns, too. But they'd all checked on the way over that any gun they were bringing was unloaded. No one was interested in anyone being shot. James, who was supposed to carry a backpack to put the drugs and money in, forgot it. J.T.'s identity was almost immediately known to the people in the house—three young men and a woman, all in their late teens or early twenties. They recognized J.T.'s distinctive voice, and the shirt he tried to hide his face with didn't cover all of it. One of the three men in the house promptly called 911, reported the crime, and named the likely lead suspect.

A number of detectives, including Sean Soderberg and Ricky Martinez, did rounds of interviews with the victims. It was not a hard case to solve.

One of the victims, Katelyn Nelson, said she knew J.T. was involved from the moment he walked into her bedroom on the second floor. She'd known him since sixth grade, she told detectives. They'd worked together for a while at a McDonald's. J.T. had been at the house before for parties.

"Why are you doing this?" she said she asked J.T.

The young woman, nineteen, told detectives she'd hidden her wallet underneath her when the men came in the house. They demanded it from her but never forced her to give it up. It held $600 from what she said was a recent paycheck. All they got from her room was a single dollar bill that had been on her hope chest and 12.5 grams of pot.

All of the victims said that, while scared and furious, they never thought the guns would be used. There wasn't much to steal, they told detectives, and they knew the seeming ringleader.

The police had J.T. in custody the next day. He initially denied involvement but then promptly confessed and named his three accomplices, including his younger brother. J.T. told them where he had hidden his BB gun and the University of Florida Gators sweatshirt he'd worn.

He agreed to write out a statement describing the crime and a letter of apology. The letter was in the records I'd acquired:

Dear Judge and victim's family

I, John T. Harden, is deeply remorseful for the crime I have committed, and never meant for any of this to happen. It was stupid and neglectful on my part for any of this to happen. I apologize to the victim's family, and I take full responsibility of my actions and for my involvement with the crime committed.

I wish I can go back and change everything. I'm regretful that any of this happened, and I wish I had no part in the crime that took place. I was easily misled into the actions that took place. Once again, I apologize to the victims and the victim's family, and I ask that I am forgiven for my actions.

John T. Harden.

James was quickly in custody, as well, and taken to the second floor of the Norfolk police station. He had his hands cuffed in front of him as he was interviewed. He, like J.T., briefly tried to say he had nothing to do with the break-in. He said he did not have a gun and had only stood by inside the house as the three others confronted the occupants. He said he had not bothered to cover his face "because he didn't believe the victims knew him." He admitted he had forgotten to bring the bag that was going to carry the takeaway. He said he and his brother had wound up without any part of what was taken, any of the thirty-five dollars or the marijuana.

"Scurlock basically felt this never should have been reported to the police," one detective's notes read, "because the victims were involved with drugs." One of them, he said, "has robbed many people in much the same manner."

Scurlock—five two and exactly one hundred pounds—was

charged as an adult but sent to the county's juvenile detention facility. Bond was set at half a million dollars.

JOE SMITH WAS the Madison County prosecutor when James Scurlock was charged for his role in the December 2014 armed home invasion. For people in Madison County, it seemed like Joe Smith had always been the top prosecutor in their part of Nebraska. He'd first shown up as an assistant in 1984, and was elected county attorney for the first time in 1990. He's never left or been defeated for reelection.

Smith had a public profile as something of a rural badass, an all-powerful law enforcement presence who knew everybody's business and who was unafraid of taking on all cases, big or small, violent or mundane. In 2004, the *Lincoln Journal Star* headlined its profile of him "Prosecutor of Trials of Madison County No Ordinary Joe."

The son of a meat-packer for Nelson Farms, Smith had worked his way through the Creighton law school in Omaha by tending bar at the Elks Club and the Holiday Inn. He did some criminal defense work after graduating but came to Madison County to polish up his trial skills. He never thought he'd spend the rest of his professional life there.

"I figured I'd get a couple years of heavy trial work in and then move on," he said. "But I ended up staying. I've liked it here. Nobody to impress other than doing the right thing. There's been a lot of challenges, challenging cases."

He's never doubted he's been doing God's work all the time.

"It's like no other job," he told the *Journal Star*. "It's a battle, a civilized battle. And the thing about prosecution, you're always on the right side."

When five people were shot dead in a bank robbery in Norfolk in 2002, Smith didn't shrink from the challenge, and won death penalty convictions for all three of the gunmen. He'd shrugged off suggestions the case was too big, that it would be best for federal prosecutors to run the case.

"It would have been cowardly and inappropriate not to prosecute," he said.

I went to see Smith to see how much he remembered about his office's handling of the Scurlock case. Short, unshaven, dressed in jeans and a short-sleeved plaid shirt, he was happy to talk in his office in the Madison County Courthouse. He dismissed with a sardonic smile any notion he was some outsize presence in Madison County. A little gruff and hard of hearing, and not naturally expansive in conversation, he'd pulled the papers on the Scurlock matter. He said drugs had been a problem in Norfolk for many years, and so the idea that the case involved an armed home invasion in search of drugs and drug money, he said, was hardly shocking.

He remembered that he had pulled Scurlock's papers together after Scurlock was killed in 2020 and sent a set of them to Don Kleine. Smith thought Kleine might use them to explore Scurlock's potential propensity for violence as he decided whether to attempt to prosecute Jake Gardner. He said he was unsure whether Kleine shared the file with Fred Franklin once he was appointed as special prosecutor. He did say Franklin never reached out to him to inquire about the details of Scurlock's criminal record in Norfolk.

I wanted to know if Smith stood by his decision to have Scurlock prosecuted as an adult, and not a juvenile. He said he did. He said he was sure Scurlock, when he was charged at age eleven for the theft of the video games, had been offered his office's help in straightening out his life.

"I mean, we'd already, by my view, been very fair with him," he said.

I asked him to confirm Scurlock had gone through the office's diversion program, but when he asked an assistant to check she told him he was wrong.

I said I'd looked at the case, and while it was clearly a serious matter, it had also been a kind of knuckleheaded episode. Scurlock was sixteen; could he have been more effectively dealt with as a juvenile?

"Knucklehead adventure that involved carrying a gun into a house where people could have been killed," Smith said, unmoved.

I corrected him that Scurlock was never charged with having a weapon during the crime. Smith would only concede that a charge involving a gun had never been pushed against Scurlock.

No regrets, then?

"When I look at the file and what we've done, if I have any regrets, it is that we may have been too lenient on some of the other ones," he said.

ON MAY 1, 2015, Judge Johnson held a hearing to determine if James Scurlock should be handled as an adult or juvenile. Scurlock was represented by Jason Doele, who had been appointed by the court because Scurlock's family could not afford a lawyer.

In the paperwork Scurlock's mother, Rajeanna, had filed in applying for a public defender, she laid out her financial situation: she'd worked at the Sunset Plaza Mall for just short of eighteen months but was earning just $7.25 an hour. Her monthly rent was $650, to go along with $112 in monthly electricity bills and another $21.75 for trash collection. She listed debts of $6,000 for student loans and $2,150 in medical bills.

Rajeanna would only talk with me briefly over many months of trying to contact her. She told me she'd grown up in an especially tough part of North Omaha—"Murder Town," she called it—and the family had needed public assistance to get along. She had her first child, she said, at fifteen, and there were three children by the time she was nineteen. I asked about James, her son, and she told me she hung on to the memory of him forever wanting to lay his head on her chest.

"He was," she said, "a momma's boy."

That momma's boy was now facing perhaps the most consequential moment in his seventeen years. Prosecutors wanted him jailed, and for three to five years. His lawyer wanted him treated as a juvenile, and to face no worse than probation.

One of the first questions that arose in front of Judge Johnson was whether James had been behind the entire break-in idea in Norfolk. He'd said as much in his interview with detectives, but his lawyer, with one of the detectives in the case on the witness stand, wondered if the detective believed it was really true.

"I didn't know if he was scared or if he was trying to, you know, make himself into, present himself to be, a bigger individual or important individual, bigger, badder person; I didn't know," the detective said.

Scurlock's lawyer pressed him.

"I'm just trying to get a sense of when you're talking to him in this interview room if you think he's trying to be a tougher guy, for example: 'This was my idea to do the robbery.' Did you get that sense that he was trying to be a bigger kid than what he actually was?"

"I thought that was probably—that was one possibility," the detective said. "I didn't know if that was it. I thought it was also a possibility that he was just trying to in a sense not be a snitch, a rat, or say anything."

"Something in your gut at least told you that that's probably not exactly the truth or the full truth?"

"Yes," the detective conceded.

Scurlock's lawyer was able to get the detective to admit there was no evidence Scurlock had a gun during the robbery. But the detective refused to concede that meant much.

"He was still one of the ones who went unlawfully into this place, opened the doors, unlawfully went into this place and knew what everyone was going to do and knew that he was going to possibly be taking stolen items that were taken under, you know, threat of death, basically, and leaving the residence with them. I would say that makes him an active participant."

Scurlock's lawyer called Rajeanna to the stand. He asked her if during her son's days in Norfolk schools teachers had ever raised any concerns about him. She said she'd once been called because he'd broken a window, but that it turned out to have been an apple he'd thrown while horsing around in class. She testified that no one had raised issues about his attendance or grades.

Scurlock's mother was asked why she thought it was appropriate that he be treated by the court as a juvenile. She said she doubted he'd have been the ringleader. He was immature, maybe, and had gone along. She said she had rarely, if ever, seen her son be violent.

"If he's transferred to the juvenile court and you were asked to be actively involved in his case, whether it involved coming to court hearings or participating in programs or family therapy or whatever the case might be, would you agree to do that?" her son's lawyer asked her.

"Yes."

"Do you think that would be beneficial to you and your son?"

"Yes."

The prosecutor was offered a chance to explore that idea with Rajeanna.

"Are you aware that if he's put on probation, he will be out I guess in the community and will not have that same structure that he has while he is currently more or less incarcerated?" the prosecutor asked.

"Yes."

In Nebraska, judges are tasked with factoring fifteen different considerations in deciding whether someone should be prosecuted as a juvenile or an adult. The considerations cover a range of things—prior bad acts; the likelihood of future crimes; the use of violence; the chances that counseling and other treatment options would work.

The prosecutor wanted to talk about Scurlock's prior conviction—the theft of the video games. He argued the two crimes—an eleven-year-old taking games out of an empty house and a sixteen-year-old participating in an armed break-in—were all but the same.

"I would note that, you know, without the presence of the firearms, the crimes then and now are relatively the same: entering the residence of another to take goods that are not his own," he said.

The burglary in 2009, the prosecutor argued, disqualified Scurlock from the county's diversion program—an option other than imprisonment that might involve something like specialized programs or even the county's alternative school.

In making a pitch for incarceration, the prosecutor argued, "I think that everything else being equal, a term of incarceration would provide a start to reality for Mr. Scurlock and demonstrate that the types of crimes that he's committing is only going to lead to a very desolate future.

"When this crime was committed," the prosecutor added, "he was just shy of being seventeen years old, you know, a year later he would have been eligible to serve in the military and other very adult activities, and I think he's more than old enough at that point to understand the seriousness of his conduct and to comprehend that his actions were both illegal and dangerous."

As further evidence of Scurlock's threat to the public, the prosecutor introduced an amateur music video Scurlock had appeared in. It was a recording done in Norfolk and included many of the staples of gangsta rap—boasting talk of guns and drugs and money. In it, Scurlock still looks like a child, radically younger and smaller than the others in the video. The gun in his hand appears to be the size of his head.

Given his turn, Scurlock's lawyer made an argument for probation. He tried to make J.T. the bad guy, saying James had just been hanging around with his "twenty-one-year-old brother and his thug buddies." His mother loved him, but James had gone through much of his young life "severely lacking in structure and supervision.

"I think his mental age is much less than his chronological age, whether sixteen at the time of the crime or seventeen now," the lawyer said. "I think his maturity is much younger than even a mature sixteen-year-old would be, even though we all remember at sixteen we did stupid things and said stupid things."

One by one, the judge went through the fifteen factors. He kept score, literally totaling up factors on Scurlock's side and those against him. But for the judge, it did not seem like a close contest.

"This was premeditated; this was planned," the judge said of the break-in. "Whether or not the defendant planned it, the defendant was aware of it.

"Treatment of the type this Court believes would be anticipated for the defendant should he be convicted would be a long-term treatment to deal with anger and recognition of failure and breakdown of moral choices."

And then the judge delivered the math that would effectively send James Scurlock behind bars for what could be years. Maybe it was just. Maybe it was one more familiar sentence in the cycle of incarceration that so many Black Americans have been derailed by.

"I have eight factors that, out of fifteen, go against the defendant's application for waiver of transfer to the juvenile court. I have, at best, two in your favor, Mr. Scurlock, and so as such it will be the judgment of this Court and order that your application to waive jurisdiction of this matter to the juvenile court of Madison County, Nebraska, is hereby denied."

Two months later, at sentencing, Scurlock's lawyer made a final plea for something like leniency.

"He's only seventeen years old," the lawyer argued. "He's got his entire life ahead of him. His criminal history is minimal other than the fact that he has a prior burglary."

Scurlock might have had friends who were in gangs, but he was not a member of any, the lawyer said. He'd used marijuana but never been cited for driving while impaired or the like. He was such a bumbling accomplice in the robbery, the lawyer said, he not only forgot to bring the bag for the stolen goods but had first tried to enter the wrong house. His time in detention between his arrest and his sentencing had included lots of schoolwork, and support from his teachers.

"He's shown that he can succeed with someone having a thumb over him and the necessary supervision," the lawyer said.

J.T. had already been sentenced to ten to fifteen years. It was the longest term any of the four received. J.T. said he was okay with the outcome, telling me he had taken the lion's share of the blame and the prison time to help spare his younger brother.

J.T. was first sent to the Tecumseh State Correctional Institution, the only facility to house death row inmates. He arrived there shortly after what had become known as the Mother's Day Riot. Some four hundred prisoners took control of the facility, lit fires, shot guards, and murdered two of their own. Over his years behind bars, J.T. told me he intentionally got himself placed in solitary confinement. He felt safer there, and developed a daily routine of eating, reading, and exercising that kept him sane.

He wrote to James from his prison cell as his brother awaited his own fate. "What's up, little man?" he began. "I wish the best for you come sentencing day because I wouldn't wish this shit on anyone. Real nigga shit. It's hard in here sometimes, but I take it in one day at a time and keep pushing it with a smile on my face."

J.T. wrote that he was the youngest inmate in the prison he'd been sent to. There were gang members, but few incidents of violence so far. He said he would put money in James's jail account when the time came. He promised James he'd find a place for him to stay when he got out.

"But whatever you do, go in there with your head held high and do your time," J.T. wrote. "Don't fall for nobody's bullshit. I got you no matter what. Love always, J.T."

In court, the judge asked Scurlock to stand.

"All right, Mr. Scurlock, is there any reason why judgment should not now be pronounced?" the judge asked.

"Oh, no," Scurlock said. "I've been in jail for a while."

The judge said he'd concluded Scurlock's "character and attitude" made clear he was "likely to commit another crime.

"It will be the judgment and sentence of this Court that on Count One, burglary, a Class Three felony, that you be sentenced to an indeterminate term of not less than three nor more than five years in an institution under the jurisdiction of the Nebraska Department of Corrections. Good luck to you, sir."

I FIRST CONTACTED Mari Agosta in the fall of 2020, just a couple of months after Scurlock's death. I had little idea how she would react. She'd lost the love of her life, and the father of her first baby. But news of Scurlock's assault on her had surfaced after he'd been killed. She first indicated she would speak with me but then went silent, and stayed that way for months.

Almost a year later, I sat in the living room of Mari's modest apartment in Omaha. We'd reconnected via text. I learned she was still very much a part of the Scurlock family's life. James Sr. helped look after Jewels, her daughter, and he and his girlfriend helped Mari get to work every day.

Mari had still been wary of me when I reached out a second time.

"I get that you have a story you are writing, but I'm not in the biggest hurry to share or talk about the life I had with James," she wrote to me. "I've been busy. I can get overwhelmed easily."

With time, it became clear she wanted to talk. She not only felt comfortable remaining a part of the Scurlock family but found it fascinating. There have been, and will be, she said, issues with some or many of the members. It might all be in her own book someday, she said, with a smile.

"I think I was in a very dark place," she said of our first interaction in 2020. "It's time. I need to speak up about my story."

We spent several hours together in Omaha. Mari is petite, and she was pregnant with a second child. Jewels, closing in on two years old, ran around laughing, climbing on her mom, and trying to get at the letters Mari held in her hand—letters James had written to her over the years.

Trying to report the life of James Scurlock had been challenging. He was young when he died, with a half a century or more of life ahead of him, whatever he would have made of it. He'd spent parts of his limited number of years behind bars, which was part of his story, but far from its entirety.

In Mari, I felt I had found someone with the legitimate claim to have known him best. Or if not best, then in a way no one else had. She had cried with him at the birth of their child, and suffered under his temper and violence. She had joined his family but also been one of the few people outside his family with whom James had ever really connected. She listened to the lyrics of his vivid raps and as well to the insecurities of a young man who for much of his life had felt rejected by one parent or the other.

After meeting on Facebook, Mari and James got together around Christmas of 2018. James had done his time at the Nebraska Correctional Youth Facility in Omaha. The facility can hold more than a hundred young people, from adolescents to those twenty-one years old. Inside, Scurlock earned his GED and eventually won his release. Outside, he held a number of jobs, sometimes doing roofing work with his father.

It was, in fact, Christmas Day that Mari went to first meet James. She'd opened her presents, and was supposed to go to an aunt's house for dinner. She wound up staying the weekend with James and his family.

She remembers hugging him for the first time. *I'm going to be around this person for a while*, she remembers feeling. He asked if he could kiss her, and she consented. *He's the one*, she thought.

"And after that, I swear, we spent every day together," she said.

Life inside the Scurlock clan wasn't always easy. There were, not surprisingly, mutating sets of allegiances and agendas, for good and not so good. There was competition for attention and affection, jealousies and alliances. It could be taxing navigating it all, and Mari came to think the person most exhausted by it was James. But there was always a place to stay, and then there was a baby.

Mari and James first learned she was pregnant through an at-home test. It had been bought at Family Dollar, Mari said with a laugh, and so they were unsure whether to trust it. Her water broke when she and James were in a car together, and she made sure to have him stop at Wendy's on the way to the hospital. It might take a while, and she was hungry.

"I'm not going to cry," James said to her.

But he did.

"I knew you would cry," she told him.

I asked Mari what she loved most about James.

"Out of everything that he went through," she said, "he still had a good heart."

That heart, she said, beat hardest for others, fueled his loyalty to J.T. and his attendance at Qwenyona's fundraisers, and his openness and even devotion to his imperfect parents. With the birth of Jewels, Mari thought, maybe that heart could beat hardest for James.

"I think he knew he deserved happiness," she said. "And that's what I think he was trying to find—self-happiness."

Mari has no real idea why James was at the protest on May 30, 2020. Could it have been for righteous reasons? Maybe. For opportunistic ones? Perhaps. Could one motivation—anger at a Black man's murder by police—have fed another, a desire to smash things, tear up the world, vent a lifetime's worth of frustrations and fury at a criminal justice system in which he'd been ensnared? Possibly.

Mari was in Lincoln, starting her new job, when she got word of the killing on Harney Street.

"What do you mean, he's gone?" she shouted into her phone when told by James's sister Hali. "Are we talking about the same person?"

Mari got back to Omaha, and spent the night with her parents. Her mother, for whom she was grateful and yet with whom she had long been at odds, expressed confusion about the protests that had wound up with James dead. "Why are people so angry?" the white mom asked the Black daughter.

Her mom was sincere, Mari thought. And her mystification telling. Her mom, she understood in that moment, was the problem.

"There's so many others who don't understand," Mari told me. "And that's why someone died that night. Because we are angry and people don't understand."

Mari said she had kept twenty-seven letters James had written her, almost all of them when he was locked up. One of them ran to seventeen pages. She was willing to share some of them with me. They are, of course, filled with the expected and repeated declarations of love and regret. And they are just snippets, nothing more, but also nothing less. And it may well be that the letters to Mari, excerpted here, are the single greatest archive of James Scurlock in his own voice:

> *I don't know if it's my pride or just me being shy, but I could never tell you how I feel in person. . . .*
>
> *The first thing I do is pick up the pen and write you. It's kind of like talking to you. I can't sleep worth shit in this damn place, this damn plantation. . . .*
>
> *I promise I'm going to keep you happy. I will not break your heart. I'm not that type of guy. I feel like I owe you and I don't even know why. Baby I don't ever want to break up. I want to last forever. If we have problems, I'm down to work through them. . . .*
>
> *The only thing I ask from you is to give me the same energy I give you. But like I said, if that is asking too much, let me know. So I can let you go before I get too deep and hurt myself. You are the only one I want. I'd rather be empty hearted than to be brokenhearted. . . .*
>
> *I hope I ain't writing too much and I hope you can read cursive too. LOL. . . .*
>
> *Better be getting them good grades too, baby. I say this all the time, education is important and key. I was a straight A and B student, baby. I swear, ask my dad, he will tell you. I ain't playing about my grades. Even though I was bad as fuck, my grades was always on point period. . . .*

This is about to be a long ass letter too, by the way, because this is my last envelope, so I might as well use the rest of my paper, right? Yep, I'll answer that for you.

I get butterflies when we kiss. I feel comfortable when I am around you. I don't feel like I have to hide anything from you at all and I love that feeling. I just want to be all you need and want to build with you and grow old and have someone I can really call my own. I just really want to be happy. I don't want my heart played with this time because that shit is getting old. . . .

I know I can be a handful, but shit, I'm your handful. I'm all yours at the end of the day. I just need to know if you are going to be all mine. I'm kind of nervous to give you my all because I'm scared to be hurt again. I'm tired of being hurt. . . .

I hope you like that pic I drew for you. It's the flower of Beauty and the Beast. You're the beauty and I'm the beast. Oh yeah, baby, I think I am going to stay sober for a while and possibly get back into working out. I hope people don't think I am boring. I just want to change for the better, and when I am comfortable with my change, I turn up again. But for right now, I got priorities. I want to make my mom proud of me for once. I gave her a rough life with all this jail shit, and I'm starting to feel bad because she wasn't really in my life because of it. I can't keep doing this to her because I know it makes her sad. I just got off the phone with her and she wasn't surprised or mad because she's so used to it by now, and that's what hurts her the most. I can't believe I let my anger do this to me again. I'm done putting my mom through bullshit and you are new in my life and I damn sure not about to do this jail bullshit for you. It's time to do better and what I say I mean. We're about to have a fun ass relationship. On God, I told my mom that I wanted to marry you. . . .

I want a tattoo that represents you. I would get your name, but I promised my mom I would get hers first, but it is going to be in Arabic. I want to get a tattoo of a queen of spades and get my queen protects me because dead ass you is my black queen. You're going to help me stay out of trouble and basically you protected me from throwing my life away to the system.

There was no particular order to it as yet. But she was not worried. The work at writing it down had been cathartic and rewarding. She said she'd done some of writing herself, but that so far it was just a collection of mere fragments of thoughts.

"It's nothing that's disrespectful to anybody. It's just the truth that I think I want to get out there. His truth is what I want to get out there. Our truth."

She shared some of what she'd written with me.

Here's one passage: "Driving past the last house I saw you in makes me feel so many emotions. The last blunt I smoked with you. The last hug I gave you. The first time I forgave you. Little did I know that was our last encounter. That was my goodbye, and it was too soon."

She'd chosen to believe James was, in his deadly grappling with Jake Gardner, trying to do good.

You were fighting for more than yourself and I understand that now.

There is no guide on how to deal with death. Everybody takes their journey alone. No matter how many people surround me I am still drowning in my pain. Some people deal with more demons than others. His last words haunt me. I hear them as whispers in my sleep.

Much of what she'd written was painful—hard to feel, hard to write, hard for me to read.

I have no hate in my heart for no one except none other than Jacob D. Gardner. That's the first and last time I will say his name.

She discloses she sought some refuge in self-medicating:

At a point drugs were the only way I could breathe. In the end I was unsatisfied with who I was becoming, so I gave them up. No matter how much I tried to drown myself in the things I thought could make me happy, there's nothing that could replace what was taken from me. I assume I have abused drugs to the point where they affect me more when I'm not on them. Consumption of complete and utter loneliness.

She riffs on what seems wrong with the world James inhabited:

Justice. That's just a word to me. A powerless empty ass promise of a word. Corrupted with greed, need for power, and money. Something the weak-minded or just plain ignorant will never understand. I think as a society we give the government too much power. We are supposed to be built on the foundation of human rights and fairness, but it's confusing as to why money, a piece of fucking paper, makes wrongs disappear.

And she writes of a hunger for James:

I wanna be returned to the earth. I wanna be returned to you. . . .

I cried out for you that night. Did you hear me? Why did you not come? . . .

Juju was the only one who could be as quiet as me and understand it. I heard his heartbeat as he heard mine. He was just as much of me as I was him. I hate the shit I put him through more than the pain of what he put me through. My love for him outweighed any possible thing you could think of. Now I'm just empty.

"Just Call Me Jake"

FOR THE U.S. SECOND MARINE EXPEDITIONARY Brigade, the run through the Iraqi city of Nasiriyah in March 2003 was not expected to be terribly eventful—if not a cakewalk, then at worst a modest challenge for America's ground forces on the way to Baghdad.

Jake Gardner was a member of the brigade, driving a light armored vehicle, and he and his fellow Marines had met scant resistance after crossing from Kuwait into Iraq. If anything, Gardner and his unit were eager for combat after weeks spent staging in the Kuwaiti desert.

The United States had cited Saddam Hussein's alleged possession of weapons of mass destruction as cause for its invasion of Iraq, and soldiers had been trained and equipped to confront the use of chemical weapons. In the rural desert heat, they spent hours in their protective gear, sleeping at night with their gas masks on.

"To this day, I don't know how any of us mentally held it together," said Matt Brill, one of Gardner's best friends. "One hundred and twenty degrees. Dust finer than powder. It was absolutely miserable. You are just waiting to die. You accepted it."

One of the men in the unit, James Dunckley, wrote of the experience to his wife—a mix of anxiety, excitement, and boredom:

> *We're getting ready to do more maneuver training at two o'clock. I hate doing it. It sucks. We just ride around and get out for security.*

Once or twice, they've been setting up movies all night for us. We watched Varsity Blues *last night. Boy, we have no support out here. So you and my family will have to be my supply. Please send two canteens, three skivvies shirts, three skivvies shorts for plastic antibacterial, baby wipe containers for D cell batteries. Two bars of soap, one five gallon Powerade or Gatorade.*

Dunckley could only exchange letters occasionally, and he had to watch what he said in them about his location and any plans for invasion:

They monitor the mail, including our letters. That's why I can't tell you where we are or what we're doing. Even if I did, they would black it out. Anyway, what I can tell you is the desert is a unique but beautiful place. The desert is fair, but firm. If not respected, it'll take you as fast as you came.

As the moment of attack grew closer, Dunckley seemed ready, confident:

I wish they would let us do our job and come home. All this crap about being here at camp and everyone acting crazy gets old. I came to do a job and nothing will stop me from doing it. The sooner we get started, the better. We're doing our combat upload for the vehicles. It was supposed to leave the next day. Then we'll await the order to go in, headed right for Baghdad. We're not to make any stops along the way. We'll be doing a lot of house to house fighting. That which never felt real now feels more real than ever. The reality of what we're about to do has hit home. We are no longer training.

Once inside Iraq, the Marines rolled mostly unchallenged. That didn't mean there weren't hard lessons to learn for young men at war for the first time.

Gabe Writer, a light-armored vehicle driver Gardner had helped train, remembers coming upon a handful of Iraqi men in the early hours of the invasion. While they seemed harmless and were not in uniform, Writer and his fellow Marines put them in plastic handcuffs, only to then wonder what they would do with their prisoners. The Marines released them and moved on. The Iraqi men would later ambush Marines coming behind. They'd hidden their guns, and retrieved them when released.

"We never did that again," Writer said.

The ease of their advance, if welcome, was unsettling to some of the Marines with Gardner.

"It never felt like a fair fight," said Aaron Flynn. He said the encounters with civilian fighters led to a certain internal questioning of what the United States was doing.

"I remember sitting with Jake and being introspective and trying to understand why this was happening," Flynn said, "why we were fighting these people, because so many of them just seemed like normal people."

Nasiriyah, a city of half a million on the banks of the Euphrates River, stood between the Marine brigade and Baghdad. The idea was to secure the two bridges that took you into the city and move as quickly as possible through the streets and buildings and get on with the race to the country's capital city.

While Nasiriyah was home to the Iraqi Army's Third Corps—constituted by its Eleventh Infantry Division, Fifty-First Mechanized Infantry Division, and Sixth Armored Division—it was not clear to the Americans if any Iraqi forces would fight, or how hard if they did.

What happened in Nasiriyah wound up being one of the ugliest and deadliest series of days of the war: intense urban street fighting; deadly mistakes that produced deaths and American hostages; U.S. airstrikes on their own soldiers; an enemy that fought from schools and hospitals and thereby sacrificed their own civilians; a full range of weather plagues: staggering heat; repeated sandstorms; driving rain.

The Americans gave as good as they got, inflicting heavy casualties and damage on Iraqi forces, those in uniform and those not. Matt Brill remembers the moment amid the unexpected and difficult urban fighting when the rules of engagement changed.

"It was, if anything moved, shoot it," he said. "Everything got killed; everything was destroyed."

An official Marine Corps history of the fighting in Nasiriyah was unsparing in its listed litany of mistakes or miscalculations for the Americans. There had been no reconnaissance of the city before the Marines charged into it; intelligence sources and planners at higher levels felt sure resistance in the city would be light; there were no artillery preparations and no air attacks on the city before the Marines tried to sprint through it; and if the resistance was supposed to be minimal, why had commanders pushed the Marines so hard in the run-up to the fight, depriving soldiers of sleep?

But the history also lauds the fighting that got done, and the United States' hard-won success in passing through Nasiriyah and making it to Baghdad in what felt like a flash:

> *Marines continually risked their lives to save others who were wounded or stranded. Junior officers and noncommissioned officers set the example and held their units together through the confusion of combat and shock of heavy casualties. They made difficult decisions under fire and refused to quit or withdraw until they had accomplished their missions. There were numerous cases of Marines continuing to perform their duties with determination even after they were wounded. Marines battled heat, driving rain, fatigue, fear, confusion, and a numerous and resourceful enemy—and performed gallantly.*

For Gardner, the most intense sequence of the fighting happened on the northern edge of the city. He and those with him had made it through Nasiriyah, and stopped to rest before carrying forward. A ring was formed, with the bigger tanks and trucks—"the big bulls,"

Gabe Writer called them—protecting the commanders and lighter vehicles inside.

What followed was the most intense and prolonged firefight of Gardner's tour in Iraq. His dad, Dave, remembers it lasting twenty-eight hours. Writer says it was thirteen. Sean Huze, another Marine there, said it was fifteen hours. Whatever, it was brutal, and felt unending.

"You grew up a lot in those fifteen hours," Huze said.

It was pitch black; that much everyone remembers. The Americans had gear that allowed them to see; and what they saw both confused and appalled them. There were uniformed Iraqi fighters, but also buses were being loaded with men, women, and children. They were given weapons and sent forward. It could be hard to tell who was who, and even harder to say if it mattered.

In the morning light, the Americans took in what they'd inflicted, on soldiers and civilians.

"You guys popped your cherries last night," one senior officer said to Gardner and his colleagues.

Aaron Flynn didn't love the crude humor.

"Aftermaths like that," Flynn said of the morning scene, "were really challenging and hard to have your nineteen-year-old mind fully process."

The Marine units Gardner was a part of became known as "The Destroyers," and a lot of what happened in Nasiriyah made its way into American popular culture. The Battle of Nasiriyah would be featured in the 2008 HBO miniseries *Generation Kill*; the ambush of the 507th Maintenance Company was re-created at the beginning of the 2003 NBC TV film *Saving Jessica Lynch*; the Battle of Nasiriyah was cited as a major factor in a Marine's PTSD in episode 2 of the 2010 PBS series *This Emotional Life*.

Once through Nasiriyah, Gardner and the other Marines raced to Baghdad without similar hurdles. There were, though, repeated and unnerving firefights. Ambush to ambush, Writer said.

"You're driving, just trying to sneak into a town, and all of a sudden bullets just riddle off the vehicle," Writer said. "RPGs landing in front of you, exploding right next to you."

"A lot of surrendering. But getting shot at every day," said another Marine with Gardner. For Matt Brill, the threat of chemical munitions didn't fade amid the firing of bullets and mortars. He clutched with white knuckles the pills he was supposed to take in the event of a chemical attack.

Writer remembers Gardner's sense of resolve along the incursion to Baghdad, and then deeper to Tikrit, Saddam's hometown.

"Maybe he was a little scared or stressed or tired," Writer said of Gardner. "But he always told us, 'We're here. Let's do this. We'll get through it.'"

In Tikrit, Gardner and the other Marines got to walk through Saddam's palaces. There were eighty bedrooms in one, Flynn remembers being told. Marble swimming pools, too.

"This is not Michael Jordan money. Not Kobe Bryant," Flynn said. "A whole other level of wealth."

The palaces were set against the abject poverty of the ordinary people living in Tikrit, and so Flynn and Gardner allowed themselves a sense of pride and satisfaction at the U.S. success in taking down Saddam and his soldiers. A bad guy had been toppled. Poor and oppressed people might have a new life.

But across the weeks of combat, the encounters with the Iraqis, their overmatched fighters and the victimized civilians, Flynn and Gardner became consumed by doubts about the purpose and integrity of their mission.

"They were just going around to villages and putting people on buses and sticking AK-47s in their hands and sending them right at us," Flynn said of the Iraqi authorities. "In the morning, there's just carnage."

"Was it really this just cause we had been led to believe it was?" Flynn said he asked along with Gardner. "I can specifically remember talking with Jake about how to handle the extreme situations and just understand the grieving process and the kind of psychology behind the extremes of combat. There was no counseling or nobody coming to tell us how to cope with this. Our heads were kind of in the same place, starting to question why we were there."

SUE BEUTLER MET Dave Gardner at the checkout line of the supermarket she was working at in El Paso, Texas. It was Thanksgiving and Dave was buying a TV dinner. She asked if he'd like to join her family for the day's big meal. He couldn't, but the connection had been made. That was November 22, 1973; they were married on November 22, 1974.

Jake Gardner was their first child, born in El Paso. Dave's family was from there, and his father ran a heating and cooling business. Sue had been born in Norfolk, Nebraska, the same meat-packing town where James Scurlock spent some of his early years. Her stepdad had been transferred from Nebraska to El Paso, and she had come with him.

Dave's father was a Korean War veteran, and a deacon and treasurer at a local Baptist church. The father ran a property management enterprise as well as the heating and cooling business, and Jake would often accompany his father making the rounds of upkeep and repairs across El Paso.

Jake Gardner was enrolled at the Northeast Christian Academy, a tiny private school. His class was made up of three boys and seven girls. He became a Boy Scout, loved animals, and got into tae kwon do. And from almost his birth, he was his paternal grandmother's favorite grandchild. She picked him up at school while Sue worked at any number of supermarkets—Albertsons or Bag and Save. Jake adored her in return, her homemade cooking no small reason why. When Dave's father died, Jake sacrificed his seventh-grade summer to go live with his grandmother and keep her company.

But Sue missed her family back in Nebraska, and both she and

Dave were worried about El Paso's school system as Jake, along with his younger brother, were approaching middle school and high school.

Sue and Dave's decision to move to Omaha was traumatizing for Jake. The move meant they'd have to give up their dogs. When the time to go came, Jake hid crying in his closet with the dog he'd been given for Christmas.

Dave and Sue had done their research on schools in Omaha, and they moved into a place within one of the city's very best districts. Jake did middle school there, and then went on to the district's top high school, Millard West.

There he met Joe Rowland, one of eight children and a kindred spirit. Jake and Rowland were close pals through high school, and they would later enter the Marines together under what was known as the buddy program.

I spoke at length with Rowland during one of my trips to Omaha. He described Jake Gardner as a kid who seemed to fit in with everyone at Millard West, maybe because he didn't fit perfectly into any of the various groupings or cliques—the nerds or the jocks, the potheads or the cheerleaders. He said Gardner often stood up for bullied kids even if it meant "getting his ass whipped."

Rowland's sister Wendy was in Gardner's grade. She dated a Black student at Millard West, and paid a price for it: Her friends and others at the school ostracized her. They wouldn't so much as look at her in the school hallways. But Gardner not only stood by her; he threw in with the boyfriend. They and others together rode dirt bikes and smoked cigarettes and tinkered with cars.

"Never a moment's doubt," Wendy said of Gardner's support, "never a moment's hesitation."

Rowland and Gardner, each coming from families of modest means, always had a job in high school, and for a while they both worked at a local movie theater. Rowland said Gardner was an inveterate hustler at the concession stand where he worked, a master of persuading people to get the large drink instead of the medium, to buy the Twizzlers to go with the Mike and Ike. There was nothing in it for him; he wasn't working on commission. He was just a natural salesman.

"He had a way of making friends with people that he had no interest in, who didn't know him or anything," Rowland said.

And Gardner had a spine when it came to doing the right thing.

Once, the boss aired out Gardner and another employee for some failing involving shoveling snow outside the theater. The other kid left in tears, fired. Gardner gave an impromptu lecture to the boss about loyalty, the hours he had put in, the quality of his work. The boss backed down, and Gardner kept his job. Rowland watched it, mouth agape.

Gardner found a way to get his dad into the theater for free, and the two bonded over movies—*The Big Lebowski*, *Pulp Fiction*, Robin Williams, Adam Sandler. But Gardner was nothing special as a student; he loathed homework. When he graduated, he was pretty set on the Marines. He enjoyed, especially in front of his Navy dad, the crack about how the Marines were technically a department of the Navy—the men's department.

His mother wasn't laughing.

"Marines are the first ones in," she told Dave and Jake through tears.

IF YOU WANT to make an impression at Marine Corps boot camp, show up short, weighing maybe 140 pounds, and have a giant Superman tattoo emblazoned on your chest.

"The drill sergeants, well, they had a target for the next thirteen weeks," Dave Gardner said of his son and his outrageous tattoo.

One of the Marine recruiters who came to know and employ Gardner said the tattoo was consistent with Gardner's very enlistment. He saw Gardner's entry into the Marines as an act of defiance: "'The little guy can't do it.' It was him giving a big middle finger to the people who said you can't."

Gabe Writer met Gardner, and instantly liked him.

"He walked tall, real proud, big smile on his face," Writer said. "That was Jake Gardner. Ready to go."

Most recruits called each other by their last name, just like their superiors. Not Gardner. "I'm Jake," he said. "Just call me Jake."

The soldiers in training were grouped by alphabet. Gardner would become close with any number of young men whose names began with *G*, including an Armenian American whose grandfather had been enslaved by the Turks in the early twentieth century.

"I didn't like him at first," the former Marine said of Gardner. "A little short guy always pushing the limits."

But he ultimately grew fond of Gardner's willingness to question authority even as they, as Marine recruits, were supposedly being broken of the trait.

"Why, why, why, the fucker was always asking why," the former Marine said of Gardner. "He earned a nickname other than Superman: Lance Corporal Why."

Soldiers sought Gardner out for his counsel.

"An enlightened guy to talk to," said a Marine in boot camp with Gardner whose heritage was a blend of Mexican and Native American. "A down-to-earth hippy. He didn't judge anyone."

One of Gardner's best and most lasting friends was an African American kid from the Omaha suburb of Bellevue. He'd enlisted in the Marines because he'd emerged from high school without a lot of discipline or purpose. He'd dropped out of college and, looking for a lifeline, fell in love with "the legend and the lore of the Marines." Boot camp, he said, "broke us down and put us back together."

He and Gardner talked University of Nebraska football, and the Black Marine said he over time came to all but live in Gardner's barracks.

"We just clicked," he said.

Matt Brill, a Jew originally from Queens, New York, would befriend and fight alongside Gardner in Iraq. Brill's father had been a Marine, although Brill never learned that until he'd signed up himself. "Destiny in my blood," he said ruefully. A former high school linebacker, Brill said the Marines were a good fit. He was used to pain and to being told what to do.

Brill and others with him among the "straight-leg" infantry who did not become armored vehicle drivers liked to mock colleagues such as Gardner as "Hollywood Marines."

James Dunckley, however, found the boot camp experience galvanizing and fortifying, as a soldier and a Christian.

"I don't think boot camp has changed me all that much," he wrote to his wife, Jennifer. "But I'll let you be the judge of that. It did make me grow up. Also, it allowed me to get my head together and figure out what I want out of life. It also showed me how I have a tendency to shy away from responsibility. I've learned to be a better leader. I'm a servant of God and I will serve him wherever he wants me to go."

If anyone was asking themselves why they had joined up, the question was settled on 9/11. In their barracks Gardner and others watched the Twin Towers fall.

Rowland told me what it felt like in America at that moment: "Nobody cared what color you were. Nobody cared what your political background was. We really gelled as a country."

THE TERRORIST ATTACKS of September 11 also tugged at the patriotic heart of a young aspiring actor named Sean Huze.

Huze grew up poor in Baton Rouge, Louisiana, although by middle school his family had graduated to what felt more like the middle class. His parents were both speech pathologists, and compelled Huze to read as a child. "You had to read Mark Twain before you could go play," he said.

He wanted to be an actor, and at twenty-five or twenty-six he'd shown potential. But with the toppling of the Twin Towers, Huze decided to go fight, and become a Marine, and he wound up in Iraq.

"Spring break 2003," he joked darkly. "Lots of sand; not a lot of water."

Huze was in the same battalion as Gardner, and was there for the prolonged firefight at the northern edge of Nasiriyah.

"Couldn't look in any direction without seeing death," Huze said.

Back from Iraq, Huze made a rare request of his superiors: Could he take a brief leave to pursue a creative idea? He wanted to write a play about Nasiriyah, about what he and the other Marines had seen, done, endured, become. His commander granted the request, and Huze borrowed $3,000 from his grandfather, a World War II veteran, to finance his efforts.

Huze produced a one-act play called *The Sandstorm*, and it opened in a small theater space in Los Angeles. If there were few seats, there was considerable interest, and sixty people crammed into a place meant to hold thirty.

"I wanted to take them into our world for an hour regardless of their personal feelings about the war," he said. "And I wanted to try and make sure they hadn't forgotten or shook off that experience when they had their coffee the next morning."

The Sandstorm involves a mix of infantrymen and their leaders, and the Battle of Nasiriyah is its central event.

"My goal, conscious or not," Huze said, "was me trying to reconcile who I was before, who I was there, who I was after."

It allowed him to work through, in quiet hours of writing and visceral moments of acting, what no one in Iraq in 2003 had the time or luxury to attempt. "You try to work shit out in the moment," he said of the actual combat, "you are going to get your grape popped.

"There's a lot of truth in *Sandstorm*. But putting it on other characters was somewhat freeing," he said. "You could dig deeper. Expose more while feeling less exposed."

In one scene, a soldier back home tries to come to terms with the fact that a child had been killed amid the street fighting in Nasiriyah:

> *Big fuckin' war hero. Everyone's so proud, and hell you actually believe you accomplished something. I was fucking Teflon for about the first month. Nothing over there seemed to follow me you know? Then that damned kid kept popping out in my mind. What did he do to deserve to die that day? He couldn't have been more than four or five. Couldn't have any wrong in him at his age. Wrong place, wrong time . . . ahhhhh bullshit! It can't be that simple. It's gotta be wrong for that child, that fucking baby to die! Someone has to be blamed and we pulled the goddamn trigger.*

One of the characters in *The Sandstorm* is, like Jake Gardner, a driver of one of the light armored vehicles critical to the march by Marines from Kuwait to Baghdad. He talks of having to deal with the prospect of chemical weapons. Warning alarms went off a lot:

> *My mask and gloves went on and almost instantly the sweat began filling the eye compartments of my mask. I tried to calm down as the restrictive air flow sent me into an instant panic. As my heart pounded away in a rapid staccato, my breaths became more and more shallow. And I did the unthinkable. I broke the seal of my mask. As the air hit my clammy skin, I instantly began to calm. I knew I should put my mask back on, but couldn't bring myself to do it. The fear was too great. From that point on I never used my mask effectively. Time after time we'd get the alert and time after time I risked it. So, folks are all pissed off about there not being any weapons of mass destruction. Shit, not me. My ass is damn lucky there were no WMD over there.*

How otherwise good young men were turned into something more like monsters through the demands of a dehumanizing and increasingly illegitimate war made for some of the most arresting and hard-to-watch scenes. Again, this one involves a Marine in the exact job Gardner had:

> *Sitting on my LAV, I tore open an MRE and drank from my canteen. Just then I caught movement out of the corner of my eye and with one motion, dropped my canteen and raised my M-16. There was a pile of half a dozen or so Rags and one was still alive and kicking. Well, maybe not kicking. I jumped down and walked the 10 feet towards their sandbag bunker. I kicked away the two AK-47s and pointed my weapon at the man's chest. I had full intentions of sending this fucker straight to Allah until he started weeping. I paused long enough for him to raise his hand and make the gun symbol with his thumb and forefinger. He pointed it at his own head and then put both his hands together like he was praying. I got it. He was begging me to put him out of his misery. . . . The more he wept and pleaded, the more I enjoyed my meal. See, I'd lost friends over there already. No one showed them any mercy, so why the fuck should I give any to this motherfucker? He kept begging to die, and I smiled, knowing he'd die soon enough. But he'd suffer in the meantime. And I'd eat.*

Nearing the end of the play, a character ruminates on all of it, losing friends in firefights, taking the lives of others, fearing losing one's own, being asked to carry it all inside and go back to a life in the United States:

> *I don't mean in some general sense like we all know one day we're going to die. I'm talking about feeling like it was imminent. Like within the hour or at most the day. Knowingly placing yourself in harm's way. It's not a natural act. I don't know if it's courage either, but it's something. That's what I was dealing with the night before we hit Nasiriyah. Word was coming down that we were going in sometime between that night to dawn. It was a mess. Nas had already garnered the nickname "Dodge City" and we knew of several Marine and Army casualties. It was rumored that the poor bastards that had been taken prisoner were paraded through the streets naked and then shot execution style. All this shit was swim-*

ming in my head. My mind trying to process this and still focus on what I had to do within the next few hours . . . The city would light up as mortar and artillery rounds impacted. The power was down there so it was only illuminated by the explosions and fires. It was almost beautiful. We talked about our kids, his little boy and my daughter. I talked about my wife and my parents. Talked about high school, little league, pee-wee football, all those wonderful experiences in life that go by so fast that you never stop to appreciate while they're happening. Father, son, brother, friend. Track star, quarterback, Marine. The things we use to define ourselves, who we are, what we are. Boom! Just like that. And you're gone. Fucking mist and a memory is all that's left. . . . There were four of us on my crew. I was the oldest at 27 and the youngest was 18. Just beginning our lives yet here we were, possibly in our last hour. A part of me screamed out against the insanity of the situation. It should be simple. People there want to kill me, I don't want to be dead, so don't fucking do it! But we did. We pushed right into that town and lit everything up that moved. The fear gave way to adrenaline and a part of me was actually enjoying it. And then it's over. The death, the destruction is left for others to deal with as we rolled on to our next objective. And I searched my soul for how I felt about the death that I brought that day. Searched for some sort of human feeling of regret or compassion. Searched and searched and came up with nothing. Nothing man! Maybe the only casualties weren't the ones lying dead on the streets of Nasiriyah. Maybe some of us are walking dead, soulless shells of the men we were.

I talked at length with Huze. He'd gone on after his return from the war to find parts in several movies, including the film *In the Valley of Elah*, a story of soldiers who served in Iraq starring Tommy Lee Jones.

"*Sandstorm* doesn't take a position on the war," Huze told me. "It's working shit out through art."

He told me that while he is proud of the acting work he got, life has been a struggle over the last eighteen years.

"I don't think I've had a day out of the Marine Corps when I totally had my shit together," he said. "What's going on externally is not what is going on internally."

He lost his home, got in a business dispute that so destabilized and enraged him, he contemplated violence. He did a stint in jail for contempt of court.

"Holy shit, I was insane," he said of the legal dispute. "Filled with murderous rage. Eliminate my enemy. Eliminate the threat.

"The USMC is very good at turning civilians into warriors," he said. "They are really shitty at turning them back into Joe Blow."

He recalled how it always felt awkward, or worse, when people back home would acknowledge what he'd done for his country.

"What exactly are you thanking me for?"

To this day, he said, the struggle for normalcy is real and at hand. Always.

"Iraq is as fresh as if it happened yesterday," he told me. "Perceiving threats that aren't there. For threats that are, conditioned to respond with overwhelming force. We are trained to quickly escalate."

He ended one of our chats with an acknowledgment of the size of the assignment of reacclimating.

"How to get quiet. How you get peace. If you figure it out," he told me, "give me a ring."

BACK FROM HIS tours in Iraq and Haiti, Jake Gardner made his way to Humboldt County in Northern California. It's hard to say all that he carried with him inside his heart. But he had suffered one, likely two traumatic brain injuries, one overseas during the sprint to Baghdad, the other as a consequence of the brutal beating he took outside the bar in North Carolina.

A number of his Marine buddies were converging on Humboldt County, to heal, to rethink their life's ambitions, to sleep among the redwoods and listen to the Pacific. Humboldt State University offered a special program for veterans that allowed them for free to take classes that would prep them for entrance into a full four-year college.

The leader of the effort was Ben Gevorgyan, Gardner's first and fastest friend from boot camp. In all, eleven Marines would spend time in Humboldt County, including Aaron Flynn, Gabe Writer, and Matt Brill.

Ben had grown up in a mixed neighborhood in North Portland, Oregon. He was both erudite and troubled, the son of a Portland State University literature professor. Ben told me he was doing book reports in eighth grade that were the equivalent of what his dad's college students were turning in. His was a liberal household, but he also spent summers logging with his grandfather in Alaska, and that gave him a taste of a workingman's perspective.

Ben, whom I met and corresponded with repeatedly, likes calling himself a "hook-nosed Armenian" with olive skin, and a familiarity with ethnic hatred. His paternal grandfather had been enslaved by Turks. Ben said with sarcasm that his ethnicity and background made him an odd best friend for a supposed white supremacist.

His Armenian grandpa's tale is a remarkable one, as Ben told it to me: "My grandfather was the youngest of a family of fifteen in Armenia when the Armenian genocide happened and his family was all murdered. He was nine years old. The last time he saw his mother she was dying of thirst in the desert. Someone came up to him at nine years old and hammered a nail through his hand and tied a rope to it and took him off to go be a slave. And he was a slave from the time he was nine to the time he was sixteen, when he escaped and wound up in an American orphanage. He got a wrestling scholarship to the University of Colorado and became a doctor of veterinary medicine."

Ben's own story is one of violence and tenacity, too.

Ben had got into dealing marijuana in Portland, often in its Black neighborhoods, and he left home at fifteen. He became a wrestler, too, one of the few white kids who were a part of a prominent, mostly Black wrestling program in Portland. His parents divorced;

his wrestling coach killed himself, and Ben wound up being stabbed in the back with an ice pick at a party in Portland. He'd see himself criminally charged for assaulting his estranged dad. He did ten months in a juvenile detention facility.

He'd always wanted to join the military. It might save him from himself, and his surroundings. Service ran in the family. He said his great-uncle was with Merrill's Marauders in Southeast Asia in World War II, a special operations jungle warfare unit led by Frank Merrill. Ben said his uncle earned three Bronze Stars, three Silver Stars, three Purple Hearts, and a battlefield commission from sergeant to captain.

Ben's felony assault charge barred him from joining the Army. But the Marines were willing to listen. He remembers his exchange with his recruiter:

"Do you like to fight?"

"I guess so."

"You want to leave tomorrow?"

Ben did well on his tests as an enlistee, which led to another brief, wiseass exchange with his superiors.

"What do you want?" he was asked, meaning what kind of unit did he want to apply for.

"Marine Corps infantry," Ben said.

"Did you not hear me?" the officer asked, baffled that someone who had tested as well as Ben would want the hardest and dirtiest job.

"Marine Corps infantry," he said again.

"This kid's an idiot," the officer concluded.

"Off I went," Ben said.

In the end, Ben would not fight in Iraq. He badly injured his back in a Humvee accident during training, and was eventually discharged. He said he watched Day 1 of the ground war in Iraq from a hospital bed. He suffered over the coming months from a kind of survivor's guilt, one that worsened, he said, when people, including those he'd enlisted with, started getting killed.

Ben was not sure what to do with himself, having been robbed of his chance to go to war. His older cousin, it happened, ran a big cannabis operation in Alaska. He gave Ben a little box with fifty small marijuana plants.

"Ben, dirty hippies are making millions in California," his cousin told him. "If you can't do it, you're a total piece of shit."

Humboldt County was an idiosyncratic blend of deep forests and tremendous beauty, free-love evangelists and drug-running criminals. It's home to close to 50 percent of the country's remaining old-growth redwood forests. In the mid-2000s, though, the medical marijuana market had made growing cannabis in Humboldt County more legitimate, and it began to attract entrepreneurs who looked forward to a future of fully legalized marijuana.

Ben got hold of 120 acres, pitched a tent, and began what would be nine years mostly off the grid, growing marijuana and pursuing other side businesses, and extending an invite to his fellow Marines to come join him.

"If all you know is how to kill and destroy, a lot of these guys weren't in any condition to start going to Safeway and taking orders from the dairy manager," Ben said. But connecting with the land, and the idea of cultivating life, even plant life, held comforts.

"Just the physical act of becoming a farmer and learning to nurture," Ben said, was therapeutic. "You're watering plants instead of shooting high-explosive rounds at people."

Aaron Flynn was among the first to join Ben. It took some time to settle in, he said. There were some bar fights. The Marines could be, Flynn said, "aggressive assholes." But he said they were met with nothing but kindness and empathy by most people.

Flynn said he'd taken the familiar "cocktail" of medicines the VA doled out to treat his PTSD, anxiety, and bouts of depression. "But it strips you of your personality," he said of the drugs.

Going to school, growing plants for profit, enjoying the physical beauty of the forest and ocean, he said, was restorative. As was smoking some of their product.

"Maybe we spent a little more time on the couch than we would have otherwise," Flynn said. "Maybe we ate a few more potato chips than we would have. But we were able to go to school and get our personalities back."

Gardner eventually joined as well. He brought the dog he had then, a pit bull, and lived with Ben in the tent initially. They took turns having the dog join them in their sleeping bags for warmth at night.

Ben doesn't hide that, for a time, he turned his acres into an illicit operation, selling marijuana in bulk to folks who would peddle it illegally around the country. He got busted once, he said, but paid off the local authorities to keep the charge a misdemeanor.

Ben said Jake would help him trim and harvest his marijuana plants but that Gardner had no real appetite for the illegal end of things. When marijuana laws in California were loosened, Ben and Flynn acquired one of the very first government licenses to grow and sell it.

The Marines, anyway, were good company for one another amid the redwoods. They traded both stories and doubts about their service.

"What I've found is that guys that really did a lot of stuff usually don't have a problem talking about it," Ben said of combat tales. "A guy who really did shit will tell you, matter-of-fact, what happened."

Gardner had his share to tell.

"Was he squeezing the trigger?" Ben said of Gardner's war experience. "No, but he's getting the vehicle in position when they shoot high-explosive rounds at busloads of civilians."

Some of those who gathered in Humboldt County shared a common tattoo—gotten in honor of the loss in Afghanistan of a beloved Marine they had trained and fought with named Ron Payne. For Gardner, who had one of the memorial tattoos, Payne's death was a devastating blow, one he would struggle to accept throughout his life.

Payne, a six-seven football and basketball star in high school in Florida, was killed while on patrol in Afghanistan, perhaps by friendly fire. He'd been revered and cherished within the company of Marines. Giant, soft-spoken, professional, loyal, modest, and fearless. "The perfect Marine," said Matt Brill. Aaron Flynn had been in charge of collecting Payne's belongings and writing the Dear John letter to his girlfriend.

Now in Northern California, the Marines who had served with Payne were all figuring out what they wanted to do. And how they wanted to live with the pain they'd suffered.

Flynn said Gardner was rarely without his weapon. He'd fought in a war, and then he'd fought for his life after nearly losing it in the streets around Camp Lejeune. He didn't like to have his back to the door. He cased every room he entered.

"Our experience shapes us. He had an experience when he could have been killed," Flynn said. "And that never left him—what can happen if you let your guard down."

Gardner actually listened more than he shared. As in boot camp, the Marines found him a compassionate sounding board.

"It was therapeutic to help people around him," Ben said of Gardner. "That in itself was healing for him. A shepherd of people."

Gardner dabbled a bit, both with school and with marijuana. He eventually found a place on the coast, in Mendocino. There were whales and giant trees, dramatic cliffs and sunshine. His parents up and sold their place in Omaha to join him. His father, Dave, was struggling with what eventually became a serial set of medical issues, from bypass heart surgery, to cancer, to mysterious infections. The sun felt good, a tonic for the bitter Nebraska winters.

Gardner befriended a local woman who ran a restaurant, and got bit by the idea of running his own business. She had a trove of books and videos by Tony Robbins, the prophet of positive thinking. There was *Unlimited Power*, and *Awaken the Giant Within*. Ben said Gardner ate it up and himself became a kind of self-help guru. He was going to streamline his life, have absolute focus, and will himself to success.

"He found his little chunk of paradise out there for a while," Ben said.

In the end, Gardner liked his business prospects better back in

Omaha. He and his family knew people. Omaha was a city that was growing, and diversifying. He and his parents headed back.

"It was a nice reset for him," Ben said of Gardner's couple of years in Humboldt County. "One of the most therapeutic I've seen."

MICHAEL RUSSELL WAS a young Army neuropsychologist at Fort Bragg in Texas when he first began to connect the dots on a military medical phenomenon that would consume much of the rest of his career.

Russell, the son of a Seattle cop and a mother who worked for Boeing and who could have been the model for the World War II character Rosie the Riveter, had done stints studying and caring for soldiers, first at Fort Lewis in his home state of Washington, later at Walter Reed National Military Medical Center in Bethesda, Maryland.

At Fort Bragg, Russell worked with the Eighty-Second Airborne, whose soldiers quite often wound up with head injuries after bad jumps from planes.

"Military parachutes are not great for steering," Russell said.

Russell said the paratroopers sometimes were knocked unconscious but rarely treated beyond being brought back to their bunks and told to sleep it off. Often commanders didn't want the injuries reported, for it might look as if training had been ordered in dangerous conditions. Russell could then later find himself being asked to sign off on forced discharges for some of those soldiers who'd been injured and later run into problems of misconduct of one kind or another.

The dots Russell thought needed to be connected involved the idea that the subsequent misconduct by the injured soldiers—disobedience, fighting, whatever—was related to their head injuries.

"We were really kind of ignorant about the effects of mild concussions or concussions that didn't put people in comas, concussions soldiers were told to walk off," Russell said. "The misbehavior was not a personality flaw, which is what they wanted me to say about these soldiers. It was actually a medical condition."

The kinds of mild traumatic brain injuries Russell was seeing at Fort Bragg in the 1990s would become the defining wounds of the Iraq War. They could be caused by improvised bombs exploding on Iraq's roads, or by repeated exposure to automatic weapon fire, or from a variety of accidents involving mortar fire or damaged vehicles. Undiagnosed and/or untreated, such injuries could have long-term effects on returning soldiers—problems with depression or impulsivity or concentration, even a propensity for suicide.

Russell would be a critical leader in efforts to better document, understand, and treat such injuries, and he gives considerable credit to the U.S. Department of Defense for the often-expensive improvements it has made—creating a brain bank to learn from dead soldiers, adjusting training to limit potential damage to the brain, creating a baseline test for all soldiers upon enlistment to better understand the nature and extent of damage they might incur in combat or training.

But the story of the military and mild traumatic brain injury, Russell says without qualification, is a story of blind spots, delayed action, and continuing problems with delivering fully appropriate and effective treatment. Russell, who helped create the Center of Excellence for the Department of Veterans Affairs to tackle brain injuries among soldiers, said the agency to this day is failing the tens of thousands of veterans who suffered head trauma.

I was introduced to Russell by colleagues I had worked with at ProPublica and National Public Radio. They had won a number of major awards for the unsparing critique they had done of the military's handling of brain injuries.

Among their findings:

From the battlefield to the home front, the military's doctors and screening systems routinely miss brain trauma in soldiers. One of its tests fails to catch as many as 40 percent of concussions, a recent unpublished study concluded. A second exam, on which the Pentagon has spent millions, yields results that top medical officials call about as reliable as a coin flip.

Even when military doctors diagnose head injuries, that information often doesn't make it into soldiers' permanent medical files. Handheld medical devices designed to transmit data have failed in the austere terrain of the war zones. Paper records from Iraq and Afghanistan have been lost, burned, or abandoned in warehouses, officials say, when no one knew where to ship them.

Without diagnosis and official documentation, soldiers with head wounds have had to battle for appropriate treatment. Some received psychotropic drugs instead of rehabilitative therapy that could help retrain their brains. Others say they have received no treatment at all, or have been branded as malingerers. . . .

. . . "It's obvious that we are significantly underestimating and underreporting the true burden of traumatic brain injury," said Maj. Remington Nevin, an Army epidemiologist who served in Afghanistan and has worked to improve documentation of TBIs and other brain injuries. "This is an issue which is causing real harm. And the senior levels of leadership that should be responsible for this issue either don't care, can't understand the problem due to lack of experience, or are so disengaged that they haven't fixed it." . . .

. . . The military also has repeatedly bungled efforts to improve documentation of brain injuries, the investigation found.

Several senior medical officers said soldiers' paper records were often lost or destroyed, especially early in the wars. Some were archived in storage containers, then abandoned as medical units rotated out of the war zones.

Lt. Col. Mike Russell, the Army's senior neuropsychologist, said fellow medical officers told him stories of burning soldiers' records rather than leaving them in Iraq where anyone might find them.

"The reality is that for the first several years in Iraq everything was burned. If you were trying to dispose of something, you took it out and you put it in a burn pan and you burned it," said Russell, who served two tours in Iraq. "That's how things were done."

I spoke with Russell multiple times. He was generous and candid. And he stood by what he had told ProPublica a decade earlier.

He also told me he had gone on at one point to oversee the military's efforts to limit suicides among its soldiers, both active duty and those who had returned to civilian life. The problem was growing at a rate that was approaching making it a crisis.

The number one cause of suicides among soldiers and veterans was, in clinical terms, the loss of a "love object"—a girlfriend or boyfriend, wife or husband. The second most common cause was the loss of employment or career. If a soldier had suffered three or more even minor traumatic brain injuries, their likelihood of suicide jumped tenfold.

Russell went to Iraq to dig in on the issue. He looked at the question of long and repeated deployments for often-young soldiers whose romantic relationships or marriages typically were just starting.

"You are asking them to be away from their spouses for longer than they have known them," Russell told me.

They often returned, Russell said, stressed, damaged, angry, lonely.

"A frayed rope," he said.

Russell reported on his findings and recommendations for action, chief among them shortening deployments.

"Most of my ideas got shot down," he said. "I got a little frustrated with trying to prevent suicides. Shortening tours? Too expensive for the Army." A committee was named to further study the issue.

"That's the typical Washington thing. If you had a problem to solve, you appoint a committee to study it," Russell said. "This is what they did with the suicide problem."

I told Russell about Jake Gardner's service, that he was among the very first into Iraq, the very first to encounter the range of the war's distinctive threats to their brains. He said Gardner, who fought so early, was part of a "lost generation" of vets when it came to brain injuries. He said that soldiers such as Gardner fell through the cracks of a system not ready to handle their often-hidden injuries.

"He was before we really got our act together. That cohort, they had very little in place to either identify their true injuries or treat them. People would come back and not have a scrap of evidence to take to the VA and say, 'I had this concussion.'"

Of Gardner, Russell said, "We don't know what happened in Iraq to this guy."

Russell said the Marines, as they had been historically, were particularly vulnerable to having their injuries undiagnosed and untreated.

"The Marines are kind of the orphans," Russell said, noting that their infrastructure for treating trauma was less robust than that of the other branches of the military. "They are supposed to tough it out."

Russell told me that, before his retirement, he had become interested in the question of what has come to be called moral injury suffered by soldiers. It's the cost to one's conscience of having participated in violence on a grand, sometimes indiscriminate scale. Were there moments where one was party to something terrible, outside the permissible in the code of war? Were there occasions when, while not a participant in something improper or inhumane, one didn't act to prevent it?

"The mask of civilization comes off pretty quick in combat and war," Russell said. He offered a refrain he had heard often from those who fought: "I want to kill them all. I know I came over here to win hearts and minds. I was the good liberal guy. And now I just want to kill them all."

In lectures, he used a case example. In one episode in Iraq, civilians were given twenty-four hours to evacuate a place the Americans were set to attack. The Iraqis were bombed just twelve hours later.

"A lot of people didn't stop it," Russell said. "There's a lot of people that probably have trouble sleeping at night. Or I hope so."

I thanked Russell for his time and insight. Before saying goodbye, he said with powerful plainness, "I don't recommend war."

BACK IN OMAHA, and years into his stewardship of his bars, Gardner met a woman named Cara through Facebook in late 2014. They shared comments and likes, and it felt safe and likely not consequential. But it lasted, and then moved to more advanced online engagement—messaging each other. Gardner at last asked if Cara would like to meet, maybe have coffee.

He chose the Omaha zoo for their first date, about as cliché a choice as possible in Omaha. There are not a lot of tourist attractions in Omaha, and so the zoo is on everyone's short list.

Gardner showed up with LeBron, his service dog, and struck Cara as talkative and at ease.

"One thing that made him different is there were no awkward silences. He's just such a people person. So he just talked and talked and talked the whole time."

Gardner mentioned his time as a Marine, and explained LeBron's presence as an aid for his hearing loss.

"Definitely very charming," she said. "He just wasn't nervous. It was great. It was the easiest first date I've probably ever had."

By then, Gardner's second incarnation of The Hive was a hot success. Cara, who would become the longest romantic interest of Gardner's life, initially heard from girlfriends who worried about the relationship's chance at success. Gardner was a nightclub owner, his bar's business model in some ways built around the aims of both attracting women and making them feel safe. Cara's girlfriends were frank with her: Was he a player?

It never worried Cara, mostly because Gardner seemed too busy to cheat on her. He was at the bar day and night, and often well into the night. He refused to hire a manager to lighten his load. He cared too much, worried too much, enjoyed it too much.

Mondays and Tuesdays became their days together. And there were mandatory Sunday night dinners with Gardner's parents.

"Everybody was like, don't you ever worry that he's, you know, messing around or whatever. And I never did worry about that. I mean, I used to go to the bar and I'm not a bar girl at all, but I would go just because he owned the bar and just to see him. And I just was treated like a queen there."

Cara grew up in West Omaha, one of four children in a sprawling Catholic family. She went to parochial grade school, then Millard North, a big public school with a graduating class of 650. Her mom had gone to beauty school but then raised her kids. Her dad worked for a data firm.

Cara was taken with photography, and took some college classes to study it before she broke out on her own. She started a portrait business, shooting weddings and other events.

She and Gardner had talks about marriage and children. But Gardner was skeptical of raising kids in a world he often saw as troubled, even sinister. If anyone became intimate with any of Gardner's lingering issues from Iraq, it was Cara. To her, it was clear there was enduring pain and upset. He could drink too much and say too little. But it was, she said, never enough to scare her off.

"I used to say, just go talk to somebody, and he would. But it didn't last very long," she said.

According to Kevin Moller, Gardner's partner in the bar, Gardner brought his Tony Robbins game to his operation of The Hive. He carried a notebook in which he wrote down new ideas for promotions; he traveled to Las Vegas to study how the casinos and other entertainment establishments worked to attract and maintain customers. Training for new hires was detailed and intense. The club was outfitted with high-end features—fancy bathrooms, a mahogany and granite bar. Gardner would call Moller in the middle of the night, and the one-way conversation would last hours, discussing finances and cocktails, security and gimmicks to draw crowds.

"Try, fail, adjust," Moller said of Gardner's eternal mantra.

Moller didn't dispute Gardner could be cocksure, even combative.

"Jake would tell you what he was thinking. He didn't pull punches," Moller said. "I helped try and smooth his edges."

Moller said Gardner turned The Hive's sign pink every year for

Breast Cancer Awareness Month. The bar hosted fundraisers for the Omaha Police Department's K-9 Unit. Animal welfare causes were another beneficiary of Gardner's charitable efforts.

Gardner and events at his bar were featured in the local nightclub magazine. Sue, his mother, liked to call up pictures of the events on her smartphone, pictures of her son, his hair long or in a ponytail, but smartly dressed, engaged with clientele of every race. LeBron, Gardner's dog, was a regular, typically there in his service vest in the night's early hours, then taken to Gardner's nearby apartment.

"Jake could be politically incorrect, maybe even enjoyed being so," Ben said. "He told off-color jokes dealing with race or gender or politics, but he told them in front of the people he was poking fun at. The point was to laugh, not to insult. He was a Marine. They used to train chanting bawdy and offensive jingles."

Gardner's family told me he was instinctively generous, and when I asked for examples they collected a few: he'd donated money to support a conservative student group on a local college campus; he offered up his bar for free when a relative had an emergency need for a venue for her bridal shower; he donated his hair to the Locks of Love charity; he sent some of his workers on cruises with his favorite band, 311, and sent his staff boxes of food during the pandemic.

Moller said the Yelp reviews alleging a racist door policy surfaced in 2016, after the uproar over the transgender bathroom issue. Gardner's mishandling of the episode caused a split among his staff, and some left. But Moller said the campaign against the bar seemed to be a coordinated effort. Gardner's support for Donald Trump was known. Moller said there was a thread on Reddit directing people to post negative reviews. Some of the reviews, Moller noted, came from people who didn't even live in the United States. A protest was called, Moller said, and a local TV news station turned up to capture it. Only a single protester showed up, he said.

Gardner, along with Moller, met Trump at a dinner at the Omaha Press Club well before Trump had formally declared his run for president. They were there with a couple of dozen other local businessmen. The talk, of all things, revolved a lot around issues with China's currency and its trade implications. They shook hands with Trump at the end.

Moller said Gardner was taken by him. "If he runs, he's going to win," Gardner told Moller.

Gardner would end up traveling in support of Trump. He'd have his picture taken with Trump's oldest son, Don Jr. He put the cardboard cutout of Trump up in The Hive. Gardner's former Marine recruiting partner said it was not meant as provocation, but as a principled stand about what should be possible in America.

"This is who I am," he said Gardner was declaring. "This is my business. This is who I am supporting. We're all Americans. You can support who you want and come drink at my bar."

I spoke to a handful of friends and former Marines about Gardner's support for Trump. One told me he didn't think Gardner had fully thought it through. Gardner liked that Trump was seen as an entrepreneur, but he didn't really take the time to research Trump's true scorecard as a businessman. Another said he'd taken to Trump because Gardner loved a good argument and Trump surely provoked that. Another said that if anything, Gardner was a libertarian. He was passionate about his Second Amendment right to own and carry weapons. He liked the notion of a true free market. He was a law-and-order champion, and he hated the violence that seemed to accompany so many of the rallies held by those on the left.

"He didn't like the lawlessness that was running rampant," said the former recruiter. "But if he had a true party to be with, it would be the Leave Me the Hell Alone Party."

Malia Shirley, a cousin of Gardner's girlfriend, felt much the same way. She was a member of Turning Point, a conservative organization on many American college campuses. It was before, she said, Turning Point became a more extreme combatant in the nation's culture wars. The group then stood for limited government and fiscal responsibility—passionate about policy questions, not railing against wokeness. Gardner was a supporter of the organization, though not a zealot even on policy questions. She said he thought education was the fundamental issue in America, and that he enjoyed Trump's "overtly patriotic" rhetoric.

"Unapologetically American," she said—of Trump and Gardner both.

Ben said a considerable part of Gardner's attraction to Trump had been his opposition to the Iraq War Gardner had fought in and been damaged by. Gardner hated the presidents he saw as responsible for years of what he now regarded as a bankrupt and ineffective war against terror. He loathed Bush as much as Clinton and Obama. And he saved a special dose of rage for Dick Cheney, Bush's vice president, whose company, Halliburton, had profited wildly from the conflicts in Iraq and Afghanistan.

"Jake was not a fan of the war on terror and all the killing that happened in the name of petroleum profits and war profiteering and lithium in Afghanistan," Ben said of Gardner. "Jake thought Cheney was the biggest war profiteer and criminal."

Whatever else Trump stood for or was capable of, Gardner calculated, he was the president least likely to commit America to another suspect war. And Gardner liked his status as an outsider. Moreover, since Trump was rich, if he was also corrupt, the costs for the people looking to buy him off would at least be a lot higher, Gardner figured.

"He was a departure from the traditional good ol' boy network in Washington," said Ben, who also jumped on the Trump bandwagon with gusto.

I asked Gardner's friends and family to help me understand his online post calling the Black Lives Matter organization a terrorist outfit. They said it was a bit of intentional overstatement and a reflection of a Marine profoundly appalled by the destruction that could take place at the rallies against police violence. That unrest ate at Gardner, as a businessman seeing other commercial establishments devastated, as a Marine who had fought for every American's right to passionate advocacy and peaceful protest.

Both Joe Rowland and Matt Brill, two Marines who knew and

served and lived with Gardner, said it was both of a piece with Gardner's self-help credo and a commonplace experience for former Marines. They expect from others what their trainers and commanders and fellow grunts expected of them.

"They give us these expectations of doing things right, always, and leaving things better than you found them," Brill said of the Marines and the consequences of their training.

Many people I talked to spoke of Gardner's willingness to extend himself for others. Gardner, at the VA's request, agreed to make presentations to other former soldiers about the value of service dogs. His bond with LeBron went well beyond close; the dog was essential to Gardner's nature and survival, and not just to help him because he'd lost hearing in one ear. Over their eleven years together, they spent just three days apart.

"Jake having a dog made him a wonderful person," said Gabe Writer. "It's why I have my dog. It makes me a better person."

"Jake was very good at finding the good in people," Kevin Moller said. "So good at giving people second chances."

Rowland said he believed that had Gardner met James Scurlock in other circumstances, James was the kind of young man Gardner might have offered help to as he tried to make his way in the world after a childhood of trauma and incarceration. It was a quality of generosity Rowland himself said he himself didn't always possess.

"I always say you can't want it more than they do," he said of efforts to help others. "And I think Jake felt like he could help a lot of people that just weren't willing to help themselves. And I think it worked on him. I think he got down on himself because I think he felt like he could always do more. And trying to identify what that was, wasn't the easiest thing to do."

Brill said it was clear to him Gardner had experienced frustration with the VA. The exact nature of which he wasn't sure—given the wrong meds, been misdiagnosed, been ignored. All were possible. Brill had experienced it himself. He said one of the central problems is that Marines don't like to think they need help and when they are asked by a shrink how they're feeling, they instinctively say, "Just fine." To get help requires instead that you answer honestly, and describe for shrinks your worst days, which might be every day.

"The stronger you are," he said, "the less willing you are to do that."

Gardner's parents agreed to share with me the most recent communications Gardner had had with the VA. The records show that he'd first been assessed in 2004, at the end of his service. He was awarded several hundred dollars a month. Two years before his fatal encounter with Scurlock, Gardner was assessed again. And in early 2020, the VA at last spelled out his injuries and afflictions.

"Service Connection for traumatic brain injury has been established as directly related to military service," the letter begins. "I have reviewed all of the relevant medical evidence in the service treatment records. The veteran has a somewhat complex medical history with significant mental health disorders, including PTSD, major depression and anxiety. He also reports multiple traumas to the head while in the military, two of which stick out as being most significant. He had a loss of consciousness on two occasions, one for about 10 minutes and one over half an hour. He was noted in the records to have signs and symptoms associated with a traumatic brain injury, particularly during the polytrauma clinic exam on September 27, 2017. It was also noted in 2004 that he had a broken jaw, which was a component of the assault that took place that caused the most significant brain injury."

Ben, Gardner's best friend, who himself suffers from PTSD, said Gardner across all those years basically toughed it out.

"He was a guy who was not going to tolerate feeling shitty all the time without trying to do something about it," Ben said.

Cara, his girlfriend, said Gardner gave up drinking over the two years prior to Scurlock's death. It was, she said, good for him, good for business, good for his family.

"Jake, you know, is such a goal-oriented person and wanted to be on the straight and narrow and wanted to have a successful business.

I think it was, 'I want to be present. I want to be the best boyfriend I can be. I want to be the best boss I can be. I want to be the best friend I can be. I want to be the best son I can be.' I think it was across-the-board. And he was so proud of it, too."

He and Kevin Moller, his business partner, had even begun to contemplate whether cashing out might be wise. If they could get a good price, maybe they'd sell the bar and brainstorm the next chapter. The blowback from the bathroom gender debacle gnawed at Gardner. Some would never see him or his place the same way.

Maybe a break from Omaha might help with his lingering issues of anxiety and depression. Gardner saw the ugly toll it took on others like him. In fact, Gardner for years wore a ring emblazoned with the insignia for a group called 22Kill.

The group's website states its mission and its choice of words:

> *Why the name 22Kill? First of all, let's start with the easy part, 22. In 2012, the US Department of Veteran Affairs released a date of report for suicides among veterans and active military members. The total numbers indicated that an average of 22 die by suicide every day. 22Kill was started in 2013 with a mission to raise awareness to this number. We are well aware that there are debates about the accuracy of this number, and there is certainly validity to the arguments. A recent report from 2018 with more accurate data shows that the average is actually 19.8. The mission remains the same. 22 was simply a number that our mission was based upon. It has become part of our brand and we continue to use that number to raise awareness to the fact that a problem exists. The fact is that suicide and PTSD are not just veteran issues, the harsh reality is that there are over 120 suicides per day in the US, and we as Americans need to educate ourselves and be willing to open ourselves up to address the issues. But why "Kill"? We get it,* kill *is a harsh word, abrasive, insensitive, however you want to look at it, so is the word* suicide. *The word and the act itself has negative connotations and most don't want to talk about it or even say the word. It's a scary subject.*

To many of us, it's just a word until it affects you personally. 22Kill is meant to grab people's attention to open up the conversation and bring people to talk about a subject that is so hard for many of us to talk about. Solving a problem begins with awareness, and awareness begins with being comfortable enough to discuss the problem.

"How Ya' Like Them Pumpkins?"

In late fall of 2020, I received an email from Ryan Wilkins. I had wanted to reach him. He was the Omaha lawyer who had prosecuted Gardner online as a white supremacist who needed to be arrested and charged. But he got to me first, and seemed eager to talk.

"Hey Joe, I'm an Omaha attorney and former high school classmate of Jake Gardner," Wilkins wrote. "Since about a week after Jake's release with no charges, I've been citizen-investigating and trying to raise community awareness around Jake's racism and criminal wrongdoing in the shooting of James Scurlock."

Wilkins said he had been a "background witness" in the special prosecutor's investigation, and that he had connected investigators "with a few other witnesses to Gardner family racism and the shooting—some who later testified before the grand jury.

"Please let me know if I can assist in your reporting," he wrote.

I called Wilkins. We spoke for close to an hour. He told me he had met Gardner in high school and had in fact been friends on Facebook with him for years. The two of them, he said, might well have run into each other at their upcoming twentieth reunion. Gardner had been treated as something of a hero at the tenth reunion, a Marine with a bunch of fancy medals from truly violent combat.

He'd come a ways since high school.

"Jake was kind of a twerp," Wilkins said of Gardner in high school. "A little squirrelly dude."

When I began to press Wilkins on how he had confirmed all the explosive material he had posted about Gardner's alleged racism, he made some startling admissions.

But first a bit about Wilkins. It turns out, Wilkins had written a memoir years earlier, a self-published book he called *Realer Than Real*. It's a story of his Christian faith, and his family's battering array of tragedies. The oldest of three children, he lost his youngest sister, Kayla, when her car was struck by a truck. His other sister, Amber, was later gravely injured in another wreck. Wilkins endured his own travails, as his first marriage fell apart and he returned from Chicago to Omaha to pick up the pieces.

In a foreword to the book, one of his friends pays tribute to Wilkins: "Over the years I've witnessed his character in moments both big and small, in success and failure, in joy and despair. Through it all, I've seen a man with a unique talent for pondering life's big questions in interesting ways.

"My biggest credit to Ryan," the friend wrote, "is how clearly he sees the truth."

The book is an endearing read. Wilkins acknowledges a degree of goofiness in himself (he's fond of the expression "nuttier than squirrel poop"), and he lays bare his shortcomings and often-deep depression as he struggled with the harm that came to his family, and the end of his marriage. "In my personal life, I felt small," he wrote. "In my marriage, I acted small.

"The source of my insecurity was the tension between my desire to be perceived as extraordinary, and my fear that, in reality, I might not be that special," he wrote.

The book lays out the basics of Wilkins's family and upbringing. His father was a South Omaha boy whose first job as he started building a family was as a bricklayer's assistant making $12,000 a year. But while it took him seven years, going to school while still working, he graduated from college and became a success in banking.

Ryan Wilkins was raised in a suburban Omaha subdivision. He wasn't that into sports but took up cheerleading. In his charming opening to the book, Wilkins sets the stage for his debut with the University of Nebraska Cornhuskers football team, including his sprint onto the field in Lincoln in "full uniform." It's not a football uniform, of course, but a cheerleader's.

He seems to have been an exceptional student, graduating with what he called a "perfect" GPA of 4.0, and earning what he said was the school's outstanding student leadership award. He did stints after graduation with the Teach For America program in Los Angeles and St. Louis. It was in St. Louis that he decided to become a lawyer, and he graduated from the Washington University School of Law.

He found himself in prestigious jobs, first with Kirkland & Ellis in Chicago, and later with the Union Pacific Railroad and another major firm in Omaha once he returned. He found love again, remarried, and had three children. It was his new wife, he writes, who "God used to resuscitate my heart and give my life meaning."

Throughout the memoir, there are flashes of admission or insight that it feels hard not to believe played some role in his decision to insert himself so publicly and provocatively into the death of James Scurlock and the case against Jake Gardner:

> "Waiting was never my forte."
>
> "I sometimes worried that I was an imposter."
>
> "I can be painfully cynical, logical and critical."
>
> "We sometimes have a stunning ability to rationalize our own bad behaviors."

At one point in the book, Wilkins talked admiringly of the pastor he had leaned on over many years. The minister was dying of cancer, but some of his final words stayed with Wilkins.

"I am very clear that God's telling me there is a window of opportunity that is closing," the pastor said. "This is a call I can no longer ignore."

Wilkins had told me in our conversation that he got involved in the Scurlock case in no small part because he felt guilty about having sat out other opportunities to say or do something in the face of what he regarded as racial injustice.

"What little I had done to confront racism," he said to me.

In a series of posts days after Scurlock's death, Wilkins had leveled a catalogue of incendiary accusations: that Gardner's father had been indoctrinated into white supremacy while behind bars for drug trafficking; that Jake Gardner had helped run drugs for his father; that Jews were not allowed in the Gardner home; and that Gardner had a swastika tattoo. The logos for his two establishments, The Hive and The Gatsby, were encoded with Nazi or white supremacist symbology, Wilkins wrote.

In my conversation with Wilkins, he could not have been prouder of his efforts. The posts, Wilkins told me, were shared thousands of times, and reached a million people.

Gardner's eventual indictment moved Wilkins to write another post, "Marching Onward–Justice for James":

> *Earlier tonight, at 5:27 p.m., I was at the Markman Pumpkin Patch with my wife and kids when I got the news: The grand jury returned four felony counts against Jake Gardner, including manslaughter (carrying up to 20 years' imprisonment), for shooting and killing James Scurlock during Omaha's May 30 BLM protests. Listening to Special Prosecutor Fred Franklin's press conference through earbuds while pushing a wheelbarrow, I fell to my knees, clapped my work-gloved hands, screamed a guttural "YEEEESSSS" through clenched teeth, and began to sob.*

Wilkins wrote of his efforts to advance the case against Gardner:

To be clear, I am not an important part of this story. So many others have sacrificed so much more for this cause. Nothing any of us can do will unwind the pain and loss Jake's hate wrought on the Scurlocks. And we still have a very long way to go. But for now, I'll let myself cry happy and hopeful tears that Omaha, this community I love, has taken a crucial step in justice's direction.

He ended the post with a burst of rather odd fury—at Gardner, at the local newspaper, at Don Kleine, the county attorney who declined to charge Gardner:

And to Jake Gardner, his white-supremacist lemming friends, Don Kleine, and the World-Herald *and Omaha media who took an ostrich-head-in-sand approach to the voluminous, credible, first-hand evidence undermining Jake's self-defense claim that I've been spoon-feeding you since June, I have two questions:*

Do you like pumpkins? Well how ya' like them pumpkins?

Megan Hunt, the state senator who had embraced the idea that Gardner was affiliated with white supremacists, chimed in again.

"Healing ourselves of white supremacy is so difficult and takes so long because it requires us to confront ourselves," she wrote. "For white supremacy to be persistently rejected, it first needs to be unlearned. Sometimes over and over. We wish unlearning racism could be as simple as denouncing a white hood, a burnt cross, vile language. But we have to address where supremacy begins, not just where it ends."

Wilkins, as he was publishing his posts, attracted a fair number of skeptics. People called his claims unproven and dangerous. Others were offended by his sense of satisfaction at Gardner's indictment.

"I hope you cheer as hard when the mob turns on you," someone wrote on Twitter.

Another called his posts "speculation and fiction."

Wilkins engaged online vigorously. He cited his credentials as a lawyer, and his command of the rules of evidence.

"It's all true," he wrote of his research. "Tens of thousands of people have read it, and no one has challenged a single fact."

That wasn't true.

Brenda Beadle, Don Kleine's top deputy, knew the Wilkins family. Their families went to the same church. Beadle had even supported Wilkins in a bid he had made to be elected to the Board of Regents for the University of Nebraska. She felt sad for his family and its tragedies, and thought a jingle Wilkins had created for his campaign was clever.

But Beadle was beside herself about what Wilkins was posting online. Beadle had seen a friend of hers support Wilkins online, and she called her and told her to stop. Wilkins was wrong. Kleine and she had looked into the Gardner family's history as they weighed whether to charge him. Wilkins was terribly, even dangerously wrong.

Beadle said she then did something she'd never done before. She contacted Wilkins about an active case to tell him he was wrong and that he should rethink what he was alleging in public. He didn't want to hear it.

When Wilkins posted his joyous piece from the pumpkin patch after Gardner's indictment, Beadle could think of only one word: "Unhinged."

I had wanted to reach Wilkins—to check on his facts. On the phone with Wilkins, then, I made clear I was interested in determining if any of what he had written was true, and how he had made sure that it was. I began by asking if he had recognized the stakes involved when making the kinds of claims contained in his posts.

"I had some concern," he told me, but he added that he had concluded he could defend everything he wrote.

I told him I'd had three of my most seasoned colleagues at Pro-

Publica scour Texas prison records for evidence that Dave Gardner had ever done time for drug running. None showed Dave Gardner was ever in prison for such a crime. Wilkins told me he had done next to nothing to check Dave Gardner's alleged criminal past. "How could I check that?" Wilkins asked. "I don't think I'm capable of finding that out. I don't know what to say."

As for the Nazi codes in The Hive's logo, Wilkins said he had heard of organizations like the Southern Poverty Law Center and the Anti-Defamation League and their work on white supremacists but had not thought to consult the organizations or others like them.

"It did not occur to me that I could pick up the phone and ask the SPLC," Wilkins said. "Maybe I don't feel important enough."

I spoke with two of Gardner's colleagues associated with The Hive. They showed me that the logo for The Hive had been used since its earliest days and first incarnation. That logo—the one in the giant window of the bar and on the sign hanging above it, the one used in advertising, the one that had been printed on T-shirts over the years—didn't even contain the images Wilkins had highlighted. Those images had only appeared in a short-lived promotional gambit that involved handheld LED fans in the bar that patrons could play with. The fans displayed a kind of hologram of the bar's logo. The supposed coded Nazi numbers Wilkins cited only appeared as a consequence of double imaging in the hologram.

So, the supposedly brazen act of boasting of Nazi allegiances at The Hive appeared not in any prominent or long-standing logo for the bar, but in some fleeting visuals created by devices almost no one used in the bar. Remarkably, Gardner's colleagues told me the promotional idea of using the LED fans had actually been the brainchild of Robert Bradshaw, the same Black former employee of The Hive who supposedly had disclosed their sinister secret to Wilkins.

MARK PITCAVAGE IS a senior research fellow at the Anti-Defamation League, and over the years he has authored a variety of reports on white extremist groups in the United States, including, "New Hate and Old: The Changing Face of American White Supremacy."

When Jake Gardner shot James Scurlock and allegations began to fly online that Gardner was some sort of white supremacist, indoctrinated into extremism by his drug-running racist father, Pitcavage paid attention.

Pitcavage, whose titles at the ADL have included director of investigative research and director of fact-finding, said he saw no evidence online that Gardner was what others alleged he was.

"The guy had some issues with people," Pitcavage said of Gardner. "But I could not confirm any ties to white supremacists."

By 2020, the threat of white extremists was an uncontested national concern, their dormant menace rekindled amid the raw racial rhetoric that powered Donald Trump's rise to the White House. The number and popularity of white supremacist websites and chat rooms exploded. Federal authorities released alarming reports of dramatic spikes in reported hate crimes. Avowed racists not only felt comfortable being publicly identified; they were running for elected office.

Pitcavage's 2015 report for the ADL—"With Hate in Their Hearts"—sketched out the freshly dangerous landscape:

> *Modern white supremacist ideology is centered on the assertion that the white race is in danger of extinction, drowned by a rising tide of non-white people who are controlled and manipulated by Jews. White supremacists believe that almost any action is justified if it will help "save" the white race.*
>
> *The white supremacist resurgence is driven in large part by the rise of the alt right, the newest segment of the white supremacist movement. Youth-oriented and overwhelmingly male, the alt right has provided new energy to the movement. . . .*
>
> *The alt right also possesses its own distinct subculture, derived especially from the misogynists of the so-called "manosphere" and from online discussion forums such as 4chan, 8chan and Reddit.*

> *Though aspects of the alt right date back to 2008, it was Donald Trump's entry in 2015 into the 2016 presidential race that really energized the alt right and caused it to become highly active in support of Trump. This activism drew media attention that provided publicity for the alt right and allowed it to grow further. The alt right interpreted Trump's success at the polls in November 2016 as a success for their own movement as well.*
>
> *After the election, the alt right moved from online activism into the real world, forming real-world groups and organizations and engaging in tactics such as targeting college campuses. The alt right also expanded its online propaganda efforts, especially through podcasting.*

Yet Pitcavage could not place Gardner in that emboldened universe of the nakedly racist. Not in its online forums, not in any criminal record.

"I tried," he said. "I looked and I couldn't find anything with merit."

Turns out, Fred Franklin and his investigators were also trying. And as Franklin put witnesses before the grand jury, he looked for a link between Gardner and white supremacist groups. That effort by Franklin came to include his investigators talking with Pitcavage.

It made sense for Franklin's people to have contacted Pitcavage, for he was not just a scholar of white extremists; he'd often been a partner of sorts with law enforcement. An online biography of his lays it out:

> *Dr. Pitcavage has been actively involved with training law enforcement on terrorism and extremism issues for over 24 years, working closely with the FBI and many state and local agencies. He has trained nearly 18,000 law enforcement officers, prosecutors and judges; assisted in a variety of criminal investigations; and served numerous times as an expert witness in federal and state courts.*

Pitcavage said he was straight with Franklin and his investigators: he could not connect Gardner with the white supremacy movement or its many and varied actors, from the politically ambitious to the violently disposed.

Remember, Ryan Wilkins's theories were pretty detailed—the *H* in "The Hive" was really a 14, the honeycombs in the logo were also the number 88, and together the numbers 1488 were "*The rebel yell for militant white supremacy.*"

Pitcavage calls the theory baseless.

"No credibility at all," he said.

Again, he should know.

Pitcavage has for years helped oversee the ADL's database of hate symbols.

"This database provides an overview of many of the symbols most frequently used by a variety of white supremacist groups and movements, as well as some other types of hate groups," the ADL says on its website.

The database has no fewer than nine categories of symbols: General Hate Symbols; Hate Acronyms/Abbreviations; Hate Group Symbols/Logos; Hate Slogans/Slang Terms; Ku Klux Klan Symbols; Neo-Nazi Symbols; Numeric Hate Symbols; Racist Hand Signs; White Supremacist Prison Gang Symbols.

In 2019, the ADL updated the database, adding the "Okay" hand gesture—the thumb and index finger completing a circle, with the three other fingers pointed downward—as an official hate gesture embraced by white extremists.

"We believe law enforcement and the public needs to be fully informed about the meaning of these images, which can serve as a first warning sign to the presence of haters in a community or school," Jonathan Greenblatt, the ADL's CEO, said in a statement.

In interviews, Pitcavage has been clear in saying white extremists employ a variety of strategies and aims in using such symbols—to instill fear, to secretly connect with each other. Some groups have sworn off images such as swastikas and chosen less obvious symbols with which to identify.

People who use hate symbols often want their ideologies known, but not so much that they'll be criticized or shunned, Pitcavage told CNN in 2019. Most people, he told CNN, aim for what Pitcavage called a "controlled display"—a swastika on their back that's only visible when they take off their shirt; or a tattoo on the inside of the lower lip. But, sometimes, followers of hate groups will obscure symbols altogether, so they only make sense to people who have similar ideological literacy.

None of that lined up with Gardner's logos for his bars. There was no evidence, Pitcavage said, the alleged symbols would have served as some kind of business draw. It wasn't a biker bar; it was one of the city's most diverse dance clubs, with salsa and reggae nights. And if it wasn't a draw, why would a bar owner run the risk of being discovered as a racial extremist?

"Literally, there would be no point in doing something like this," Pitcavage said.

The ADL's Center on Extremism eventually did a full and formal investigation into Gardner's shooting of Scurlock, and in a final report titled "Murder and Extremism," the ADL declared that the media, law enforcement, and its own Center on Extremism had failed to find evidence that Jake Gardner or his father were connected to, or advocates of, white supremacy.

I TOLD WILKINS on the phone that I had spoken with Pitcavage. It was hard to tell how it registered, but Wilkins soon said he was "not really comfortable with the turn" our conversation had taken.

I told Wilkins I was impressed by his willingness to talk, and that I was sympathetic to any alarm he was feeling about what he had written. But I told him the conversation had taken no turn. I was just trying to find out what was true.

Wilkins said his involvement in the case owed to his disappointment in the local and national media. His writing was something he was "doing on the side."

"This isn't my job," he said.

Wilkins said he would be concerned to learn that what was in his posts was not true, and that he'd be open to writing again if he became convinced the material was false.

"These are fair points of criticism," he said. "I did my best."

After the interview, Wilkins would never meaningfully engage with me. I had come to learn that the claim he'd made about Gardner having a swastika tattoo was untrue. I wanted to know how he reconciled his published assertion that Jews weren't allowed in the Gardner household with the fact that one of his best friends was a Jew from New York, Matt Brill, whom he'd met in the Marines. I laid out my findings to him; I invited him to show me his proof; I said I'd be happy to talk with the supposed Gardner family members he had relied on or the alleged friends who had told him of Gardner's swastika tattoo. But Wilkins refused to meet with me or talk more. He sent several messages insisting everything he had written was true. He did, though, alter the texts of his prior online postings, removing some of the more extreme claims.

For me, Ryan Wilkins was among the most interesting actors in the Omaha tragedy. Smart. Devout. A lawyer with an impressive résumé. A father. What had possessed him to do what he did, with as much enthusiasm and so little thought? It was as if, guilty and determined to make amends, he had decided to jump headlong into a complicated, racially charged case as a way of at last "doing something." With the Internet at the ready, he appeared to have blown through every guardrail—personal, legal, spiritual—to possibly libel a family he did not know.

It made me recall one of the observations about himself Wilkins had made in his memoir: "We sometimes have a stunning ability to rationalize our own bad behaviors."

But in examining the infamous and ubiquitous claims that Gardner was a white supremacist, I also badly wanted to talk to Jennifer Heineman.

Heineman was the university professor who had posted online Gardner's phone number in the hours after the shooting, alleging he came from a family of bigots and was a white supremacist. She'd alleged he had a violent past, with multiple assaults against others. She'd repeated the allegations at length in her appearance at the state senate hearing days after the shooting, and she had been a source Ryan Wilkins had used to support his multiple postings.

I had spoken with any number of the Gardner family members to understand Heineman, and how well she had known Gardner, if at all. She was described to me as a second cousin on Gardner's mother's side of the family. If Gardner had ever met Heineman at a family function, it was fleeting, and likely twenty years ago or more, they told me.

I had written to Heineman as well, saying I was working on a comprehensive account of the tragedy. She wrote back calling my request "unorthodox," and then later said she had been threatened by family members for her alleged truth telling.

I wrote again:

Jennifer,

Sorry you feel that way. It is a sad and disturbing case. I have read your online commentary and public testimony and want to hear you out.

- *how exactly are you related to Jake?*

- *how much have you ever interacted with him or his parents? When and in what circumstances?*

- *if you have been threatened or otherwise harassed by*

> *family members since your public comments, who did it and what did they threaten or say?*

Call anytime.
Joe

She wrote back, copying my bosses at ProPublica:

Joseph,

*I have a PhD, I am a professor, and am a well respected journalist covering marginalized communities under the name Juniper Fitzgerald. I have covered the story of *my* own family for CNN, and I have a book due for publication in 2021 with the story included in a series of essays.*

*And yet, you speak to me like I'm a child who's just been accused of stealing candy. Or perhaps you speak this way to all hicks in the Midwest because you think we don't know any better? You want to be "fair" and do justice to the story of a well-known neo-Nazi killing a Black man? Start by exercising some fucking empathy. Do you understand the gravity of the situation here? That in order for my story of enduring masculine brutality to be heard, I have to endure *yours*?*

The world is changing. Take a class on trauma informed reporting. Give the story to a Black woman and pay her the going rate for white, male senior editors with Pulitzer Prizes, and then we'll talk. Do better. And do not email me again, Joe.

Best,
Dr. Jenny Heineman

I would not give up. And in the spring of 2022, I finally got Heineman to engage with me. I'd reached her father, and he'd notified his daughter, and she wrote to me worrying that she wouldn't be properly represented in my reporting. I'd told her father that Jennifer had portrayed the Gardners as "nothing short of wicked" in their racism and taste for violence.

In a series of emails, she sought to both explain her history with the Gardners and back off any specific claims that Jake or his parents were racists:

> *I want to be clear. My intentions have only ever been to demand an investigation into the death of James Scurlock. When you emailed me two years ago, I felt immediately like you didn't understand the gravity of the situation. I was in hiding because of the death threats I received.*
>
> *In my public statements, I only ever spoke to the broader culture of my family, which is undeniably patriarchal and racist. You seem to have a difficult time believing my own lived experiences, which of course is your right.*
>
> *Relatedly, I have never claimed to be close with Jake.*

"I do not think they are wicked," she said of the Gardners. "At the end of the day, I believe that every human is nuanced and complex. I believe that both Dave and Jake are products of generational abuse and hate and I deeply mourn that."

I accepted Heineman's communications. But I wanted absolute clarity. I asked her if she had ever, even once, seen or heard Dave, Sue, or Jake Gardner say or do something racist?

She wrote me back. She had not.

"I Couldn't Let You Take My Parachute"

FOR JAKE GARDNER, HIS LIFE IN Omaha was over upon his release from jail that Sunday night in May. After his phone number had been posted on social media, he got hundreds of death threats. He counted them, humiliated, frightened, upended but obsessed with his portrayal as a white supremacist. He'd been in deep financial waters before the shooting; his bar had been trashed. His idea of selling it was dead.

"Jake Gardner was convicted by social media before the shell casing of the bullet that killed James Scurlock hit the ground that night," said one former Marine.

Gardner, in fleeing Omaha, had opted not to go back to Northern California, but to go instead to his friend Ben's house in Portland. Gardner was given the spare bedroom in Ben's basement. Ben, split from his wife, had his two children in the house every other week. The pandemic was in its first, explosive months, and the kids were doing school remotely.

Gardner's initial routine upon his arrival was simple, rote, and unhealthy: he stared at his phone, reading the unending accounts of his supposed life, his alleged character, his presumed actions and thinking the night he shot Scurlock dead. He took pills to help with sleep, but they were not terribly effective. He stayed up well after his friend went to bed, and was up before the sun in the morning, always checking the portrait of himself online as a racist psychopath.

Ben worried and begged him to turn off his phone. What good was there in reading nonstop about how you were the worst person on the planet?

Ben forced Gardner to at least go out occasionally, to a local dog run or for donuts, a Gardner favorite. The mask Gardner had to wear for COVID protection helped keep him anonymous.

Gardner realized it could seem silly, but he was hurt profoundly by the conduct of his longtime favorite band, the Omaha group 311. He'd loved the inclusive quality of the band's image and its music. They were an Omaha success story. He'd gone on cruises with the band. They donated a guitar to be displayed at The Hive. A 311 concert that included an after-show performance at The Hive was rated one of the best concerts of 2015. When one of the band's members had gone missing in New Orleans one year, Gardner had gone to New Orleans to help find and rescue him. When the band's leader disavowed Gardner, it came without a call or an acknowledgment of his longtime support for the band.

When word later came that a special prosecutor had been appointed and a grand jury would consider criminal charges, it arrived like a thunderbolt. Whatever guilt or trauma Gardner had experienced for having taken Scurlock's life had been tempered by Don Kleine's decision not to charge him with a crime. Now that sense of security was gone.

Gardner's Marine buddies, one by one, reached out, to reassure him, buck him up, offer money if it became needed.

"He sounded like he was fine. But I could tell he wasn't," said Gabe Writer. "I could tell he was borderline freaking out because he was scared. I told Jake, 'I don't think any less of you; none of us do. You did what you had to do. He made your decision for you when he attacked you. Don't back down. We will all support you. If we all have to give up our life savings to help you out, so be it.'"

One of those Gardner reconnected with was the African American former Marine he'd first met in boot camp, and with whom he'd driven cross-country back to Omaha upon Gardner's discharge.

"You know me," Gardner tried to reassure his friend. "I didn't want to kill the kid." Gardner offered to send the former Marine video of the incident. He told Gardner that wasn't necessary.

The friend hung up the phone and briefed his wife.

"He seemed defensive," he told her of Gardner. "But I have to think he was starting to feel the weight of it."

If such support had an impact, it could often seem minimal. The longer the grand jury process went on, for weeks, then months, the more unsettled Gardner became.

"He sounded very hopeless," the former Marine recruiter said. "I said, 'Please, tell me he's talking to a counselor.' He's got to be talking to someone."

The recruiter had a sense of how destabilizing all the online attacks and coverage could be. He'd read enough of it over time that he began to wonder if maybe Gardner somehow indeed was the racist he was being portrayed as, that somehow, over close to two decades, he'd missed it, or it had been hidden from him. But then he would catch himself, and disconnect from the Internet.

"I had to stop. I had to tune it out," he said.

Matt Brill touched base, too. He and Gardner had fought in Iraq together and healed in Humboldt County after. Brill had made his own choice not to carry a weapon as he battled his personal issues with PTSD over the years.

It was hard for him not to wish Gardner had done the same.

"I believe he had a right to be out there. I believe he had a right to defend himself," Brill said. "Do I think he needed a gun? Probably not. When you think you are in the right, when the chemicals in you are pumping and you think you see things so clearly, it's such a fragile thing and so complex. We react so differently in so many different ways to so many of the same situations. But I do support Jake in killing that dude that night."

Brill didn't enjoy saying so, but it was exactly how he felt.

At one point, Gardner decided to return to Omaha. There were things he wanted to retrieve, and some people he had not been able to say goodbye to. The return, though, would have to be carefully planned. Gardner did not want to risk being seen, and maybe set upon. A night with friends was arranged, and Gardner came and went, flying to and out of Kansas City. The one night he spent with his aunt in Kansas City, he wept, apologizing for having so badly disfigured the lives of his family members, his parents most profoundly.

When Dave and Sue Gardner bought the house at 3066 S. 72nd Street in Omaha, it was going to be their retirement home. It was a distinctive structure in a quiet neighborhood, with a giant circular window in front and a glide-like staircase from the first to the second floor—shallow, wide steps that made it feel like you were floating upstairs rather than climbing. There was a giant deck off the back, with a yard and an ample shade tree. There would be plenty of space for future grandkids to play.

"Not a place I ever expected to leave," Dave said.

But they were as sure as their son that their Omaha days were over. Sue had got a text in the days after the killing: "If we can't find Jake Gardner, we know where his momma is. She's the woman who raised the racist."

Sue's bosses at the Hobby Lobby store she'd worked at for a decade told her it was best not to come in for a couple of weeks after the shooting. They were trying to be sweet, she said, and offered to put Sue and Dave up in a hotel for their safety. They just needed to look out for the welfare of those who worked with Sue at the store.

One of the Gardners' neighbors on S. 72nd Street, people the couple had been friendly with since they moved in, chose to drape a sign over their fence: "No justice, no peace."

Dave vowed never to speak to them again, but plenty of people, alert to the possibility that the Gardners might not be long for Omaha, found more or less polite ways to say they'd be interested in buying the house at 3066 if it was going on the market. The home didn't last a week once it was listed, and sold for above the asking price in an all-cash deal.

"Our safety, our future, no matter what happened, it was never going to get better," Dave Gardner said.

On August 1, just two months after their world was turned upside down, the Gardners gave up their house keys and set out to drive to join their oldest boy in Oregon. Gardner's younger brother and his wife came, too.

Once his parents and brother had come to join him in Oregon, Gardner was a bit more reassured and reflective. He began to read the Bible as he had as a young boy in the private Baptist school in El Paso. He found a way to get to the Pacific coast with LeBron and his parents. He began to write out his life story. It was a hell of a story, he thought.

Gardner told Ben that he'd joined the Marines at the perfect time, with 9/11 a fresh national wound and with a war to fight, and he'd come out of it decorated for his valor. He'd become the owner of a hugely successful nightclub in his hometown. It was a lot of life he'd squeezed into thirty-eight years, he said. He said he felt blessed.

"He was hoping not to lose everything he had built," Ben said.

But optimism was hard to hold on to. Gardner had read the Ryan Wilkins post alleging his father had been an imprisoned drug runner and white supremacist. He'd been so unsettled by that and the array of claims—his family was a collection of racists; his bar was some kind of secret redoubt for white supremacists—that he actually found himself, with embarrassment, asking his father if the claim that he'd been imprisoned for drug running was true. He was ashamed of himself as soon as he asked.

Cara, Gardner's girlfriend, went to see him in Oregon during those summer months. In phone calls over the first weeks, she said Gardner could sound upbeat. His lawyers had told him Fred Franklin, the special prosecutor, was a fair man.

"Hey, Babe, how are you?" Gardner would say or text. "How was your day? I love you."

His confidence could seem a little forced, she said, done for her benefit. But the effort was appreciated and, she thought, cause for hope.

Her visit in July was timed for her birthday. Gardner had no income, and his finances back in Omaha were distressed as well. But he found a way to stage a set of birthday treats—a trip to Cannon Beach on the coast, a show of old military airplanes, a dinner out. Gardner spoke of a variety of ideas about his next life chapter. He told Cara he wanted to go off the grid for a while, disappear and decompress. But he was nursing ideas, too. One involved opening a bar or club for disabled veterans in Colorado.

"Jake definitely didn't let me really see the super sad, scared side of him," she told me. "He didn't want me to worry. I think he just put on a strong, good face for me."

Gardner even sent a note of apology to Frank Vance, the owner of the pub underneath The Hive whom Gardner had ignored or antagonized over the years.

But things dimmed after the weeks dragged on. In Omaha, there were repeated rumors of an imminent grand jury announcement. But then the rumors went bust and the summer of uncertainty stretched on. Jake assured Cara she'd be the first person he called once the announcement actually came.

One bright development involved Gardner's introduction to a man named Don Olson. Olson came from hardy Norwegian stock who had settled in Wisconsin in the 1830s and made an improbable success out of tobacco farming, ultimately becoming a chief supplier for the famous Dutch Masters brand of cigar.

His family was highly educated, full of lawyers and dentists, but Olson would become the first to study neurology, qualifying early for medical school and emerging with an appetite and talent for brain surgery.

While in the Air Force, he helped lead a program training pilots how best to withstand interrogation and psychological abuse if captured behind enemy lines. Hard experiences during the Korean War made such preparation more urgent as America's later involvement in Vietnam deepened.

Olson returned from the Air Force and took up his studies in neurosurgery, eventually becoming one of the few surgeons in the United States to master the nascent art of conducting surgery by accessing the brain through the nose.

Asked to become a part of the medical staff for the Wisconsin National Guard, Olson did, but when a National Guard unit was implicated in the killings of protesters at Kent State in 1970, Olson quit. He said it took sustained recruitment by the Reagan administration years later to get him to return.

For the next several decades, Olson, given the rank of full colonel in the Army, would play a role in the treatment of brain injuries of all kinds, including trauma. He pushed the early use of CAT scans and magnetic resonance imaging to identify injuries, and developed protocols for soldiers to convalesce effectively once returned home.

"What you were beginning to encounter was the phenomenon of traumatic brain injuries that didn't require surgery, but required some significant level of care," he said.

Olson over the years toggled between private practice on the West Coast and work for the military. He was, he liked to say, subject to recall by order of the president.

Most recently, Olson had become taken with a treatment called transcranial magnetic stimulation. It's a noninvasive form of brain stimulation in which a changing magnetic field is used to direct an electric current at a specific area of the brain through electromagnetic induction. An electric pulse generator, or stimulator, is connected to a magnetic coil, which in turn is connected to the scalp.

Olson believes the treatment has the potential to create a degree of mindfulness for the patient, a way to address the lasting effects of trauma and the stress, anxiety, and depression that can accompany it.

Olson thinks the VA should seize on the treatment option, buy the machines, put them to use. But he has been frustrated over the years by the VA. He said his efforts to try to work with the VA to better tackle brain-injured veterans were rebuffed and undervalued. The suspicion of the VA felt by many veterans—its bureaucracy and inaction and occasional incompetence—is warranted, he said.

In his retirement, Olson had bought land in Oregon and started a winery, ten acres set high in the Dundee Hills in the Willamette Valley. Olson named it Torii Mor, using an ancient Scandinavian word for "earth." Pinot Noir would be his specialty.

Olson was friends with Ben's family, and when Olson met Gardner he liked him instantly, and knew enough about his service to guess at his lingering challenges. His Marine buddies and others mentioned PTSD. They acknowledged he was struggling with the events in Omaha.

"I never sat down with him like a doctor," Olson said, "although I was getting feedback around him."

Gardner came out to the vineyard and met with Olson. Olson sensed his acumen for business, and for managing a staff. He made a proposal: Olson wanted to get into the spirits end of things, and wanted to add a distillery to his enterprise in the Oregon hills. He thought Gardner could run it for him.

Gardner was intrigued. It was hardly a foreign undertaking for a guy who'd run nightclubs for almost two decades. He could live out near the property, maybe on it. Quiet, beautiful, tucked away from the rest of the world. Even more basically, it was a job, with income, two things that were no longer sure bets given his now quite public reputation.

Gardner did not fully commit. Maybe the vineyard was an option if it all worked out; but he also spoke of just disappearing for a while.

"Mom and Dad are here now too, they are settling in their rental house and on the hunt for a community they want to buy their retirement house in," he wrote to a Marine pal. "Hopefully we'll all be close in the end. I'm going almost to Canada to get a conversion van and will be doing just that, converting it into a tiny house on wheels."

Gardner said he was uncomfortable living the anonymous and circumscribed life he was living as he awaited Franklin's grand jury investigation. It reminded him of the hyper-vigilant life he had led as a Marine.

"I like being loud and obnoxious and having everyone pay attention to my adventures (especially with LeBron)," he wrote to his friend. "Just have to adapt and overcome. I promise, it will all work out. Not in some weird karma way, but in the way that I followed the law exactly and was justified in defending myself. I'll have this van inhabitable as a tiny home by September. I'm gonna work here until winter is over, then I foresee myself getting on the open road with the van and the old dog."

Once September had arrived, there had been some troubling scuttlebutt. Kevin Moller, Gardner's business partner who had been outside The Hive the night of the killing, had been called by Franklin to testify before the grand jury. Moller said one of Franklin's investigators had shown up at his home prior to his appearance and told him he could keep his name out of the media if he'd just testify that Gardner was a racist. When Moller appeared before the grand jury, he said it lasted more than two hours and during it Franklin had berated him and accused him of lying about what had taken place that night.

As an announcement grew close, Gardner texted with a Marine colleague back in Omaha. He said he was more nervous than he'd been headed to fight in Iraq.

"How you holding up?" Gardner's friend asked.

"So stressed," Gardner wrote back.

"Fingers crossed, man," the friend wrote. "Even if they hand down an indictment, they still have to prove beyond a reasonable doubt it wasn't self-defense."

Gardner used a heart emoji to show he appreciated his friend's text.

"Your friendship has always meant the world to me," Gardner wrote. "I'd go to war with you 100 times over and I'm sure we'd both always make it home. Thank you for everything. Mainly your support, unconditional love and the friendship you've given me. Those things are priceless to me and I'll never forget them. Semper Fi, brother."

The Marine pal told Gardner the city was bracing for Franklin's eventual announcement.

"Omaha is prepping for a riot," the friend wrote.

"It looks like it," Gardner acknowledged.

That struck the two of them as possibly good news. Maybe the preparation by the authorities was because they knew Franklin would not charge and they'd have to be ready for unrest in Omaha all over again.

Then Gardner's friend ended the exchange: "Keep your head down, but on a swivel.

"Spirits up. Breathe in deeply and exhale slowly. Taste the air. Feel the wind."

On September 15, Gardner gathered with his family to watch a livestream of Franklin's announcement. Upon hearing of the indictment, he got up, turned off his phone, and walked away.

"It's like all the life in him was just sucked out," said his father.

"You could see the pain in his face," Ben said. "'They're going to kill me in jail.'"

Gardner asked Ben to help him shave his head. He joked darkly he was having his Britney Spears moment. Ben handled the back of Gardner's head to complete the buzz cut.

Gardner and his parents talked about what it could all mean. He had good lawyers, but they would cost considerable amounts of money. If he was held even overnight in jail, would he be victimized? There would clearly not be a more high-profile, controversial inmate in Nebraska's detention system. For Gardner, it all raised a dreaded prospect for a Marine, the family's oldest son, and self-made businessman: he was a liability.

"No Marine ever wants to become a burden," said Matt Brill. "If we hide our feelings and the battles we deal with daily, it's ultimately not to become a burden."

Gardner decided to move in with his parents at the Airbnb they had rented in nearby Hillsboro, Oregon. He packed the few things he had brought from Omaha, including a 9mm Springfield pistol.

Worried, Ben snuck into the spare bedroom and removed the gun from its carrying case. Gardner had cracked a beer after Franklin's announcement, his first drink in close to two years. Not wise, Ben thought.

When Gardner unpacked at the place his parents rented, he was furious that the gun was missing. He called Ben and cursed him out.

"You know these people want to kill me and my family," he screamed at Ben. "You've left us totally defenseless."

Ben drove the gun to Gardner. When he handed it over, Gardner thanked him. "You know I couldn't let you take my parachute," he said.

His Marine buddy knew what he meant. Gardner wanted the option to pull the chute on his life, to end it.

Ben told Dave Gardner his son had his gun back. "You need to take custody of that," Ben told him.

Gardner's lawyers arranged with Franklin for Gardner to surrender on September 21 in Omaha. The lawyers, Monaghan and Dornan, had enough pull with judges in Omaha and corrections officials that they also arranged for Gardner to be sped through a court appearance and released on bail without having to spend time behind bars.

Gardner had called Cara from his father's phone soon after Franklin's announcement. He told her he'd shut his off.

"I remember him just saying how much he loved me. He was just like, 'I'm so sorry this is happening,'" she said.

Gardner dismissed Franklin's claims he'd uncovered some damning communications that implicated him as a person bent on shooting someone that night. But he was despondent about the turn the case had just taken.

"I remember him saying you're never going to see me again," Cara said. "And I was like, what?"

"I didn't, I guess, take it as seriously at the time, because I knew he was just shocked and freaking out," Cara told me. "And I was like, it's okay, we'll get through this, you know, whatever. And anyway, it wasn't a long conversation. And so we hung up and about an hour later, his mood had completely changed. He called me again and was like, 'No, it's okay. I talked with my lawyers and I feel better. And um, you know, I'm gonna, I'm going to fight this. It's going to be fine.'"

Two days later, on Thursday, they talked again. Jake asked Cara to make sure they talked at length on Friday and Saturday. He wasn't sure of his lawyer's promises that he would not be behind bars. He feared it could be a while, and that anything could happen.

"So I want to make sure that we can have this opportunity to talk and everything," Cara said Gardner told her. "I thought it was kind of weird. I think Jake had just made peace with what he was going to do. And, uh, you know, that's why his mood completely changed."

Cara said she had seen Gardner try to reconnect with his faith during the summer. He had come to like watching sermons on religious channels.

On Saturday night, hours before Gardner was to get on a plane for Omaha, Ben joined him and his parents. They had talked about going out to dinner for steak and drinks. But they ordered in instead. Ben had arranged with a friend, a federal marshal, to accompany them to the Portland airport in the morning so that Gardner was safe.

The four of them spent the night watching a string of Adam Sandler movies. Gardner sat between his parents. Gardner had lost weight as he awaited his fate. His face was gaunt and defeated, furrowed by concentric rings of sorrowful anxiety. His smile, with which he once reassured his family and promoted his bar business, was now the forced effort you might see from someone in their last days of hospice care.

He told his father not to worry himself to death. He told his mother not to smoke herself to death. He told Ben, with a wink, not to eat himself to death.

Sue stayed up with Gardner until 5:00 a.m., holding his hand. She told him she'd come to him after he got released from custody back in Omaha. She'd bring LeBron with her.

In the morning, Gardner texted with Cara. It was Sunday. Gardner asked Cara to make sure she went to church with her brother.

"And I was like, 'Oh, I will.' And then I said, 'Are you okay?' And he said, 'Yeah, I'm fine.' He's like, 'I'm just watching my sermon. I was just wanting you to know that I was thinking about you.' And then I said, 'Are you all packed up and ready to go?' And he said, 'Yeah, I'm almost ready.' And that was it."

Gardner's father was awake in the house. The two talked. When Dave Gardner went to the bathroom, Gardner left the house. His father found his wallet, his dog, LeBron, and his opened and empty gun case. Dave Gardner called Ben. Ben jumped in his car. It was thirty minutes from Portland to Hillsboro.

Ben called 911. Dave got on the phone with the local police. Police records detail what happened next, with Ben referred to as Benedict:

> *Once on the phone with Dave, I asked him if Jacob did in fact own a gun. Dave replied he was positive Jacob owned a Springfield 9mm firearm. When I asked Dave how he knew Jacob had it on his person, Dave stated he looked all over Jacob's room and was unable to find it. Dave added Jacob did not take his phone, wallet or any other items when he left the house. I asked Dave to describe what he last saw Jacob wearing. Dave described Jacob as wearing a light green sweater, blue jeans and a 49ers hat. Dave also informed me he last saw Jacob approximately an hour ago. While on the phone with Dave, Benedict sent me a photograph of Jacob. In the image, Jacob is wearing a light green sweater with the letters USMC written across the front. At the time the photo was taken, Jacob's head was shaven.*
>
> *After speaking with Dave, I briefed Sgt. Kelsey and several other officers assigned to the call with the details I collected. Once our meeting concluded, I called Dave to collect additional informa-*

tion. While speaking with Dave, I received an incoming call from Benedict. I ended my conversation with Dave and began to speak with Benedict. Benedict immediately informed me he found Jacob's body.

When I arrived at 356 SE 9th Ave, I found a white male adult, later identified as Jacob Gardner, in a seated position leaning on the South side of the building. Jacob had what appeared to be a gunshot wound to the right side of his head. There was blood present on the ground near his body. I could see the butt of a black handgun in his right hand. I did not see any signs of life. I did not touch or move the body. I did not touch or move anything in the area around the body. I secured the area with police tape and began a crime scene log. I photographed the scene and the body with my department issued phone and later uploaded the photos into evidence.

At 1408 hours, Kate Makkai, Matthew Straub and myself entered the scene and made our way to Jacob. I noticed immediately that the view from the street/sidewalk had been blocked. I learned that Matthew had placed a quick shade on its side to provide privacy. As we made our way around the quick shade I observed a male in a seated position and slouching to his left. He was against a brick wall. He had blood coming from his head and pooling around him. I saw that his right hand was partially obscured by his body and inside his hand was a pistol. The cigarette butts and empty pack was collected and it was later determined that the brand was the same brand that Sue had purchased for Jacob earlier. The pistol was removed from Jacob's hand and when the magazine was removed, 12 rounds remained. There was also one live round in the chamber. It appeared that a single gunshot from the right side of Jacob's head had exited the left side and ricocheted off the brick wall.

Ben had found the body, and had made sure Sue, who was out looking, did not see her dead son. "Did you find him, Benny?" she asked through tears. "No," he responded. "Go back to the house."

After police interviews and hours with Gardner's devastated parents, Ben had to head back to Portland. In his car, there was something left in one of its cupholders. He reached in. It was Gardner's 22Kill ring.

Gardner had left one other thing for his family and Ben to find. Gardner had dug up an old quote from Rubin "Hurricane" Carter. Carter was the Black boxer who'd been wrongly convicted in a murder case and done years in prison though innocent. Denzel Washington had played Carter in the movie version of his life.

The quote read: "To live in a world where truth matters and justice, however late, really happens, that world would be heaven enough for us all."

"A Fascinating Case to Try"

JAKE GARDNER'S DEATH DID NOT QUIET Omaha.

Conspiracy theories were soon floated that Gardner's suicide was a hoax and he was alive and well and still on the run, protected by white supremacists. Scurlock's father publicly adopted the theory. Democratic Party leaders in Nebraska, including Ja Keen Fox, thought Don Kleine still needed to be punished for not charging Gardner initially, and they began to draft a formal censure of him, alleging he had helped "perpetuate white supremacy." Kleine, in response, worked to have Fox fired from his job with a local foundation. Ben Gray, a longtime Black city councilman from North Omaha who had stood by Kleine, was targeted for unseating. The pastor of a local church declined the Gardner family's request to hold a memorial service. He told the family he didn't want his church burned.

Megan Hunt, the state senator who had embraced the story line put out by Ryan Wilkins that Gardner was a white supremacist, took what seemed like a victory lap.

"The indictment of Jake Gardner would never have happened without the community, the people who stood up for justice and demanded action from city officials," Hunt wrote on Twitter. "Jake Gardner is gone, but the white supremacist attitudes that emboldened him are still with us today."

The notion that Gardner's death had been staged and that he was alive and on the run gained a dark momentum.

One Facebook post alleged Gardner was "on a boat to Ireland right now." In the comments section, the person wrote that Gardner was a white supremacist, and linked to the June 19 article by Ryan Wilkins.

"Unless I see a body," wrote another, "I believe Jake Gardner is under witness protection with a new identity."

Someone else quickly agreed: "Y'all done made a whole new lie. Body—or it didn't happen."

"Suspect he will be 'cremated' quickly," alleged yet another.

James Scurlock Sr. said he never believed Gardner would show up for trial and that to him it just made more sense that he was alive and being assisted in a new secret life. In fact, James Sr. said such an outcome, however outrageous, might have felt better than Gardner avoiding trial by killing himself. With Gardner's suicide, James Sr. said, the family felt cheated that there would be no formal accounting for Gardner's actions.

"I don't know. I just felt like the way everything had been going, I just felt like maybe they had given him a new identity, given him a new start. I think it would've just made the math add up more, I guess, if they would've just helped him just get away with it rather than him committing suicide."

Fox, the activist who had led the protests at Don Kleine's house, did not seem to doubt Gardner was dead but was glad for it. His choice to kill himself was evidence that he had believed he was immune from justice, from the indictments that shocked him when they eventually came down.

"We're safer with him gone," Fox said. "His white supremacy made him believe so certainly that he would escape this consequence that he wasn't able to deal with reality."

Conversely, the fringe right was quick to deliver its verdict on Gardner's suicide.

"Omaha bar owner who became political prisoner for defending himself commits suicide," read the headline of one online posting. *The New American* had this take: "Iraq Marine Vet Commits Suicide after Indictment for Shooting BLM Thug in Self-defense." "Murdered by wokeness," someone wrote.

One post by someone in the Oregon town where Gardner shot himself articulated a fuller critique of the painful turn of events and the coverage of the case by the media:

> *James Scurlock, a man with a long, violent criminal history, loaded up with meth and coke, jumped on Gardner's back and began choking him out. All of this on video. Gardner shot in self defense and Scurlock died. Of course news reports highlighted skin color though it was irrelevant unless you think Scurlock, a black man, attacked Gardner because he was white. Attacked by a criminal, his businesses gone bust, cut off from raising funds for his defense, he came to Hillsboro and took his own life. Summed up by reports here in the Northwest as "white bar owner kills Black man."*

Gardner's family was not silent either. His aunt Janet, his mother's sister, appeared on a popular conservative talk radio show in Omaha hosted by a man named Scott Voorhees.

Voorhees welcomed her to the show by saying he was "honored" to have her. Voorhees described the protests that took place in the streets of Omaha in May as criminal, dangerous riots. Janet had lived for years in Omaha before moving to Kansas City. Her children were still in Omaha. Voorhees asked her what it was like to find Omaha in the state it was in.

"I wouldn't come back if you paid me. They are dancing on his grave," she said of Omaha's reaction to Gardner's death. "This stuff is not going to fix race relations. I don't know what's happened to our country."

It got quite raw.

"Jake was deemed a racist and horrible and a murderer from the start," she said. "How many Black men kill Black men? They don't go out and riot for the Black children that are lost. Nobody ever said Black lives didn't matter. I don't recall a movement about how Black lives don't matter." Yet, she said, "it doesn't look like all Black lives matter to them. It came down to a white man and a Black man and people feed into that and eat it up."

Gardner, she said, had been "so proud of Omaha." "It's horribly sad what Omaha did to him. The city destroyed that man's life. The citizens, the politicians, everybody had a hand in it."

Janet claimed local TV stations were complicit, too. They refused to show the interview Gardner had done with a Black on-air reporter with whom he had served in the Marines, she alleged. She said a TV interview with her children for a fuller portrait of Gardner had been edited to remove the fact that Janet's daughter had spent the night of the shooting in the hospital parking lot praying for James Scurlock.

"Justice hasn't been served," she went on, sometimes breaking down. "An American war veteran, a true hero, a loving son, brother, uncle, has been taken from us. His blood is on the hands of the mob community in Omaha. It is a sad day in America when an ex-con thug is considered the hero compared to a veteran who served his country, came back to Omaha, opened a business, served the community, and he's the bad guy?"

Gardner's aunt said her nephew had taken his life to spare his family and hometown from further hurt and division.

"For the city of Omaha, if you can believe it," she said.

Voorhees said he would post information where people could safely donate to the Gardner family and any legal action they might pursue. He wondered what it must have felt like for Gardner when he feared his city would burn because of him if he hadn't been convicted. Voorhees said the persecution of Gardner and family is "something you are going to see multiple times during your lives. Civil unrest. Us against them. Police officers and criminals.

"I ask that people look at all the evidence when looking at this story," Voorhees told his listeners. "We convict people in the court of public opinion and it's all we seem to care about. Make sure you explore all the evidence."

Voorhees asked how Janet wanted her nephew remembered by Omaha.

"I'd like them to remember his face, his smile," she said. "He had an infectious smile."

Janet closed by saying that her nephew being called a racist "broke his heart."

"I hope we can find our way back to each other—no Black, no white, no left, no right, no Democrats, no Republicans," she said. "We're all under one God."

Amid the mix of mourning, celebration, and conspiracy theorizing, Fred Franklin, the special prosecutor, decided to hold another news conference. There was no legal requirement he do so. Gardner's death had made his indictment moot. In his earlier presentation announcing the charges, Franklin had refused to discuss what the grand jury had heard as evidence, citing laws regarding grand jury secrecy.

No one, then, knew what he was prepared to say or do. Tom Monaghan, Gardner's lawyer and Franklin's onetime boss, said Franklin had next to no experience dealing with the news media during his career with the federal prosecutor's office. The U.S. Attorney was the only one who spoke when announcing developments in investigations or cases. The office did not even have a hired spokesperson.

Franklin, back in the legislative chambers where he had announced the indictment of Gardner, could not have got his presentation off to a weirder start. Making perhaps the soberest and most consequential appearance of his career, he wanted to talk about the NFL running back Gale Sayers.

"Good afternoon. Before I get to the Gardner matter, I just want to acknowledge the passing of one of the living legends who lived in Omaha. Some of you all know that I'm a huge Chicago Bears fan, and Gale Sayers is one of my all-time favorite football players and the running back who I personally consider to be the greatest running back in the history of the National Football League. My father would argue with me all day about the fact that he thought that it should have been

Jim Brown. But his passing is meaningful to me and I just felt like I needed to acknowledge that."

There was an awkward silence.

Franklin then articulated the needle he'd try to thread all afternoon: to honor his pledge not to disclose evidence in the case—no names of witnesses, no testimony, no names of grand jurors—but also remedy "the public's lack of understanding of the entirety of the facts and circumstances surrounding this matter, as well as my own desire to want to be as transparent as I possibly can.

"What I do intend to talk about today involves the information that was passed on to me and my team from the Omaha Police Department. And this information would have been prior to the actual grand jury convening, and the members of the grand jury receiving certain information."

Franklin said that in the run-up to the deadly confrontation on Harney Street on May 30 there were "individuals inside" Gardner's bar. He called it by its former name, The Hive. He said Gardner was inside with three handguns and a shotgun. He said Gardner had been in text communication with people who were keeping him apprised of the events in the streets of Omaha via Omaha Scanner, "something I did not know existed before this case." He noted that there was video of "individuals" inside the architecture firm down the block from Gardner's bar but did not name them as James Scurlock and Tucker Randall. He said the lights inside the bar, which had once been on, had at some point been turned off.

"The text messaging, and the Facebook messaging, to and from Jake Gardner makes multiple references to anticipated looters and how they could be dealt with."

Franklin at that point veered from a narrative of what was taking place to call attention to Gardner's support of President Trump.

"I will remind you if you haven't figured it out already, the day before this shooting took place, Donald John Trump tweeted, 'When the looting starts, the shooting starts,' and the evidence is significant in terms of Jake Gardner's affinity for the president."

Returning to the scene inside and outside The Gatsby, Franklin said "vandals" had "destroyed" and "broke what they could" of Gardner's club. Again, he made no mention that two of those who had damaged the bar were Scurlock and Randall.

What came next was a damning assessment of what Gardner and others had been up to: "So, to the extent that Jake Gardner had set up an ambush inside of his business, waiting on a looter to come in so he could light him up, and that particular objective was thwarted by individuals not coming in, it would be understandable that Mr. Gardner would have had some frustration about sitting back and watching the place that he was renting be destroyed like it was being destroyed."

It seemed clear Franklin had concluded Gardner was plotting an ambush from the fact that the lights had been turned off and he was a supporter of Trump.

"He stayed inside of his business while it was being vandalized," Franklin alleged, "in the hopes of executing another plan."

Franklin then said Gardner had emerged from the bar "with some anger" about what had happened to his establishment. Franklin, without offering any material, then claimed Gardner was "philosophically opposed to the reason why the protest was taking place.

"Now I told you guys when we had this press conference last week, that the significant evidence didn't really come from a witness before the grand jury, but rather came from Jake Gardner himself, and specifically his cell phone. And I'm not going to get into specifically all of the evidence that could reasonably be construed as incriminating, but one of the things I will tell you is that one of the things that was on there was a communication concerning whether or not the 'field of fire' from inside The Hive going outside was clear."

Franklin was referring to a text exchange between Gardner and his Marine friend in Oregon. But Franklin knowingly misstated what the text actually said. The friend had asked about whether Gardner could "feel the fire." Was it a typo and the friend had indeed meant to say "field of fire"? Was he asking if Gardner could sense the heated scenes on the street? But if Franklin misstated the actual words, he seemed certain about what they suggested: Gardner was eager to shoot someone.

"That evidence is completely supportive of an intention to use a firearm to either kill or to cause serious bodily injury to whatever looter might have decided that this was a good idea."

Franklin implied Gardner was frustrated he hadn't been able to shoot a looter.

"And so the question becomes whether or not when Jake Gardner emerges from inside his business, whether he has a state of mind that is consistent with utilizing deadly force, such deadly force, that is evidenced by his own communication, or whether he came out and was just simply assessing what he's going to do about the damage to his property."

Franklin, having stated the question, did not answer it. Had Gardner emerged still thirsting to use deadly force on someone, anyone? Or was he judging just how badly his bar had been damaged? The video from the bar shows Gardner standing around talking with others in the street outside his bar, and at least once talking on his phone. There is no indication he was looking to shoot anyone.

Franklin then got back to what happened once Gardner was outside the bar, with his father and others. He scolded the journalists for failing to see what he and his investigators saw in the video that had been publicly available for months.

"I want to say this to the media. You guys have a whole lot of what's significant about this case if you would simply do the same thing that my team and I did, which is to take the video that you already have, that's already been played to the public, slow it down and enhance it, and you can see that this entire confrontation didn't start with David Gardner being pushed down. That was in response to something else."

Franklin then jumped around in the chronology of events. He said Scurlock had nothing to do with Gardner being tackled the first time. He claimed Gardner hadn't really checked on his father after he was knocked down but instead was headed after the person he thought might have flattened his dad.

"And one of the first things that happened after that was that Jake Gardner ended up in confrontation with James Scurlock."

Franklin then asserted that there was video that captured the initial encounter between Gardner and Scurlock, video other than what was recorded by the security cameras at The Gatsby.

"But that video was provided to the Omaha Police Department by an individual who was down protesting and happened to come around the corner and it captured that initial confrontation between Gardner and Scurlock. Now it's been stated that this is a clear case of self-defense. Chapter Twenty-Eight, section One-Four-Oh-Nine is the Nebraska statute that deals with the use or reliance on force in self-protection, and I just want to read just a little bit of that statute to you. It says 'the use of deadly force shall not be justifiable under this section unless the actor believes that such force is necessary to protect himself against death, serious bodily injury, kidnapping or sexual intercourse compelled by force or threat. Nor is it justifiable if the actor with the purpose of causing death or serious bodily harm provoked the use of force against himself in the same encounter.'"

Franklin said the video shot by a protester "clearly depicts who the provocateur was as it relates to the initial confrontation between Scurlock and Gardner." For Franklin that provocateur was Gardner.

"I gave the grand jurors the entire statute on the use of self-defense or the use of force in connection with self-defense," Franklin said.

Franklin then decided to address Gardner's death. He said he was sorry for the loss of life but that he took a dim view of suicides.

"I was saddened and am still saddened about Jake Gardner having taken his own life. I think it's contrary to the beliefs that I have for anyone to engage in that sort of conduct. But beyond my personal beliefs, him doing so deprived the community of being able to have this evidence play out at trial."

Franklin then took issue with something Gardner's lawyers had said in announcing his death—that it was Gardner who'd been denied the opportunity at trial to have his innocence proven.

"There were witnesses who appeared before the grand jury who I can assure you would have been favorable to the cause of Jake Gardner. Witnesses plural, and though Jake Gardner himself had a Fifth Amendment right against self-incrimination and understandably did not appear and was not asked to appear in front of a grand jury, his videotaped interview with the Omaha Police Department was played in full for the benefit of the grand jury, and at the conclusion of all of the testimony from all of the witnesses, the grand jury was apprised for what most lawyers will fully understand to be an instruction on them assessing the credibility of the witness based upon the evidence that they have heard and seen, and what that witness has had to say about what those events were. They were given a credibility instruction, and it wasn't specific to any one witness but applied to each of the witnesses."

Franklin then offered a personal anecdote.

"I was having lunch Monday with two people whose insight and wisdom I greatly appreciate, and one of them said to me, 'You know this is just a ridiculous tragedy. You have two families devastated by the loss of a son, or a brother, or a father. But that's what hate produces.' And I share that comment with you because I find it to be profound as it relates to this entire tragedy."

If hate was at the heart of the matter, Franklin did not specify whose hate was to blame—the cops who had killed George Floyd, the Omaha police who had battled with protesters, or the protesters who had trashed the city. But the clear inference was it was Jake Gardner's hate.

Franklin said he had decided to go ahead with his news conference despite not yet having all the police paperwork concerning Gardner's suicide in Oregon.

Franklin said he was no longer going to discuss Gardner or Scurlock or the case, and that he would take no questions.

"I think I've shared with you the information that is relevant to this investigation, and as a famed radio journalist used to always say at the end of his broadcast: 'And now you know the rest of the story.'"

Reporters, though, did have questions, and Franklin tried to answer some of them, his bald head glistening under the lights of the cameras, his face a mask of frustration and impatience.

One reporter asked if Franklin had found evidence of criminal behavior in Gardner's past. It seemed a reference to the claims on social media about his dad being a drug runner and him assisting. Franklin wouldn't answer the question, saying it wasn't part of his investigation.

Franklin was asked about his description of Gardner having been eager to "light" someone up. Franklin, remarkably, denied saying what he clearly had said just minutes before.

But he stuck by what appeared to be his theory of the case: Gardner had been the first aggressor and that deprived him of the ability to claim self-defense, no matter the particulars of the actual events surrounding his use of deadly force.

"For my purposes I would have been derelict of my responsibility if I had not pointed out what the state of Nebraska's law is as it relates to provocation. Given the fact that there was video evidence of the initial confrontation. I mean you can take from that what you want."

Franklin was asked if there was evidence Gardner had used any racist language. Franklin again insisted the decision of the grand jurors was not colored by whether Gardner was a racist or had used racist language.

Franklin was asked about the advice he'd given protesters about how vandalism could play into the hands of those who oppose their aims. Franklin talked about how such rioting and property damage allowed critics to dismiss the protests as familiar, out-of-control nihilism. He thought the protesters were better than that, and that they could not be reduced to a Black mob. The people who turned out to protest, in Omaha and Minneapolis, he said, were diverse.

"But what ends up happening, and to answer your question, is it always gets portrayed as if it's the Black people who are doing this. Yes, we do it sometimes, but it's not an exclusive thing with any race of people. Despite how it gets portrayed."

Franklin was asked why Gardner hadn't been arrested under a warrant, why he'd been allowed to volunteer to surrender, maybe making it possible for him to kill himself. Franklin said there had been confusion around the process for having a warrant issued, and that he had been given inaccurate information about how to get it done. He said it was fine with him if Gardner had turned himself in, but he denied he was not interested in or willing to execute an arrest warrant.

"There's a critic for everything. I don't care about that."

Franklin was asked whether he had looked into the social media presence of the people who were seated as grand jurors to see if they had any strong views or biases. He said he had not.

He was asked why he had referenced Trump's remark about looting and shooting. Franklin answered obliquely:

"I didn't have any conversation with Jake Gardner to see if he was inspired by that comment one way or another. That's for you guys."

Franklin, in the end, sounded as much robbed of an interesting career moment as torn up by the deaths of Scurlock and Gardner.

"Speaking for me personally," Franklin said, "I think that it would have been a fascinating case to try."

"So, We're with You on This"

GARDNER'S FAMILY WAS LIVID AFTER FRANKLIN'S news conference. He had lied, they said, misrepresented the evidence, come across as a guy, in an unexpected late-career chapter, who was eager to become a celebrity, an avenging champion of supposed racial justice. His theory of the case against Gardner was not just erroneous, it was patently fantastical, they felt.

Don Kleine, in a series of interviews, all but agreed with the Gardner family, escalating an already highly unusual public furor over a case that had left two young sons of Omaha dead with no legal issues left to adjudicate. He said Franklin must have pushed an agenda for the grand jury to have returned any indictments. He said Scurlock was less a victim than a violent agitator that night, out "terrorizing" people.

Scurlock's family considered Kleine's public statements to be violations of everything from good taste to ethics guidelines for prosecutors. Kleine might have had a reputation as an honorable man and something of a progressive, but to some in the city's Black community he was throwing it all away to justify a decision that he agreed to have looked at anew.

Speaking with me privately, Kleine expanded on his analysis and upset.

Kleine called Franklin's theory that Gardner was intent on harming or killing protesters nothing more than "a good story" that didn't fit the facts.

"He didn't come out of his bar and plug someone," Kleine said of Gardner.

Kleine insisted that the grand jury had seen no meaningful evidence he hadn't already evaluated himself, and Franklin's own presentation made that clear. He openly doubted whether any Omaha cop would have testified in support of Franklin's case had it gone to trial. Kleine suggested Franklin was unconcerned about what Scurlock had been up to that night. He said Gardner's lawyers would have been free at any trial to explore Scurlock's actions that night to establish a "penchant for violence." He'd looked up the law on that question the morning after the killing.

Scurlock and his friend had done $6,000 worth of damage to the office close to The Hive, and had heaved rocks and a metal beam into Gardner's bar. Scurlock's friend had flattened a sixty-nine-year-old man. Gardner had shown Scurlock his gun and told him to move on. They instead came at Gardner.

"Gardner's not the first aggressor. He's in the middle of a riot," Kleine said. "People are screaming. Property is being broken. He tells people to move on. That's not being an aggressor."

In short, Kleine said, the grand jury didn't investigate the case; it bought a theory pushed by Franklin.

"You expect more," Kleine said of Franklin's handling of the case. "He's supposed to be an officer of the court who deals with the truth and the evidence as it is."

Instead, Kleine argued, Franklin chose to satisfy the desires of those who had campaigned for Gardner's prosecution.

"We don't bow to emotions or the mob," Kleine said. "We make difficult decisions every day about hundreds of cases. And you have to look at the law and the facts. I said it publicly: it's not what the mob thinks. And God help us if that's the way we are going to act."

Support for Gardner and criticism for Franklin moved beyond the fringe right websites and random online commentators to right-wing figureheads in the national media. Tucker Carlson took up the torch. Carlson would do two segments on his nightly Fox News show, and then another longer special segment months later. Carlson got Scurlock's name wrong, and erroneously said Kleine had indicted Gardner after his initial decision not to charge him. In the heat of Donald Trump's reelection campaign, Carlson laid blame for Gardner's death at the feet of "Biden voters."

"This summer a bar owner in Omaha called Jake Gardner was attacked during a BLM riot there. A man called James Spurlock jumped on Gardner's back and put him in a choke hold. Gardner shot Spurlock in order to save his own life. It was clearly self-defense and that's what prosecutors concluded. But then Biden voters took direct action; they took to the streets. What does that mean exactly? Well, in this case, it means they gathered outside the home of Douglas County Attorney Don Kleine, and they threatened him. Their presence was a threat. And guess what, it worked. Last week Gardner was charged with manslaughter. This weekend, Gardner killed himself. See how that works. Do you want to live in a country like that?

"This should terrify you," Carlson told his viewers. "Democratic leaders have decided that everything is allowed in pursuit of power. Nothing is off-limits: 'Give us what we want or we will hurt you.' Yeah, if they can do this to him, a man just trying to defend himself, then of course they can do it to all of us."

Ann Coulter went after Scurlock, Kleine, and Franklin, and the mainstream media, selectively citing an early account of the killing by the *New York Times*. "Mr. Gardner got into a fight with one man, James Scurlock, 22. The two scuffled before Mr. Gardner fired a shot that killed him," the *Times* had reported.

"They 'scuffled,'" Coulter wrote. "It brings to mind the *Times* headline from Nov. 24, 1963: 'President Kennedy Dies in Dallas After Scuffle—Albeit at Great Distance—With Lee Harvey Oswald.' . . .

"At 22, Scurlock already had a rap sheet a mile long, including home invasion, assault and battery, domestic violence—and, of course, he was in the middle of a crime spree that very night," Coulter wrote. "Methamphetamine and cocaine were found in his urine," she went on, before concluding in exasperation and despair, real or cynically created for an opinion piece she meant to push the right's narrative:

"The country has gone mad. I always figured the first armed civilian who ever fought back would put an end to the violence exploding all over the country—the violence that police and prosecutors can't or won't stop."

In the days after Gardner's death, his family struggled to hold a memorial service for him in Omaha. They tried a local bar first but were told the establishment wasn't willing to risk hosting the event. They applied to Omaha police to hold the service at Memorial Park, a striking public space dedicated to those who had fought in America's wars. The police said they did not have the resources to provide adequate security.

The family then turned to a church in nearby Council Bluffs, Iowa, the New Life Fellowship. The pastor told the family he worried violence would accompany any service and he could not put his church at risk.

I went out to see the pastor on a Sunday morning. The church is a single-story structure with a modest parking lot and a BBQ grill out front. Inside, there were seats for roughly 150 and a blessing was posted over the exit door. I asked to speak to the pastor, who had just finished the service. I was told he somehow had instantly left with his family for lunch. I asked that he call me. He never did.

Gardner's family at last held a service at a hall run by a disabled veterans organization. There, amid ATMs and TV screens showing Keno game results, in a hall with patriotic flags and notices warning that no confetti should be used at any event, people eulogized Gardner and music played for a couple of hours. People wore bracelets in honor of members of the military who had been lost to suicide. Family members played Gardner's favorite numbers on the electronic Keno games.

But many chose not to come at all. The police presence was heavy. One relative of Gardner's told me it's the only funeral he'd ever gone to where he felt he had to carry a gun.

Gardner's parents were among those who did not attend. They were too scared to return to Omaha from Oregon. Their son's life had been threatened, and now he was gone. They feared for their own. Dave and Sue watched the memorial via a nephew's iPhone feed. Sue had written a short tribute, and her sister Janet read it aloud:

> *"Jake loved traveling. He traveled to just about every state in the United States. He especially loved traveling with LeBron. The happiest times of life were with LeBron and the people he loved. We had wonderful vacations together and such beautiful memories. No matter how late Jake worked Saturday nights, he always made time to come to Sunday family dinners and family events. Those will be some of my favorite things to remember about Jake. When Jake was young, we went to Ohio to his Grandma Margie's with my sister and her kids. My stepfather would take them fishing and riding on the riding mower around and around the farm. They all loved being there so much. Another time when Jake was younger, he thought he was catching a crab to bring home to take care of. It bit his fingers and would not let go. We ended up having to take him to the hospital that day. He just loved animals so much. His grandmother moved to Omaha with us in 1995 when we left El Paso. It was shortly after she had lost her husband, Jake's grandfather. Jake stayed with her the whole summer, so she wasn't alone. When he was in the U.S. Marine Corps, she was very sick. He was able to come home for two weeks and he stayed by her side the whole time in the hospital. The night he left her and went back to camp, she passed away. Jake meant so much to so many of us. As his mother, all I can say is he was my firstborn son. I loved him more than my own life. He loved us all so much. He went out of his way to make everyone in his life happy. I could not have been blessed with a more wonderful, beautiful, amazing son, and I will always thank God for the wonderful thirty-eight years we were given with Jacob."*

The veterans organization arranged for a twenty-one-gun salute, and the rounds were fired in the suburban neighborhood on the outskirts of Omaha. A family member scooped up the spent shell casings as a keepsake.

Gardner's family was not sure if they had legal options to pursue a claim of any kind. But they were desperate to vindicate their son's name. And they took dead aim at Fred Franklin. Ben, who had found Gardner's lifeless body in Oregon, agreed to go on the Voorhees radio show Gardner's aunt had previously appeared on.

"I don't like to use the buzzwords 'racist,' 'prejudiced,' 'bigoted,' 'intolerant,'" Ben told Voorhees. But he said those exact words "adequately describe Fred Franklin.

"Fred Franklin's motives," Ben told listeners in Omaha, "were dishonest and dishonorable."

Ben's advocacy on behalf of his dead friend went beyond appearing on the radio show. He traveled to Omaha from Portland and spent hours with a local TV reporter. He explored hiring a lawyer for the family. Maybe there could be a malicious prosecution case. Or a wrongful death filing. Any such case, he and the family knew, would require obtaining the transcripts of the grand jury proceedings. If, as Don Kleine had alleged, Franklin pushed an agenda to the grand jury, the transcripts would likely be dispositive.

And then Ben did something extraordinary. He secretly recorded a conversation he had with Don Kleine and his deputy, Brenda Beadle. Once in Omaha, Ben got Kleine and his deputy to agree to meet with him. He bought a recording device and held it in his pocket under the conference room table when he was in Kleine's office. He'd researched that Nebraska was what's called a one-party consent state, meaning as long as one party to a conversation knew it was being recorded, doing so was legal. Beadle was there in person. Kleine, in chemotherapy treatment for his prostate cancer, joined by video.

Ben shared the recording with me.

What Ben captured was a genuine rarity, especially for journalists: an unvarnished, unrehearsed, wide-ranging, and specific discussion by prosecutors of a controversial case. Kleine and Beadle covered a vast amount of ground, revealing previously unknown facts, taking shots at Scurlock and the politicians who lined up behind his cause, and offering commentary on the state of politics in Omaha and the country at large. They both declared they were on Gardner's side. And Kleine stated that he had referred a complaint about Franklin's treatment of a grand jury witness to the U.S. Attorney's Office for possible investigation.

I listened raptly, and had my breath taken away. Not because anyone seemed malicious or villainous, although some might see them as such. But because, for once at least, people were being absolutely honest.

Ben got right to it with Beadle and Kleine. His aim, he said, was "exposing" Fred Franklin. Kleine responded by expressing sorrow: "First, just let me say how sorry Brenda and I both are for your loss. I can't even imagine the emotion."

Ben brought up Gardner's military service, and told a story about what happened when his friend Ron Payne was killed in Afghanistan. Ben said the other soldiers in Payne's unit in Afghanistan were so demoralized only one thing might cheer them up: Jake Gardner. His presence was requested but turned down by his commanders in Haiti, Ben said. Kleine listened and said he thought Gardner had been treated unfairly. He also wanted to talk about his own feelings of victimization.

"I was called a white supremacist because of my defense of Jake," he said.

"We need to put the pressure on people to hold Franklin accountable for what he's done," Ben pressed on. "Because in my opinion, omitting evidence that blatantly shows a man's innocence to convict him based on whatever motive he harbored in his heart against an innocent man is tragic. And I believe that he needs to be held accountable for that."

"Well, we agree," Kleine said.

Kleine asserted that Franklin's very first press conference announcing the indictment was intended to make Gardner seem racist even while Franklin was saying it didn't matter.

"He kept saying this inflammatory kind of thing about Jake. And that's troubling to me," Kleine said. "We believe he obviously had an agenda. We have to be able to prove he misled his jury. And the problem is we don't know what the evidence was that was presented."

Ben said if Gardner had wanted to light someone up, as Franklin had asserted in his second news conference, he had the weaponry and artillery to do that.

"We're infantry Marines. We all are gun enthusiasts. We all have souped-up AR-15s. You know, if you wanted to go cause a mass casualty situation or go target people, that would be the tool that would be in the toolbox."

That didn't happen.

Kleine then disclosed that he had made a referral to federal authorities about Franklin's handling of a witness. The witness, Gardner's business associate, had claimed one of Franklin's investigators had effectively threatened him in an effort to get him to testify that Gardner was a racist. The same investigator allegedly taunted Gardner's partner after his suicide. The associate, Kevin Moller, had come to Kleine asking what to do. Ben said he understood Moller had met with the FBI.

"I'm the one that contacted the U.S. Attorney to start that," Kleine said.

"Thank you, Mr. Kleine, thank you," Ben said.

"I feel bad for these grand jurors now, because I'm sure they would have done the right thing had they got the evidence before them," Kleine said.

Of the indictments Franklin won, Kleine said, they were "not supported even by the evidence he presented. So that's what troubles me about this grand jury. It's like, what were they told? What happened in there? I can't believe all these people came to that conclusion without being pushed that way or told something that they shouldn't have been told."

It was Kleine who then returned to the question of Franklin being held responsible. He encouraged Ben to air his grievances in the media, see if he could rally public opinion. "And then if the public gets outraged enough," Kleine said, "then maybe something will happen here."

Ben brought up the posts written by Ryan Wilkins, the Omaha lawyer with an eagerness to insert himself into the case. Beadle mentioned she knew the family and had tried to get Wilkins to disavow what he had written. She and Kleine said investigators had gone hard at the allegations Wilkins had made about Gardner's father being a convicted drug runner indoctrinated into white supremacy behind bars. They found nothing.

Kleine and Beadle said the misinformation was the work of crazy radicals, including Ja Keen Fox.

Kleine said those who had marched near his house were guilty of trespass and harassment, and lamented that the city prosecutor sat on his hands. Ben asked him about the Democratic Party's move to censure him, and joked that Kleine would be welcome to get behind Trump as an alternative. Kleine then revealed he intended to switch parties and join the Republicans. Of the local Democrats, Kleine said, "I can't be a part of a group or organization that supports that kind of conduct.

"When I was a young person and I became a Democrat, it was a lot different. It was a lot of hardworking, God-fearing people who were pro life and everything else. Now, things have gone so crazy with that party. It makes me sick, and I should've done it a long time ago."

"Everybody's so afraid to stand up for what's right," Ben responded, "and that's got to come to an end."

"It has to," Kleine agreed.

Ben asked Kleine if he would issue a statement warning other prosecutors not to give in if they found themselves in similar circumstances.

"I said, publicly, it's not what the mob thinks," Kleine said. "So

I'll be happy to say anything in that regard the more I get asked. I don't have any problems saying that because it's the truth."

Kleine then baldly said how unfair it was to compare Gardner to Scurlock.

"He's a combat veteran; he served his country; he served his country well. And to compare him, I'm sorry, I can't help it, to James Scurlock, who was convicted of home invasion robbery and went to the penitentiary for it at a very young age, who beat the hell out of his baby's mother and got ninety days from our office when we convicted him of that domestic violence assault.

"It's just unbelievable; it's hard to take it in," Kleine went on. "I get called a white supremacist because I refuse to call James Scurlock a victim. That's what all this is; they're saying, 'Well, he's a victim. You need to call him a victim.' I said, he's not a victim."

"He's an assailant," Ben offered.

"Yeah. Oh, so we're with you on this. My heart breaks for you guys," Kleine said.

"We are personally invested in this from Jake's standpoint. I hope you know that," Kleine declared. "We made a decision and we're being criticized about the decision we made. We know we made the right decision to begin with. It wasn't a hard decision. So that's where we're at. So, we're with you on this. We'll brainstorm."

Then Kleine, a lifelong Democrat, whose parents championed John Kennedy, said he feared what would happen if Trump didn't win reelection. Who would Biden appoint to be U.S. Attorney in Omaha "to appease these people"? he wondered.

"Brenda and I both say this: You live in a great country where everybody can have an opportunity. Okay, we need to keep striving to make sure that happens, that people have those opportunities. People better realize how good they have it here. If you started going to some other places and see how their criminal justice system works or their economy, what kind of opportunities people have, you're going to be there on your knees, thanking God that you can live in a country that we have here. And it blows my mind because these people are going to ruin it for all of us."

Before Ben left, Beadle shared something more with him. She knew that Scurlock's phone had been taken into custody by police the night he was killed. It had been reviewed, and she said his text messages revealed that Scurlock had set out that night intending to rob someone. He'd been tipped off that someone had $700 in cash. He'd also gone on to joke about how he was knowingly spreading sexually transmitted diseases to women he was sleeping with.

That information had never been made public, had never been shared with Scurlock's family. Beadle said it had been offered to Franklin but that he had declined to make use of it.

Whatever Ben had come for in his surreptitiously recorded session with Kleine and his deputy, he felt he'd come away with material he could use as he worked to clear Gardner's name.

"You Need to Be Careful"

IN THE WEEKS AFTER GARDNER'S DEATH, Ben and the Gardner family had met with a local Omaha lawyer, David Begley, to talk options and strategy. Begley took $3,000 up front, and laid out his sense of the opportunities and challenges ahead.

"The adversary system, that is, a trial, is how the truth comes out in America," Begley wrote to the family. "With Jake's death, there will be no trial. But part of the truth may well lie in Jake's grand jury testimony.

"I told you that generally grand jury testimony is secret. There is, however, the provisions of Neb. Rev. Stat. Section 29-1407.01 (4) which reads, 'Upon application by the prosecutor or by any witness after notice to the prosecutor, the court, for good cause, may enter an order to furnish to that witness a transcript of his or her own grand jury testimony or exhibits relating thereto.'

"Right now my theory for good cause is that Jake is now deceased and his voice needs to be heard regarding his defense of self-defense. This is true in light of both his suicide and the fact that Don Kleine declined to prosecute."

Begley told the family the attempt to get the grand jury material might be a legal long shot. There was little precedent for it in Nebraska. But then he took care to say something that would end his relationship with the family:

"I want to be crystal clear on this point: I will not, under any circumstances, allege that Fred Franklin is a bad lawyer, bad person or a dishonest person. I know Fred because he was in my freshman law school class at Creighton. More importantly, he was an Assistant United States Attorney for many years. That's an important and responsible job. Therefore, I have to presume he is acting in good faith and honestly. I do not think it prudent and wise of you to make those allegations although I know you are upset with how this was handled.

"I will advocate for you and Jake Gardner, but this is a difficult case," Begley told the family. "I need to be careful. You need to be careful."

Of course, the family thought. In Omaha, it could seem like every second lawyer you met went to Creighton. The local bar was insular. Aggressively going after Fred Franklin, whatever the facts, would be in bad taste. The family seethed and forfeited their $3,000.

What followed was yet one more jaw-dropping turn.

Franklin and the Gardner family issued warring public statements, both delving deeply into the dispute over the case's particulars. Franklin, perhaps unsettled or enraged by some of the criticism of his work, went beyond his discussion of the evidence at his second news conference, and went through the charges one by one. The family, with Ben's help, issued a blistering response, laying out what they said were Franklin's lies and misrepresentations. And the exchange involved more than disputes over evidence and possible motive and Nebraska's governing criminal statutes, with Franklin defiantly defending his character and the family accusing him of a cynical miscarriage of justice done so he might make a name for himself and profit from his celebrity in certain circles.

Franklin's statement began with him noting that he had indeed received a formal death certificate for Gardner. He seemed intent on ending the disturbing conspiracy theories about Gardner's death. He ended it by expressing his disappointment that Don Kleine, someone he'd known for years, had accused him of having an agenda based on the color of his skin.

Franklin said "given the community interest in this case," he was issuing, in effect, his own report on the grand jury inquiry.

Franklin's decision to effectively publicly prosecute a case against a dead man felt unheard of to me. On one hand, it's always good to have more information. But it seemed unusual to the point of maybe seeming desperate. And perhaps dangerous. Would anyone trust Franklin's version of the grand jury proceedings knowing that the official record of those proceedings would likely remain secret forever? And in his statement, he disclosed specific eyewitness testimony, the very sort of protected material he had sworn months before he could not legally discuss:

> *On Friday May 29th, an Omaha protest against racial injustice and the police killing of George Floyd in Minneapolis occurred* [Franklin's statement began]. *The object of the protest was something to which Gardner was philosophically opposed. The protest did not move into the Old Market area that Friday night. However, Jake Gardner stated that he sat "outside" his Old Market businesses armed for 4 hours in anticipation of problems from those associated with the protest.*
>
> *On Saturday May 30th, Gardner again returned to his closed business. This time, he was joined by his father, and two other men associated with the operation of the Hive/Gatsby's. They had with them at least four firearms including three handguns and a shotgun. One of the four was also armed with a tactical styled knife. Jake Gardner was not the only one of the four who had possession of a firearm.*
>
> *As the protest moved from downtown Omaha east towards the Old Market, Gardner, this time from the inside of his business, monitored the movement of the protestors from what he texted was his "police scanner." As the protestors came closer to Gardner's businesses, he caused the inside lights of the business to be turned off, making the space appear to be unoccupied to someone on the out-*

side. Additionally, though officers with the Omaha Police Department were literally seconds away and on every corner surrounding his business, Gardner called Emergency 911 claiming that his business was being shot at. (Omaha Police later concluded that there was no evidence that shots were fired in or around Gardner's business Old Market that night by anyone other than Jake Gardner.) On that 911 call, Gardner also stated in part to the 911 operator, ". . . that [he] just wanted to call in and make sure that [he] was on the record for this." Gardner did not specify what the "this" was for which he wanted to be on record. (It begs the question, was Gardner alerting the 911 operator that he wanted the "record" to document an anticipated need to return gunfire in self defense, since he reported that his business was being shot at?)

Gardner and those with him remained inside the Hive/Gatsby's with the lights off for approximately 15 to 25 minutes. During this space of time, video evidence shows the absence of anyone entering or attempting to enter the business, though it does show approximately 9 individuals engaging in window breaking and acts of vandalism of The Hive/Gatsby's. (The County Attorney at his press conference announcing his decision to decline filing charges referenced earlier acts of vandalism engaged in by James Scurlock. He was correct, however, when he also stated at that same press conference that acts of vandalism by Scurlock were irrelevant in the proper assessment of possibly charging Jake Gardner.)

Gardner certainly would have been free to argue that he was simply there to protect his property. Except, he didn't protect it. He did not stand in front of the businesses, with or without his firearms, as a deterrent to looters or vandals. There is no evidence that he did anything to stop the vandalism that was occurring while he was inside his business with the lights off. He allowed the vandalism to occur while awaiting the entry of looters, so as to use his firearms on them, at least that is one of the conclusions that could have been reasonably drawn from that evidence. And so as to be very clear, no one associated with the protest, looters, vandals or any other person, ever entered or attempted to enter The Hive/Gatsby's. No part of the confrontation between Gardner and Scurlock took place inside of Gardner's business. Nothing about the confrontation between Gardner and Scurlock involved Gardner engaged in the protection of his business.

From the front exterior of the business, a close review of the surveillance video from Gardner's business (previously shown on news reports), depicts an individual attempting to throw a traffic barricade into the window of the building on the southwest corner of 12th and Harney. That individual was being videotaped by an acquaintance. (These two individuals were white males from Elkhorn, Nebraska. The person doing the videotaping has been erroneously reported by some in the media as being a female.) Jake Gardner's father observed that activity and confronted the individual doing the videotaping and assaulted him twice by pushing him. Another person, who did not know either Gardner's father or the person who was being pushed by him, crossed from the north side of Harney and stopped the assault by Gardner's father by pushing him down. The young man from Elkhorn being assaulted by Gardner's father was interviewed by a team member with the Office of The Special Prosecutor. He indicated that he was grateful for the person coming to his assistance and in fact shouted a "thank you" to that person before they both left the immediate area. The point is to illustrate that Gardner's father was NOT randomly and indiscriminately attacked, as has been suggested. He was pushed down by someone who had come to the aid of a young man videotaping and being assaulted by Gardner's father.

Jake Gardner did not see his father pushed down but was immediately alerted to that fact while his father was still on the ground by one of the individuals with whom he was inside his business. The surveillance video clearly depicts Gardner watching the person who had pushed down his father running away east on Harney street.

Another video clip from a citizen cell phone provided to the Omaha Police some 4–5 days after the County Attorney announced his decision, depicts the initial encounter between Jake Gardner and James Scurlock. This video depicts an area east of Gardner's business and importantly, out of the field of capture for the surveillance video for Gardner's business. Because Gardner saw the person who had pushed his father running away east on Harney, he well knew that the person with whom he was then engaged, James Scurlock, was not the individual responsible for his father being pushed.

---

*The video clip is short, only 12–13 seconds. Nonetheless, it depicts Jake Gardner advancing towards James Scurlock, who is engaged in a true retreat, walking backwards 7 or 8 steps, before Gardner can be heard at the end of the clip saying, "What the f*ck are you going to do?" Scurlock's voice is not heard on the clip. The clip does not depict Gardner then brandishing his firearm. However, other evidence clearly demonstrates that he had the same 9 MM handgun inside his waistband during this initial encounter.*

THE TERRORISTIC THREATS COUNT

The Grand Jury Indictment includes a felony count of Terroristic Threats. When I announced the Grand Jury's decision, I specified that the Terroristic Threats count referenced the conduct by Jake Gardner in his threats of violence while brandishing and displaying his handgun. This conduct occurred prior to Gardner being jumped and prior to him having fired any shots. Yet, comments from supporters of Gardner persist in declaring justifiable "self-defense," as if the Terroristic Threat count was nonexistent. I am not suggesting that there was no defense that could have been asserted on Gardner's behalf as it relates to the Terroristic Threats count. I am strongly suggesting however, and solely for the sake of discussion, that to the extent that Gardner was justified in asserting self-defense in relation to his having been jumped, that justification would not have retrospectively applied to his earlier terroristic threats conduct. In other words, the claim that Gardner's conduct was justifiable self-defense would NOT have applied to his terroristic threats conduct. The evidence suggests that Gardner was threatening the use of deadly force and was doing so prior to having been jumped.

There came a point in the confrontation between Gardner and Scurlock when Gardner's father walked from in front of his son's bar business east towards where his son and James Scurlock were situated, and assaulted Scurlock by pushing him, the same as he had done earlier with the young man from Elkhorn. He then immediately walked away, while receiving a pat on the back from Jake Gardner.

Whatever was intended by Gardner's father pushing Scurlock, it is clear that the hostility was immediately escalated. At this point, Gardner is observed by witnesses to be in an agitated state and ready to pull and use his firearm. One such witness is a white male in a dark hoodie depicted in the surveillance video standing to Jake Gardner's immediate right. The video depicts him being pushed by James Scurlock. This individual was interviewed by my investigative team. He related that he did not know anyone involved in the conflict prior to that evening but that he had engaged in some discussion about the protest with Jake Gardner earlier that evening from across the street in front of another closed business.

The witness stated that he inserted himself into the conflict between Gardner and Scurlock in an effort to de-escalate it. He stated that when Scurlock pushed him, that he did not interpret Scurlock's actions as an attack or assault on him but rather as a statement from Scurlock to him to stay out of the fray. But importantly, he also stated that Gardner presented as agitated and eager to use his firearm and that he was very afraid that Gardner was about to pull his gun out again and use it. He was present and had observed Gardner when he initially displayed and then brandished his gun.

Another witness interviewed by my team includes a 20-year-old Hispanic female who initially jumped Jake Gardner from behind and took him to the ground. (There have been erroneous reports that Gardner was initially jumped and taken to the ground by two people, including Scurlock.) The surveillance video from Gardner's business clearly shows Gardner being taken down from behind by a single person, not two. When asked why she intervened, she stated that she had been observing an agitated and erratic Gardner from behind, knew from the comments of other bystanders that he had a gun, and believed that he was about to pull and use it. This is essentially the same observation made by the white male in the hoodie.

THE 2ND SHOT . . . ATTEMPTED FIRST DEGREE ASSAULT

After Gardner was jumped and taken down by the 20-year-old woman, Gardner pulled his gun and fires a first shot which appears to have just missed the torso of the woman, traveling between her legs as she is attempting to get off of him. Just after that, Gardner can be seen turning towards a tall black male near his feet, tracking him with his firearm in hand, and discharging his weapon for a second time. Gardner missed the tall black male with this shot. This is the Attempted First-Degree Assault count in the Indictment.

GARDNER'S CLAIM OF FEARING FOR HIS LIFE BASED ON BEING IN A CHOKEHOLD

As Jake Gardner brought himself off of the ground and turned towards the direction of the woman who had tackled him, he got off of the ground and in a position consistent with readying to shoot. Scurlock then broke away from engagement with Gardner's father and jumped on the back of Jake Gardner. Though the video evi-

dence is not definitive, it generally shows Scurlock attempting to pin Gardner's arms against his body so as to prevent him from extending his right arm and hand, where he initially held his gun. Arguments can be made that Scurlock, in jumping on Gardner's back, was attempting to assault Gardner. Arguments can also be made that Scurlock was acting defensively to prevent Gardner from engaging in additional shooting.

The Omaha Police took Gardner directly to the Omaha Police station after the shooting. Gardner told the Omaha Police that Scurlock had him in a chokehold and was threatening to kill him. The police took frontal and side profile pictures of Gardner while at the station. The pictures show no marks or bruising on Gardner's neck, chin, or shoulder area. Additionally, citizen cell phone video from a person standing directly across the street reveals only the voice of Gardner being heard. And Gardner's voice is loud and clear. He repeatedly and loudly yells at Scurlock to get off of him, something generally not able to be accomplished while being choked.

Under Nebraska's self-defense statute, Jake Gardner would have been required to prove both that his use of deadly force was in response to an imminent threat of death or serious bodily injury AND that he was NOT the initial aggressor in the conflict. As noted earlier, the best evidence of who the initial aggressor was came from the citizen cell phone video depicting Gardner as the aggressor, while Scurlock took 7 or 8 steps backwards, retreating from Gardner. That incident, along with Gardner brandishing his gun, and Gardner's father assaulting Scurlock by pushing him, is a reason why Scurlock may have been confrontational with Gardner during the scene depicted on the video shown at a prior press conference. Prior to Gardner firing his first shot, Scurlock had not engaged in any act constituting a threat of death or serious bodily injury towards Gardner. The evidence suggests that Scurlock wanted to fist-fight. Moreover, Scurlock was not on Gardner's property, but rather on a public sidewalk in front of a business adjacent to Gardner's, a place he had a lawful right to be.

After Scurlock was shot, Gardner, his father and the other two individuals with him immediately went back inside the bar, where surveillance video depicts Gardner having collected three of the four firearms present and giving them to his father. His father then hurriedly departed from the premises through the back door with the shotgun and two of the three handguns just prior to the arrival of the Omaha Police. Gardner's father is seen on video loading the guns into the rear of a vehicle and then driving off. The gun used to shoot Scurlock remained on the premises and was provided to the police before Jake Gardner was removed.

MY "AGENDA" AND THE DIFFERENCE BETWEEN THE GRAND JURY'S DECISION AND THAT OF THE COUNTY ATTORNEY

I have been accused of having had an "agenda" concerning the presentation I made to the Grand Jury investigating the shooting of James Scurlock. I did have an agenda. My agenda was for my team and I to review the investigation including approximately 60 interviews conducted by the Homicide Unit of the Omaha Police Department, seek out the existence of any additional evidence, and to follow that evidence to assess whether any of it was consistent with potential violations of Nebraska Criminal Statutes. It took my team and I nearly two months to thoroughly review that evidence and determine what was relevant.

I did NOT have any agenda as to any outcome, understanding that fidelity to the process mandated that the relevant evidence be followed and presented, rather than to pursue a predetermined conclusion, based on an allegiance to a political party or racial affiliation, or especially on uncorroborated statements by Jake Gardner to the Omaha Police.

Once the evidence from the investigation was reviewed, rel-

evant portions were presented to the Grand Jury for their consideration and ultimate determination as to whether to charge or not. To be clear on this point, it was the Grand Jury who had the authority to charge, not me as the Special Prosecutor. But more importantly, the Grand Jury was NOT deciding the guilt or innocence of Jake Gardner. The Grand Jury did not assess the likelihood of success at trial. They were only deciding if the evidence was sufficient for Gardner to be charged. Stated simply, the Grand Jury was not assessing the end game for this matter, something apparently done by the County Attorney given, his early and committed belief in a potential self-defense claim. Rather, the Grand Jury was only looking at whether there should be a beginning. In our system of criminal justice, criminally charging someone is NOT the same as determining one's guilt or innocence. Indeed, after the Grand Jury indicted Gardner, I announced that he was still presumed innocent.

The Gardner family took several days but then issued their own point-by-point rebuttal. In the family's response, they drew upon their access to the bar's security footage to build a time-stamped case. They made a raft of accusations of misconduct or criminal activity against Franklin and his investigators. And they chose to disclose the, if true, damaging information about Scurlock's true plans that night that had been shared with them by Don Kleine's office:

On May 30th, 2020, Jacob Gardner, a bar owner weathering the turmoil of coronavirus, and a decorated Marine Corps combat veteran, went to his business that was in the path of violent riots. His intention was to sound the alarm in case his business was set on fire. He was armed with a handgun, and a shotgun containing non lethal ammunition as was his right according to Nebraska State law 28-1202 which allows a business owner to carry weapons in defense of his person, property or family. At 22:28:00 on the high resolu-

tion video footage from the Hive Lounge security cameras, James Scurlock and others begin to break out the windows of the business while Jacob Gardner took cover behind a concrete wall within the business. At 22:42:00 Scurlock and others return and break more windows. From inside, Jake pulls the fire alarm, and calls 911 to report the sounds of gunshots, and his windows being broken at 22:42:15. At 22:43:30 an unknown male attempts to gain entry to the business through a broken window. Instead of shooting the intruder, Jake pumps a non lethal round into his shotgun. The sound of the shotgun being pumped startles the intruder, and he retreats back out of the broken window hastily.

James Scurlock was killed by Gardner during his third attack on the Hive business in 30 minutes. During Scurlock's first two attacks on the business, he simply broke windows. However, during his third attack on the business Jake Gardner was on the street with his father photographing the damage caused during the first two attacks after the street had cleared at 22:49:00. Jake's elderly and infirm father weighed just 140 lbs due to the second round of chemotherapy he was undergoing. More rioters began breaking windows in the building next to the Hive lounge. The elder Gardner, a 69 year old Vietnam Veteran with a clean criminal record, pushed one of the assailants in the group breaking windows at 22:55:00. A member of James Scurlock's entourage, Tucker Randall, violently tackled the senior Gardner to the ground. Jake Gardner ran up the street and placed himself between the advancing violent mob, and his beaten father. He is heard on audio and video recordings saying, "If you didn't push the old man just move on, we don't want any problems." Jake walks backward with his hands up in a surrender posture for approximately 20 feet before showing his lawfully concealed handgun, while keeping the muzzle pointed at the ground, to the advancing mob of rioters that includes James Scurlock. Jake Gardner showed the weapon in hopes of dissuading the advancing group of rioters from any further attacks on his person, family, or business. He reholsters his weapon, and continues backwards for an additional 30 feet at which time he is attacked from behind by Alayna Melendez, and Tucker Randall (James Scurlock's accomplice in criminal assault and vandalism). As Jake Gardner is being punched and kicked on the ground he manages to pull his pistol and fires ONE warning shot to scatter his assailants. The first two attackers withdraw at 22:58:01, and Gardner rolls over onto all fours with his back to the mob in an attempt to get back up after the beating he suffered. At 22:58:04 James Scurlock, a violent multiple felon (previously convicted of armed home invasion and assault on a pregnant woman), jumps on the already down Jake Gardner and performs an MMA move called a rear naked choke with a leg hook. It is a move designed to kill Jake Gardner. As Jake slips closer and closer to unconsciousness he is witnessed in the 780p surveillance, and heard in audio recordings from other videos pleading for Scurlock to stop his attack. "Get off me, get off me, please get off me." At 22:58:22 Jake Gardner saves his own life by reaching over his shoulder and firing his second shot over his shoulder killing the assailant James Scurlock.

After a review of all pertinent evidence by every Omaha PD detective and the Omaha DA, it was decided unanimously that Gardner acted in self defense. Sadly, after 36 days of protests in front of DA Don Kleine's home, common sense was abandoned in favor of mob rule justice, and the case was turned over to "Special Prosecutor" Fredrick Franklin who had no interest in justice or truth, but rather only to score a blow against a known innocent man simply because of Jake's race and political affiliation.

During and after the grand jury, Frederick Franklin has falsified evidence, hid evidence favorable to Mr. Gardner, and shamelessly slandered Jake Gardner as a white supremacist. These claims by Frederick Franklin are not only meritless, but easily found false by the review of the extensive and high quality video evidence. His claims reveal his agenda. Fredrick Franklin's conduct has dishonored the justice system, and makes a mockery of what it means to be an officer of the court . . .

Release the grand jury transcript, justice for Jake, Semper Fi.
The Gardner Family

The competing arguments, closing arguments if you would, were each littered with mistakes and dubious characterizations. Each side spun words and sentiments and facts to win the day and salvage reputations—for Franklin, his own, for the Gardner family, their son's.

Yet it may well be the closest thing to litigating the case as Omaha will ever see.

Justin Wayne, the lawyer for the Scurlock family, considered a small variety of his own legal possibilities—suing Gardner's estate, or filing ethics complaints against Don Kleine, maybe even suing him for defaming James. But he opted to stand down. Money had been raised for the family in the aftermath of the killing.

And in the end, the Gardner family would have no luck in finding the kind of representation that might have yielded what they most wanted—the disclosure of grand jury material that could possibly equip them to consider a legal move against Franklin.

The family, frustrated with the Omaha lawyer they first engaged with, wound up opting to go with another lawyer, John Pierce, who had been involved in the Kyle Rittenhouse case in Wisconsin. Rittenhouse was the seventeen-year-old white teenager who killed two people with a high-powered gun during protests over a police killing of a Black man in Kenosha.

The family liked the aggressive and unrepentant tack Rittenhouse's lawyers had taken, doing combat with not only the facts of the case against their client but also the political climate they claimed was behind his prosecution: Black Lives Matter partisans pushing to defund the police, the rise of cancel culture, and efforts to oust Donald Trump.

According to the Gardners, Pierce, at least initially, told the family he'd push Jake Gardner's case with no-holds-barred and zero fear of reprisal. They said he was confident it would, in the end, be a blockbuster case.

But weeks, then months followed with no progress and barely any contact between Pierce and the Gardner family. The family said he'd promise filings were just around the corner only for nothing to happen. Gardner's parents said they were visited just once in person by Pierce. Their subsequent calls often went unanswered, family members said. No one could say if anyone else close to Gardner or with information on the events of May 30, 2020, was interviewed.

Meanwhile, Pierce's own fortunes had become a public matter. He withdrew from the Rittenhouse case after prosecutors filed a lengthy motion alleging his personal finances were so troubled he might be in the case simply to resolve his outstanding debts.

Pierce and another lawyer, Lin Wood, had helped form a nonprofit organization called the #FightBack Foundation, which they declared would be used to "bring lawsuits to check the lies of the left." The organization had raised some $2 million during the early stages of Rittenhouse's prosecution. Wood would gain a degree of infamy for his role in challenging the results of the 2020 presidential election that removed Trump from office.

In July of 2021, Ryan Marshall, an associate with Pierce's firm, told the family a lawsuit seeking justice for Jake was imminent. Three weeks later, Pierce filed a suit in federal court in Omaha. The twenty-two-page filing named both Fred Franklin and Don Kleine as defendants:

> *Defendant Franklin conspired with Defendant Kleine . . . to make false and misleading statements to the media which violated Jacob Gardner's Sixth and Fourteenth Amendment rights to a fair trial and due process of law by implying Mr. Gardner's guilt, implying he was a racist, and inflaming the community regarding the case. These recklessly biased and false statements by Defendant Franklin also caused Jacob Gardner to lose all faith in the justice system and*

end his own life for fear of an unfair trial. Defendant Kleine . . . had knowledge that these wrongful statements were going to be made to the media, and negligently or knowingly failed to prevent them. The Douglas County Attorney's Office and Douglas County, Nebraska, created a wrongful, unconstitutional policy in allowing Defendant Franklin to make the wrongful statements which deprived Mr. Gardner of his rights and caused his death.

The suit took on Franklin's various claims during his two extensive news conferences about the case:

The statements made during the press conference caused Jacob to be "surrounded by a dark cloud" of depression and be in extreme emotional distress regarding both the loss of life that had occurred and his fears for a fair trial and his own safety and that of his family. Mr. Gardner stated that he was more nervous than when he was in combat in the military. He was dismayed by the statements that it was a "slam dunk" case and was reasonably fearful that people were going to hurt him or his family. Immediately after the press conference, Jacob told friends he had "lost all faith in the justice system" and should "walk into the woods and kill [himself]." As a result of the extreme mental anguish suffered by Jacob because of the false statements made by Defendant Franklin and his loss of a chance for an impartial jury, Mr. Gardner committed suicide on September 20, 2020. As a combat war Veteran suffering from PTSD and Traumatic Brain Injury, Jacob was especially vulnerable to emotional trauma. The Defendants are still liable for damages when a preexisting condition results in a greater harm. It is reasonably foreseeable that a prosecutor's publicly making false or misleading statements about a defendant, particularly in connection to a highly publicized criminal case, can cause such defendant severe mental and emotional distress, and that such distress can cause such defendant to engage in self-harm, up to and including suicide. Plaintiffs have suffered great loss of consortium, society, comfort, and companionship, pecuniary damages, mental distress and emotional damages due to the loss of their son.

The lawsuit generated a modest number of stories in the local papers and on Omaha television. The Scurlock family's lawyer said it was a meritless and malicious filing meant chiefly to subject the Scurlock family to more anguish.

Any number of lawyers in Omaha, some connected to the case, others merely interested, dismissed the filing as a dubious, even incoherent claim. Kleine and Franklin had conspired together to rob Gardner of a fair trial? Lawyers for Kleine and Franklin turned in withering motions to have the case dismissed, with prejudice, meaning it could never be brought again.

It all left Gardner's parents in tears. When Pierce and Marshall got involved in defending some of those arrested for their role in the assault on the Capitol in Washington on January 6, 2021, their reputations took a beating. Pierce repeatedly failed to show up in court, and he and his office offered shifting and conflicting reasons for why. Marshall had appeared instead, and was later accused of having pretended to be a lawyer when in fact he wasn't.

Days after the lawsuit was filed, and exasperated at what she considered the lack of adequate coverage by the local media, Gardner's aunt Janet took to *The Scott Voorhees Show* to plead for help. In her prior appearance, Janet had been introduced only as Gardner's aunt. She was too afraid to have her name mentioned.

This time it would be different.

"I'd like to clear up who I am," she said. "I'm going to use my name this time.

"I would like to take a moment to address Governor Pete Ricketts and our request to get the grand jury transcripts unsealed," she said, reading a statement. "This is a terrible tragedy that has happened, but then the city sacrificed an American hero, who acted in self-defense, and we believe people should be able to look at everything that Franklin did. We need everyone's help to do this. I am asking all of Jake's Marine brothers to please email or write your letters to the governor and I am asking all veterans to please help your brother veteran and email or write the governor. I am asking every citizen of Omaha, even if you're against Jake, please email or write the governor. Everyone should want the truth, and if you are so certain that Fred Franklin did nothing wrong or did not have an agenda, let's all take a look at it."

"I'm Really Not Sure How Many Different Ways I Can Say This"

I FIRST CONTACTED FRED FRANKLIN EARLY IN the fall of 2020. I'd already had a couple of conversations with Justin Wayne, the lawyer for the Scurlock family, and it appeared he had told Franklin he felt I could be trusted.

I was surprised and pleased. I could find no evidence Franklin had been interviewed at any length by local or national media—before his appointment, during the grand jury proceedings, or in the aftermath of the indictments and Gardner's suicide. Which, to be honest, seemed predictable, even natural. There were legal limits on what Franklin could talk about, and there were I suspected a raft of reasons he'd just as soon have the entire episode behind him. Any relationship he had with Don Kleine had fallen apart. Franklin had been pilloried by right-wing media outlets, both powerful national organizations and menacing fringe outlets. His long-standing friendship with the Scurlock family's lawyer, Justin Wayne, had been strained by the perception that he'd delivered the family what it wanted, facts be damned. Much as Kleine's decision not to indict Gardner felt to Black Omaha like an inside job, Franklin's decision to prosecute Gardner struck White Omaha as an equally tainted outcome.

"I felt like we couldn't even stop and talk in the street," Wayne said.

Even some of Franklin's closest friends and professional admirers had cringed at his performances before the cameras. They felt he had declared it didn't matter if Gardner was a racist, only to then insinuate again and again that he was. Franklin's referencing of Gardner's "affinity" for Donald Trump struck them as gratuitous. His advice to the protesters about how best to serve their just cause felt like he was taking sides.

One of Franklin's critics was a government lawyer who had worked in the same office as Franklin. His name was Christian Martinez, and he had come to know Gardner over his years in Omaha. Martinez wrote a personal letter to the Gardner family after his death. In it, Martinez said Franklin's handling of the case was "reprehensible" and "disingenuous." He said Franklin's reputation in the office was not that of a particularly gifted or brave prosecutor.

"Unfortunately, regretfully, Mr. Franklin chose to pursue indictments for crimes that he knew would never, ever support a guilty verdict at trial," Martinez wrote to the family. "This was wholly outrageous and unethical, and as a result of what has occurred, I want you to know that Mr. Franklin's name is mud amongst the law enforcement community."

In our first extended conversation, Franklin told me his full backstory, from childhood through his work with the U.S. Attorney's Office. He was warm, introspective, honest, if careful, in discussing life in Omaha for a Black family, and for him as a prominent professional.

We talked again weeks later, after his exchange of public statements with the Gardner family. We spoke for well over an hour, this time specifically about the case. Once more, I was kind of shocked, and fully eager. I had a million questions.

Franklin tried to answer quite a few of those questions. He initially told me he didn't think Don Kleine's decision not to charge Gardner and the grand jury's findings were "mutually exclusive."

"I don't know what Don Kleine's thought process was," he said. "He could have made a determination on his likely success at trial."

Franklin did seem frustrated at points with how hard I was

pressing him. "I'm not interested in engaging with the Gardner family's point of view," he told me. He later broke off communications. I wrote to him, texted him. He stayed silent. But he sent word through Justin Wayne, the Scurlock family lawyer, that he feared any portrait I painted of his handling of the case would be unflattering.

Throughout our conversations, Franklin, as he had at his news conferences, seemed to want to hold himself apart from the grand jury's actions. In indicting Gardner, the grand jury had only concluded there was evidence a crime had been committed and that Gardner was the one who had committed it. Franklin wanted to be seen as some sort of neutral chaperone for the grand jury, there to apprise them of the relevant laws and let them conclude what they may.

"The only thing I did was to advance the decision the grand jury had made," Franklin told me.

It's not really, of course, a sustainable position to try to adopt. I'd covered criminal justice for parts of four decades. Prosecutors decide who testifies, and who doesn't, and they control the nature and extent of the answers given. The evidence put before the grand jury—say, videos of a possible crime—is chosen by prosecutors. While grand jurors are empowered to ask questions of their own, prosecutors get to decide what questions may simply be inappropriate.

Perhaps most important, the standard of proof set for the grand jurors—probable cause to believe that a crime was committed—is not the standard governing prosecutors. They are duty bound not to proceed with any case if they don't believe they can prevail at trial, where the standard of proof is "beyond a reasonable doubt." However much Franklin might want to say the indictments were simply the work of the grand jury, his actions meant he not only concurred but felt even more strongly about the case against Jake Gardner. He just didn't seem to want to say so.

I had read, and reread, Franklin's detailed statement concerning the charges against Gardner. It contained a spectacular misstatement of the basic legal concept of burden of proof at trial. It assigned a sinister color to everything the Gardners did that night, while depicting Scurlock and his friend Tucker Randall in the most innocent light. Randall was never charged, for his action in the office on Harney Street or his flattening of Dave Gardner. Franklin's omissions were often as striking as what he included.

In short, Franklin's own discussion of the facts and evidence stood in stark contrast to his portrayal of himself as a background figure simply equipping the grand jury with information and staying out of their way.

Franklin had asserted that Gardner had set up inside his bar along with his father and two other men, lying in wait for the chance to shoot someone. Franklin made clear an orchestrated ambush had been set up. In fact, Gardner had been there alone at the outset, and was joined by his bartender when the bartender got hopelessly ensnared in the street traffic amid the protests. Gardner had called 911 and later pulled the fire alarm in the bar, setting off lights and noise. Gardner's father didn't arrive until much of the damage had been done to the bar, and after he had managed to get his younger son's car to safety. The idea, then, that a crew of people had strategically gathered inside the bar and dimmed the lights as part of a conspiracy to entice looters to freely attack just didn't line up with the facts.

Franklin's depiction of Gardner's call to 911 was also hard to accept. He suggested that Gardner, his bar being trashed by a marauding group of protesters in the street, should have, instead of calling 911, gone out and found a cop nearby to come help him. Franklin said there were cops everywhere, not bothering to mention they were effectively under siege, arresting people with weapons, and firing tear gas in answer to the bricks being thrown at them. Franklin also made clear he believed Gardner had falsely reported that his bar "was being shot at," part of a calculated ruse to justify shooting someone, which Franklin alleged Gardner was determined to do.

The 911 recording makes clear that was not exactly the case. Gardner reported that a mob was outside his bar, breaking its windows and throwing bricks and debris into it. He later said he was pretty sure a gun had been used to shatter one of the windows but that he couldn't swear to it.

Here, again, is the relevant exchange:

Gardner: "I've got some people breaking in all the windows right now. It's Twelve-Oh-Seven Harney Street."
Dispatcher: "Twelve-Oh-Seven Harney. Are you on scene there or are you viewing this from a camera?"
Gardner: "I'm inside the window being broken right now."
Dispatcher: "That The Hive?"
Gardner: "Yeah. Correct."
Dispatcher: "How many people? More than ten?"
Gardner: "Yeah, for sure. There's like a whole mob of them. I have no idea. They're throwing things through windows. I just wanted to call in and make sure that I was on the record."
Dispatcher: "Okay. Anybody inside injured? Need a rescue squad?"
Gardner: "No, we're good. We're kind of pulled back from the windows. I'm pretty sure they used a gun, so we pulled back pretty far so that nobody got injured and then we parked behind a brick wall."

And then later:

Dispatcher: "Okay. Did you see a gun? Just hear it?"
Gardner: "I heard it. Safe to say, if it was a rock being thrown there, I'd be surprised. It was a pop."

Franklin's position was that Gardner, in saying he wanted his report of the violence against his establishment to be "on the record," was creating some sort of cover story.

"It begs the question," Franklin wrote, "was Gardner alerting the

911 operator that he wanted the 'record' to document an anticipated need to return gunfire in self defense, since he reported that his business was being shot at?"

Couldn't the answer to that question be some version of, "Damn right." Might Gardner have worried, gun or no gun, that the mob outside might soon become more dangerous, perhaps a threat to his safety, and that he might have to do something drastic? Franklin does not even nod to the possibility. If Gardner wanted to create a cover story that his bar was shot at, why wouldn't he have simply told the 911 operator he definitely saw a gun?

Of course, Gardner shot no one who was vandalizing his bar, despite his life's work at risk of being ruined. Franklin concluded that Gardner was disappointed he had not been able to shoot anyone. Not that he had a shred of evidence that was so. The idea Gardner might instead have been relieved he hadn't had to shoot anyone, again, was dismissed, if it was considered at all.

Franklin in his statement claimed that Don Kleine had concluded Scurlock's behavior that night vandalizing the architecture office on Harney Street was irrelevant to his reasons not to charge Gardner. It's just not true. Kleine had concluded the exact opposite. He'd researched the case law, and he explained to top police officials why Gardner's defense lawyers could legitimately cite Scurlock's conduct that night as establishing a "penchant for violence." Kleine was calculating his likely success at trial, just as the ethics guidelines for prosecutors demanded. Kleine had opted at his first news conference not to show the video of Scurlock and Randall inside the firm's office at the request of Black leaders.

Franklin sought to undermine any claim Gardner was at his bar merely to protect it by stating "there is no evidence that he did anything to stop the vandalism." "He did not stand in front of the businesses, with or without his firearms, as a deterrent to looters or vandals," Franklin said.

Franklin, it seems, thought it would have been more responsible for Gardner not to wait out the assault at his bar by taking shelter inside it, but instead walk out into a rolling riot with his gun, to halt it all.

Really?

Franklin then followed that with what can only be read as a pejorative non sequitur.

"Nothing about the confrontation between Gardner and Scurlock," he wrote, "involved Gardner engaged in the protection of his business."

Of course it hadn't.

"It had everything to do with his father being knocked down," Franklin told me.

Yes, exactly.

While Scurlock had participated in damaging Gardner's bar—something that goes unsaid throughout Franklin's statement—he and Gardner came together after Gardner's father had been leveled in the street. No defense of Gardner's shooting of Scurlock would have relied on a claim he was protecting his business. It would have asserted he feared for his life after someone—someone he could not see, much less actually identify—had jumped him, and was choking him in the street.

Franklin characterized Dave Gardner's shoving of the protester filming the vandalism on Harney Street as assault. Tucker Randall's flattening of the sixty-nine-year-old cancer survivor was a push.

"The point is to illustrate that Gardner's father was NOT randomly and indiscriminately attacked, as has been suggested," Franklin wrote. "He was pushed down by someone who had come to the aid of a young man videotaping and being assaulted by Gardner's father."

When Dave Gardner later pushed Scurlock in the scrum in the street, that was another assault, in Franklin's eyes. Scurlock's similar shove of a bystander in the encounter was a push merely meant "as a statement from Scurlock to him to stay out of the fray."

Franklin further argued that Gardner should have known Scurlock was not the person who knocked his father to the street. He claimed this, he said, because the video from the bar "clearly depicts

Gardner watching the person who had pushed down his father running away east on Harney Street."

How Franklin had any idea where Gardner, his back to the video cameras, was looking or what he was seeing or what he was concluding about what he was seeing is never made clear. It's just asserted. Gardner never made such a claim in his interview with police. What the video does make clear is that Gardner, after asking the crowd who had floored his father, told people to move on if they had nothing to do with it.

Franklin, in explaining the terroristic threat count against Gardner, cites Gardner's "threats of violence while brandishing and displaying his handgun." In truth, Gardner never said anything about using his gun against anyone. He never brandished his weapon. He took it out of his waistband, held it at his side, and returned it to his waistband after his business partner told him it wasn't worth it. The most Franklin alleges Gardner said was, "What the fuck are you going to do?," though he fails to make clear whom he was asking that of. And Franklin neglects to mention that, as Gardner later backed up, he told people to "keep the fuck away" from him.

Franklin enlisted the testimony of an eyewitness to establish Gardner's eagerness to use his gun. "At this point, Gardner is observed by witnesses to be in an agitated state and ready to pull and use his firearm," Franklin wrote. How a person in the street could credibly determine that Gardner was ready to use his gun is a mystery. And, of course, Gardner didn't actually use the gun until he was assaulted and taken to the street.

Franklin said that after Gardner was tackled the first time, by Rose Melendez, "he got off of the ground and in a position consistent with readying to shoot."

This is flatly false. Gardner never made it fully back to his feet after being tackled and firing the first one or two shots from his pistol. The pistol was in his right hand, which was at his side as he tried to stand up. The gun was never raised, much less pointed at anyone. Scurlock then leaped on his back.

Franklin said in his statement that "prior to Gardner firing his first shot, Scurlock had not engaged in any act constituting a threat of death or serious bodily injury towards Gardner." And then, in the very next sentence, Franklin said, "the evidence suggests that Scurlock wanted to fistfight."

Wanting to fistfight with a man with a gun in the street during a riot was not a possible threat of serious bodily harm?

Franklin went on. "Moreover, Scurlock was not on Gardner's property, but rather on a public sidewalk in front of a business adjacent to Gardner's, a place he had a lawful right to be."

Well, yes. Jake Gardner was on a sidewalk he had a lawful right to be on, too. But it's Scurlock who jumped Gardner.

Franklin's two most egregious gaffes involved Scurlock's choking of Gardner and the question of the burden of proof at any trial that might have happened. He questioned whether Gardner could have been being choked if he was able to tell Scurlock to get off him.

"He repeatedly and loudly yells at Scurlock to get off of him," Franklin wrote, "something generally not able to be accomplished while being choked."

As prosecutors made clear in the trial of the Minneapolis police officer who killed George Floyd, Floyd had said, "I can't breathe," more than twenty times as he was slowly asphyxiated by Officer Derek Chauvin.

Finally, as Franklin laid out the supposed evidence against Gardner, he declared what Gardner would have been up against at trial.

"Under Nebraska's self-defense statute, Jake Gardner would have been required to prove both that his use of deadly force was in response to an imminent threat of death or serious bodily injury AND that he was NOT the initial aggressor in the conflict."

As any reasonably seasoned viewer of America's limitless supply of true-crime television would know, the defendant at a criminal trial has no burden of proof whatsoever. The burden of proof rests solely with prosecutors.

For me, it's hard to imagine a more embarrassing misstatement of a most basic fact of the criminal justice system.

In my second conversation with Franklin, he again insisted Scurlock's behavior that night had nothing to do with the question of whether charges were warranted and a prosecution likely to succeed. I asked him directly whether he had ever looked at the information on Scurlock's phone. Gardner's family had been told by Kleine's office that Scurlock's texts that night showed he had set out intent on robbing someone.

"I can't confirm or deny what was on James Scurlock's phone," Franklin told me.

Franklin said he had been hurt by Don Kleine's comments about his alleged agenda, and expressed outrage that Kleine had shared some details of the investigation with Gardner's supporters.

"Astounding and extraordinarily concerning," he said.

He said again that sixty people had been interviewed during his investigation. "Those people had useful information," he said. He added that Kleine might have reviewed interviews with as few as four witnesses, one of them Gardner.

Franklin told me he had access to video footage no one else had seen, and that it showed Gardner advancing on James Scurlock as he sought to find out who had hit his dad. Scurlock, Franklin had said in his statement, had initially been "in a true retreat." But he would not show me the video.

I had spent hours watching the available video of the episode, and it showed something quite different from what Franklin said had happened. Scurlock, as Gardner was going to seek out his father's attacker, was on the other side of Harney Street and behind Gardner. He can be seen racing through the construction materials to run up the block and position himself in front of Gardner. The footage would appear to eliminate any claim that Gardner had somehow targeted Scurlock as he sought his father's assailant.

But Franklin told me not only that he believed Gardner was the aggressor but also that Gardner had been confrontational in part because he knew he was likely out of range of his bar's video cameras.

"I don't want to say 'orchestrated,'" Franklin said to me, but Gardner "clearly understood his behavior was going to be the subject of his surveillance system."

I found this, frankly, breathtaking. Really, to be honest, a fantasy. A man who has seen his bar badly damaged, seen his father knocked to the ground, and who found himself in the middle of a raucous scene on the street somehow made the internal calculation about what his video system could capture and what it couldn't, and freely targeted Scurlock because he was confident the encounter would never be seen?

"That's madness," said Tom Monaghan, Gardner's lawyer and Franklin's former boss at the U.S. Attorney's Office.

Franklin and I talked as well about Gardner and the question of whether Gardner was a racist.

"I wasn't investigating a hate crime. His views on race were irrelevant," Franklin told me. "Unnecessary to filter through his life and politics to produce motivation."

Yet I knew that Franklin's investigators had spoken with Mark Pitcavage, the white supremacy expert at the Anti-Defamation League, trying to run down the claims made by Ryan Wilkins that Gardner was some kind of neo-Nazi.

And then it was as if Franklin just could not stop himself.

"The only thing I'll say about race is that Jake and his father and the others that were with him wouldn't have been down there if it wasn't a Black Lives Matter protest that was happening. And they didn't go to support what was happening. There's an argument to be made that they were unsympathetic to the protesters."

Maybe Gardner was just unsympathetic to the vandalism imperiling his business and those of others.

Which, of course, would not have distinguished him from much of Nebraska. Calls by Black Lives Matter supporters to defund the nation's police departments, as well, would not have been a policy idea embraced by the 74 million Americans who later voted for Donald Trump that fall. Kleine had told me Gardner's online postings about the protests had included him saying he understood the legitimate reason for the protests but objected to the way they were being conducted and the dangerous unrest they had produced.

Before Franklin and I concluded our interview, I made a point to ask him about the anecdote he had related during his second news conference. He'd had dinner with friends, one of whom said to him, "You know this is just a ridiculous tragedy. You have two families devastated by the loss of a son, or a brother, or a father. But that's what hate produces."

Franklin had agreed with his friend; that's why he had told the anecdote at his news conference. And so I asked him how he saw hate as a factor in James Scurlock's death. And whose hate?

"I'm not prepared to support it," he said when I asked him about the anecdote. "I won't run from it either."

I asked him about whether he had determined if racial slurs had been used in the exchange between Gardner and Scurlock. Don Kleine had said he'd seen no evidence that it was so.

"I'm not going to confirm or deny what the investigation showed on racial slurs," Franklin said.

I had actually spoken with Scurlock's cousin P.T., who had been by his side during the incident. He told me he had heard no slurs. I asked if he'd told that to the grand jury. He told me he had never been called. I couldn't fathom why a witness to the critical seconds of a fatal encounter had not been called.

ANOTHER PERSON WHO was never called before the grand jury—never even formally interviewed by the police or Franklin's investigators—was Dave Gardner, Jake's dad.

"Not once, not ever," Dave said to me. This despite the fact that the older Gardner had been there for the entirety of the deadly episode and had, according to Franklin, been the instigator of the fatal series of events when he pushed the protester filming the vandalism.

Franklin in his presentation of the evidence had suggested Gardner's father's efforts at getting the guns not used in the shooting out of the bar quickly that night was "suggestive of something." He never, though, said what exactly, and the grand jury didn't indict Dave Gardner.

"I got them out because we feared people would come into the bar after the shooting looking for revenge, and they could have gotten their hands on the other guns," Dave Gardner told me.

The Gardner family in their reply to Franklin's statement had made much of the fact that Franklin had intentionally misrepresented the words used in a text exchange between Gardner and his Marine friend in Portland. Franklin had said Gardner's friend asked if he had a clear "field of fire," bolstering Franklin's speculation that Gardner was intent on shooting a looter. The friend had shown me the text. He'd asked if Gardner could "feel the fire."

I didn't know for sure what Gardner's friend intended in his text. Could he have indeed meant to ask Gardner about his "field of fire" from within the bar and merely mistyped it? Maybe. But even if that were so, you don't, as a prosecutor, get to change the words of potential evidence without at least explaining you were doing so, and why. But Franklin had done none of that.

In our conversation, Franklin said he had no concerns about what he had done. "I was trying to make the public understand the nature of the communication," he said. "I'm one hundred percent confident a judge would have let that in.

"It was crystal clear," he said to me, "how the grand jury regarded that communication."

Of course, being able to better assess Franklin's conduct as the special prosecutor would be helped enormously by obtaining the transcripts of the grand jury proceedings. The Gardner family wanted them made public. Don Kleine wanted them made public. I wanted to see them, for sure.

I wrote to the clerk of the Douglas County Court but was told I had no shot of acquiring transcripts that he said, by law, were secret. I wrote to the judge who had overseen the grand jury investigation, Horacio Wheelock, but he never replied. I consulted with a First Amendment lawyer, and again was told the law was not on my side.

But my reading of the Nebraska statutes governing grand jury testimony suggested there might be a way to get a look at some of what happened in the grand jury. A witness who testified had the right to ask the judge to be given a copy of their testimony. One of the witnesses who testified was Kevin Moller, Gardner's business partner and the man who had gone to Don Kleine to complain of his alleged mistreatment by Franklin and one of his investigators. Examining Moller's testimony could be revelatory.

I then met with a prominent Omaha criminal defense lawyer, Clarence Mock, to gauge my chances at success. He had no connection to the case but of course had followed its twists and turns. He thought it was possible I could get hold of Moller's testimony, but Moller might well have to appear in court as part of his effort to obtain his testimony. Moller was unwilling to, fearful of the charged environment surrounding the case.

But Moller was willing to tell me the full story of his dealings with Franklin and his investigators, and to describe in detail his testimony before the grand jury.

Franklin had been assigned two former Omaha Police Department detectives to assist with his investigation. One was named Steve Henthorn, a white twenty-five-year veteran of the department who had spent years of his career in the Homicide Unit. The other was Jeff Gassaway, a Black retired detective who had spent time working in the department's Gang Unit.

Gassaway had earned a reputation as an aggressive cop, maybe too aggressive. Tommy Riley's public defenders had told me Gassaway was well known to the office as an officer to be wary of in any case.

"The kind of guy who when he says the sky is blue," Riley said, "you go outside and look to be sure."

Riley and his staff had some justification, for the veracity of Gassaway's sworn testimony in a drug case had been called into question by a federal judge.

The case involved the conviction of a college student, a young father who had no criminal record beyond a marijuana arrest and a citation for driving with a suspended license. The man had told the authorities he'd smoked marijuana three times in his life and drank alcohol on just four occasions. Gassaway and prosecutors had implicated the man, Jerome Bass, as part of a drug conspiracy, and a jury had found him guilty, subject to a harsh mandatory sentence of ten years as a consequence of federal sentencing guidelines, required punishments many judges had come to regard as extreme and unjust.

In a remarkable formal opinion, the judge handling the matter eviscerated the case brought by prosecutors and Gassaway, saying the jury had been deceived by multiple witnesses who had lied on the stand:

> *The government offered no evidence of drugs, no evidence of drug money, no wiretaps, no pictures, and no confidential informant testimony. . . . The trial testimony regarding times of drug transactions was vague; the amount of each transaction vague; and information about the sales vague. . . . There was no testimony in this case where one witness corroborated the testimony of another witness. . . . The government offered the testimony of members of the drug conspiracy and the testimony of Officer Gassaway.*

The judge then offered a scornful assessment of Gassaway's testimony in the case. The judge found Gassaway's claim that Bass had confessed to him unbelievable:

> *Officer Gassaway testified that Mr. Bass was asked if possibly he carried clothes that might have had drugs in them. Mr. Bass allegedly stated that he might have carried clothes and maybe they had drugs wrapped up in them. The question and answer were contrived*

at best. The court's experience in previous Omaha Police Department cases is that they do not record interviews with suspects, except in some homicide investigations. The jury is required to rely on the veracity of the reporting officer in recounting conversations with a suspect. There was no other witness to this alleged admission. There is no evidence in this record that Mr. Bass or anyone else carried clothes with drugs in them to buyers or suppliers. There is no evidence to substantiate this alleged statement or admission that Officer Gassaway says Mr. Bass made. The court did not find this statement to be credible, and the statement was definitely not supported by any other evidence during trial. The court has had previous cases with Officer Gassaway, and while the court is aware that he is an effective gang enforcement officer, the court has been less than pleased with some of the aggressive tactics used by Officer Gassaway to accomplish his arrests and convictions.

Moller told me he was in the yard of his home in Omaha when Gassaway, unannounced, one day arrived in his white Dodge Ram truck. Moller was scheduled to appear before the grand jury in the coming days. Gassaway said he wanted Moller to come talk with Franklin ahead of his grand jury testimony.

"We just want to see what your story is," Moller told me Gassaway had announced. "I said, 'No, I'll tell you in the grand jury.' And he just kept pushing."

Moller said Gassaway eventually grew frustrated. He said Gassaway mentioned all the protests that had gone on at Don Kleine's home. He told Moller it'd be a shame if that happened to him at his home. Moller said Gassaway told him all he had to do was say Gardner was a racist.

"Tell me about Jake's racist past, and why you are lying about it," Moller said Gassaway demanded.

"He said, 'Well, you know, we can, we can help protect you, keep your name out of the paper,'" Moller said of Gassaway.

Moller had been interviewed by detectives in the hours after the shooting, and it was clear to him Gassaway had read his interview. Gassaway now accused him of lying. Moller was astonished. He had trained many of the Omaha Police Department's officers to fight in Omaha's annual fundraising event—cops against firefighters in the ring. He had friends on the force.

"I just told him, 'Jeff, I appreciate what you did on the police force when you worked there. But I don't appreciate what you're doing now. And I'm done.'"

Appearing before the grand jury, Moller said Franklin asked him his name and phone number and then immediately wanted to talk about his boxing career. Moller had been raised by a tough and demanding dad, a former Army Ranger who'd served in Vietnam, and he'd been a Golden Gloves champion as a kid.

Moller told me it was clear to him where Franklin was going—he was going to paint Moller as some guy with a taste for violence.

"What was your reasoning for going down there that night? Were you gonna take some anger out on the crowd?" Moller said Franklin asked him. "Were you going to just go down there and use your skills and beat people up?"

Moller said he was incredulous. He asked Franklin where in any of the video he was seen being violent, even confrontational.

"I said, 'You look back through my record. I have no record for assault ever. That's not what my dad taught me. It was always self-defense. I fought in the ring where there's rules and where both people agree that that's what you're going to do. So it's as simple as that.'"

Moller told me he'd been instructed that witnesses could engage in a back-and-forth with the prosecutor. It was a grand jury proceeding, not a trial. He said he and Franklin went at it for two and a half hours.

"He had asked me a question. I'd ask him a question back," Moller said.

Moller said he and Franklin spent fifteen minutes on the meaning of Gardner having talked that night about being on "fire watch."

Moller knew it meant guard duty. His Army Ranger dad had told him that. Franklin, he said, thought it more sinister.

Moller said he was struck by how adversarial it was. Franklin was the lone prosecutor in the room. He roamed about, and often grew frustrated, even angry with Moller. He yelled at him more than once.

"I was like, could he even do that at a trial?" Moller said to me. "Would a judge allow that?"

Moller said he and Franklin had an extraordinary exchange dealing with Gardner and his gun. The video played for the grand jurors showed Gardner had lifted his shirt to show Scurlock and the others he had a gun; he'd taken it out briefly, then put it back in his waistband. Then, retreating, Gardner had raised his hands.

Franklin had a theory: Wasn't that a ruse to provoke Scurlock or the others? Weren't Gardner's raised hands an invitation to have the crowd come at him? Wasn't he trying to dupe them into an altercation so he could use the gun? Franklin asked.

Moller recalled Franklin's theorizing vividly.

"He said, 'Isn't it in your fighting training that you can put your hands up because you're actually looking to attack?'" Moller said. "'As soon as they get forward, you're going to leap forward and get them.'"

"That's the dumbest thing I've almost ever heard," Moller said he told Franklin.

Looking back, Moller said Franklin's mission in the entire episode was clear to him: "I was the number one witness they had to destroy the credibility of."

Moller told me Franklin apologized to him after his appearance. But Gassaway, he said, was not done with him. After Gardner's death, Moller said, Gassaway called him to taunt him. Moller said Gassaway sounded drunk. Gassaway accused Moller of having lied before the grand jury. He told Moller Gardner had killed himself because he knew he'd never have been able to beat the charges against him.

Moller said he went to the authorities to see about filing a complaint. He felt he'd been intimidated by Gassaway before his testimony, mistreated by Franklin in front of the grand jury, and then improperly contacted by Gassaway after his friend's suicide. He went first to Don Kleine, who sent him to the U.S. Attorney's Office. Moller told me he and his attorney met with the FBI and laid out what had happened. A spokesman for the federal prosecutor's office confirmed they had received a referral about possible witness intimidation. Moller said he was later told the investigation had been turned over to the Nebraska State Patrol. I found no evidence Gassaway had ever been sanctioned in any way.

When I asked Franklin about Moller's account, he conceded he had been aggressive with him, as well as with the bartender from The Hive who had been on Harney Street that night, and who also had testified.

"They were being untruthful," he said of Moller and the bartender. "I'm not going to make excuses for how I question a witness."

This from the man who had sought so hard to say he'd had little role in shaping the thinking of the grand jurors.

Franklin never responded to repeated questions about Gassaway's alleged misconduct. I tracked down a phone number for Gassaway and over many weeks we exchanged several texts.

"Respectfully, I'm not interested in talking about the Jake Gardner case," he wrote to me after my first inquiry.

I wrote him back:

Understood. But I'm duty bound to put some things before you to give you a fair chance to respond. I understand one of the witnesses who testified before the grand jury has now met with FBI on a complaint of misconduct on your part. Witness intimidation and improper disclosure of grand jury information. These are serious claims. I don't know them to be true. But seems like a formal inquiry is underway.

He didn't respond, but I persisted over time:

I'll be back in Omaha next week. I'm obligated in fairness to try every means to get your story. I could come to your house. But I'd love to avoid the imposition and awkwardness. Let's meet!

He then replied with his last message to me:

Joe, again with [due] respect, I do not want nor have any desire to speak. You of all people should know that I took an oath not to disclose any information pertaining to this case. If you trust the information that you have, then you proceed with your book. I do not want any further text about this and you are not welcome to drop by my house. Good luck.

I responded:

Jeff, Genuinely appreciate your taking the time to respond. And I apologize for this final text, if you continue to want no contact. I just wanted to be clear once and for all: I respect your oath not to talk about the case. But you will be a character in this book, and I think it only fair you not be reduced to a stick figure who appears briefly in a controversial moment in a controversial case. You have had a career and life in Omaha. A long career as a Black officer. You have family there. I'm happy to talk just about that, and not the case. Feels important to you most of all.

MOLLER WOULD NOT be the only grand jury witness I'd get to talk with. When I had first begun my reporting in the summer of 2020, I'd contacted Rose Melendez, the young woman who had first jumped on Gardner in the street outside The Hive. She was suspicious of me, and indicated she would not talk because she had concluded I did not already accept that Gardner was a racist. It felt dispiriting in any number of ways, and she declined to respond when I asked why she seemed to feel the way she did.

Close to a year later, I was in Omaha, and tried her again. She still had the same cell phone number, and she eventually agreed to talk. We had a meal together, and she told me her painful life story. We then agreed to meet and record an interview, and she brought along her boyfriend, Brian, who had been with her that night in May of 2020.

She and Brian had both testified before the grand jury, appearing alone of course. They described their experience to me in detail. Neither had ever before been involved as a witness in a major criminal case, and so they were neither experienced nor sophisticated in the workings of a grand jury investigation. But over several hours, they recounted for me yet one more remarkable chapter in the story of James Scurlock and Jake Gardner.

Melendez said she regarded Franklin as a kind of intimidating presence, struck by the way he carried himself, his stern voice. He seemed to her, she said, like some kind of celebrity she'd somehow found herself in the same drama with. She and Brian described a fairly freewheeling environment in the hearing room. To them, it was clear the grand jurors were divided about the case, with some asking aggressive and opinionated questions about Scurlock's motive and conduct that night and others openly seeming to line up against Gardner.

"So it was a very odd mix," Brian said of the grand jurors and the proceedings. "I thought it would be a lot more serious than it was, to be honest. I didn't think they were very qualified to be doing what they were doing."

Both Rose and Brian told me Franklin's allegiances were obvious.

"Oh, he definitely wanted James to win a hundred percent," Brian said. "He was fighting for James. I could feel his passion."

Both Brian and Rose said Franklin would cut off grand jurors if they seemed to in any way disparage Scurlock. His passion, they said, underscored his desire to get justice for James.

"He made me feel like, 'Okay, we're gonna get this done,'" Brian said of Franklin's eagerness to press a case against Gardner. "'Let's get this dude put in the right place where he needs to be. And then let's go.' He was like, 'It's kind of stupid that I've got to fight for this. But let's finish it and get it done.'"

Brian said Franklin had personally thanked him after his testimony, saying he thought it was helpful to the case. Incredibly, Brian also said he mingled with grand jurors in the hallways after, as well.

"I remember specifically the jurors talking to me, some of them thanking me," Brian said.

It was not, for me, a story I had ever heard before. A witness mingling with grand jurors still empaneled to decide Omaha's most explosive case in decades? Could it be true? If not, why would Brian make it up? In some ways, Rose's and Brian's lack of experience in a high-profile case made them more trustworthy.

Having been rebuffed by Gassaway, I reached out to Steve Henthorn, the second former Omaha Police Department detective assigned to serve as one of Franklin's investigators. Henthorn had done twenty-five years with the OPD, a number of them in homicide. After retiring, he did three years as an investigator in Don Kleine's office. I sent Henthorn a message laying out everyone I had talked to so far—Franklin and Kleine both, the Scurlock and Gardner families as well, three grand jury witnesses, and others. Henthorn was wary of me. He said so directly. He would check me out.

And then he agreed to talk with me. *Wow*, I thought. I had actually never thought it likely. But what an opportunity—a discussion, rare when dealing with grand jury proceedings, with someone intimately familiar with Franklin's investigation, and likely disposed to support it.

When we did talk, Henthorn told me he would not speak about the protected material of actual testimony or exhibits. But in a number of interviews, he shared an awful lot. He confirmed outright some things I had been told. And for me, he confirmed other things by his choice not to tell me, when asked, that I was wrong about some controversial aspects of what had happened.

Henthorn quickly cleared up some mysteries. Franklin had never disclosed how many people had actually appeared before the grand jury. Henthorn could not be precise but said twenty or twenty-five was likely right. He said there had indeed been three shots fired by Gardner and that shell casings for all had been found.

I then told Henthorn that I'd been drawn to the case by the possibility that what was a terrible tragedy had somehow been twisted into a tainted morality play. That both Gardner and Scurlock, each of whom would lose his life, had been reduced to pawns at a moment of raw hurt and suspicion in a hopelessly divided America.

"So I will tell you that I agree wholeheartedly with the way you're coming at it," he told me, "as far as you have two young men that had flaws and they came together at a point in time that ended up costing both of them their lives."

Henthorn told me he had never worked with Franklin before. He was a city detective; Franklin was a fed. He said Franklin had tried to recruit one of Henthorn's friends to serve in his investigation, but the friend had a conflict and had recommended Franklin try Henthorn. He said his friends had discouraged him from joining the case. Too hot; very little upside.

"But I just thought that it was something that needed to be done, and needed to be done properly. So, I did it," he said.

Henthorn knew of Franklin's career in the U.S Attorney's Office, and he told me straight out Franklin was not really equipped to run a homicide investigation. He'd never run one before in his two decades as a federal prosecutor.

"Fred's career was based on crime against property. Investigations are investigations, but I think there's a big difference between them and the property side, where a lot of it is, for want of a better expression, paper pushing. A lot of your evidence is just right there in front of you. You don't do as much with people and the motivations of people when they do things. I was concerned about that lack of background with him. Even though the feds generally don't do homicides, they do do crimes that involve people. He just did not have a background on that. That was a concern as far as I was concerned."

Henthorn made clear he became convinced Gardner needed to answer for killing Scurlock, that a trial on some kind of charges was warranted. But he also emphasized he had issues with some of the decisions made, and theorizing done, by Franklin, including whom to put before the grand jury and whom not.

Franklin's critics had openly questioned whether any of the homicide detectives who worked the case had actually testified before the grand jury. I'd been told only one detective actually had, a veteran of the Homicide Unit named Ryan Hinsley. And I'd been told Hinsley and Franklin had argued in front of the grand jury, with Hinsley taking the position that he believed, as he had from the hours and days after the shooting, that Gardner had acted in self-defense.

I had traded texts early on with Hinsley. He was polite but would not talk. I requested that the OPD allow me to interview him but was turned down.

Don Kleine told me he had spoken with people close to Hinsley.

"He was torched," Kleine said of Franklin's treatment of the detective. "Gone after."

Now, with Henthorn, I said what I'd heard about Hinsley being the only homicide detective to testify and about his open disagreement in the grand jury room with Franklin. I told Henthorn to tell me if it was wrong. He did not.

I then told Henthorn I had reason to believe Franklin might have called Jennifer Heineman, Gardner's distant cousin, to testify before the grand jury. The idea that Franklin had even contemplated calling her seemed unthinkable. She was not a witness to the incident; she had no communications with her distant cousin that might have somehow been helpful. She had merely made unverified and inflammatory claims about her supposedly racist family, and thereby fueled a narrative that had shaped much of the public understanding of that night in Omaha's streets. If that's what she would have been called to tell the grand jurors, it seemed not only improper but willfully malicious, designed only to inflame the grand jurors and prejudice them against Gardner.

Henthorn said he had cautioned Franklin against calling Heineman and had spelled out his concerns to him. He told me he could not say for sure whether she testified nonetheless.

"What I will say is that Fred and I didn't always see eye to eye on everything," he told me.

I asked Franklin if he had called Heineman; he did not respond.

Heineman ultimately insisted to me she had not testified. Henthorn seemed relived when I told him.

I asked Henthorn how he regarded the quality of the initial investigation done by the OPD's Homicide Unit, his old stomping grounds. Don Kleine said Franklin had bad-mouthed the work to him shortly after taking over as special prosecutor. "I think the ones that were in charge, the main ones, did a good job," Henthorn told me.

Then I asked about Franklin's claim that he had seen a video showing Scurlock, as Franklin phrased it, in "a true retreat" during his initial encounter with Gardner. The claim had been essential to Franklin's belief that Gardner was the initial aggressor.

"I don't know where that theory would have come from," Henthorn said.

Henthorn told me he personally was not persuaded by Franklin's theory that Gardner and his bartender, business partner, and dad had created a plan to stage an ambush. He told me there had been no evidence Gardner had used a racial slur at any point that night. When I asked about the "tactical styled knife" Franklin had alleged was among the weaponry inside the bar that night, Henthorn said he had no idea what Franklin was referring to. Gardner's father had admitted he'd had a pocketknife that night.

He then elaborated on Franklin's career spent rarely, if ever, prosecuting violent crime cases:

"I would say that Fred was trying to be as fair as he could be. We all have our issues. Sometimes you just don't overcome them. His experience is what it is. His cases are decided by the paper that he gives the jury. So, yeah, I would say that his lack of experience in that area was not helpful. But I would say that he tried to be as fair as he could be within the abilities that he had."

To Henthorn, however, it never felt like Franklin had an agenda. Henthorn said he was not shocked by the grand jury's decision but would not have been surprised either if they had come back the other way.

"Obviously they had a lot of things to go through," he told me. "They're not attorneys; they're not district attorneys; they don't deal with that side of things. I think it was a close call either way.

"There were things Gardner could have done numerous times along that timeline that could have changed the events," Henthorn elaborated. "So, I think he held a great deal of responsibility for the ultimate outcome of Scurlock's death."

I'm not sure exactly why Franklin stopped communicating with me. Maybe he realized he never should have talked with me at all. Maybe he didn't like my persistence.

"I'm really not sure how many different ways I can say this," he wrote to me in one of his last texts. "The issue before the grand jury was whether there was sufficient evidence to charge. The grand jury did not and could not have deprived anyone of a claim to self defense. Since it appears that I am not capable of explaining to you what the role was for the grand jury and that it was not evaluating the issue of self defense the same as would a jury at trial, I have no further comments. I wish you the best."

I tried once more:

> *Fred, I'll stand down. My job though obligates me to present you with anything that I think you need the chance to respond to as a matter of fairness. I'll keep you posted on that. As I have throughout, I thank you for your openness and patience.*

But I'm not as thickheaded as you might suspect. The grand jury's indictment is evidence a probable cause threshold had been met.

But all prosecutors have discretion. They are only to move forward with a case if they believe they have a likely chance of prevailing at trial, that they can clear the more substantial bar of beyond a reasonable doubt.

You declared your intention to try the case. Indeed looked forward to it. To me, that's the position you have to defend. Not the grand jury's action.

With great respect, joe

Silence.

There were many in Omaha's Black community who championed Franklin's role, and the outcome he had helped produce. To them, charges had always been warranted and it took Franklin to see that they were filed and prosecuted. Justin Wayne, the lawyer for the Scurlock family, told me the bitter upset felt by the Gardner family and their supporters was a taste of what Black suspects and their families had endured for centuries. Of course, Wayne was not suggesting the answer to injustice is more injustice, but he couldn't resist making the point.

One of Franklin's supporters was Greg Rhodes, the former federal prosecutor who had come out of the South Side of Chicago just like Franklin. Rhodes had told some people during the grand jury proceedings that he was a bit baffled by how long it was taking. Based on what he knew, he figured Franklin's presentation would result in the grand jury declining to hand up charges.

But when it turned out otherwise, Rhodes stood by Franklin's work. In the fall of 2021, Rhodes was nearing the end of a fight with cancer. Franklin had been given a lifetime achievement award, and Rhodes chose to make a heartfelt videotaped tribute to his friend and fellow pioneer in the U.S. Attorney's Office. He'd taken an incendiary case, put in the hours, produced an honorable outcome, Rhodes said.

In July of 2021, a nonprofit organization in Omaha called Inclusive Communities gave Franklin its "Necessary Trouble" award. The award draws its name from the legendary remarks of the civil rights icon John Lewis. The *Omaha World-Herald* reported:

> *Inclusive Communities presents the Necessary Trouble Award to inspire others to speak truth to power. It is a recognition of the bravery required by a single individual to confront injustice and take measures to advance equity, reconciliation, and the restorative process in the community. "We recognize the bravery it takes to do the right thing, even when, and especially when, it's not the popular thing," said Executive Director Maggie Wood. "From what we've learned about Fred, he has been getting into Necessary Trouble for a long time now, and that deserves to be elevated in our community."*

Tom Monaghan, the former U.S. Attorney who had recruited Franklin as part of his effort to diversify and improve the ranks of the federal office's prosecutors, was glad for Franklin receiving the award. He and Franklin both attended the memorial service for Rhodes when he succumbed to cancer. He still likes Franklin. But the case Franklin made against his client Jake Gardner, Monaghan said, had been created "out of whole cloth."

Clarence Mock, the accomplished Omaha lawyer whom I'd consulted about obtaining the grand jury transcripts, was surprised by the indictments, and not overly impressed with Franklin's various attempts to explain and justify them. He certainly wasn't buying Franklin's efforts to distance himself from the grand jury's actions.

"You are the only lawyer in the room," Mock said of grand jury presentations. "You are controlling and showing and commenting. Prosecutors have an ability to influence how the grand jury views the factual evidence."

Of Franklin, Mock said, "In a sentence, good human being and an excellent prosecutor. But race seemed to be injected into the proceedings more than it deserved to be. People don't understand the ethical obligations of prosecutors. They don't represent the victims. They represent the public and the sense of justice."

Mock has spent decades in legal combat in Omaha, and has seen other special prosecutors appointed to other cases. The risk with special prosecutors, he said, was that, consciously or not, lawyers told to take a second look at cases could go forward believing something must have gone wrong the first time. They could understand their very appointment was evidence that a correction or different outcome was required.

"A subtle but compelling urge," Mock said of the dynamic. "Compelled to do something when maybe doing nothing is the right course of action."

It was possible, he said, that Don Kleine had decided too quickly, and that Fred Franklin had overreached. It didn't make either of them evil, just human.

"All these people are honorable people," he said.

"They Can't Be Hurt Anymore"

THE FUNERAL SERVICE FOR JAMES SCURLOCK was held at the Tri-Faith Center at Countryside Community Church. Tamika Frye, James Sr.'s girlfriend, thanked those who came. Six brothers of James served as pallbearers. Three preachers spoke. There were readings from Scripture as well as a Muslim prayer.

A program had been created. It contained thirty pictures of James—with a store Santa on Christmas; flexing his muscles as a kid in the family backyard; with his baby girl, Jewels, lying on his bare chest; with his arm around one family member after another. The program offered a kind of printed eulogy:

> *James Reginald Scurlock, affectionately called Juju, was born in Omaha, Nebraska, to his father, James H. Scurlock, and biological mother Rajeanna Past and stepmother April Whiteman on February 15, 1998. James was the ninth child of twenty seven biological siblings. He was a natural protector of anyone, and very territorial over his loved ones. James was mentally fearless with a pure heart of gold.*
>
> *James was intrigued by sports at a very young age when he attended Sunny Slope Elementary. He was a natural born athlete; he joined the Omaha Saints football team and wrestled for his middle school King Science Center. When he graduated from Bryan High School in 2017, his plan was to enroll at Metro Community College that fall.*

Mari Agosta and James Scurlock were friends who would later become significant others on Christmas of 2018. They conceived their first and only child together, Jewels Aries Scurlock, in February of 2019.

James was a music head, and a jack of all trades, such as rapping, drawing, building, designing, and a plethora of many other talents. A few of Juju's hobbies were "getting lit," having fun, as well as being around the ones he loved. He had a very big personality with a silly, uplifting, unforgettable vibe, who loved making everyone laugh and was one heck of an entertainer. Juju loved being with his daughter the most! He loved her presence more than life itself. "It's all for my daughter," James Scurlock would always state.

Let us keep in mind, in the last minutes of his life, James performed as a hero to protect our citizens during a peaceful protest. We will not let his name go in vain. James was a son, a grandson, a brother, a nephew, and a father, who was loved and cherished.

The Scurlock family over my months reporting had let me into their lives with little hesitation. They gave me videos of James rapping and the letters he'd written over the years. James Sr. made me welcome at the family home on the southern border of North Omaha. James, his father, and his brother J.T. had planned to breed pit bulls as a joint family project, and so there were a handful of the dogs always about.

Over those months I spent with the family, added pain piled up. Tamika Frye, James Sr.'s partner and longtime counselor to the children, told me she lost her job as a nursing home aide when she wore a "Justice for James" pin to work; her bosses told her it upset the residents. James Sr. had been close to reaching out to the Gardner family to perhaps create a bond of sorts, but the Gardner family's lawsuit in July of 2021 offended and wounded the Scurlock family and no outreach happened. Tamika and James Sr. told me of the regular awkwardnesses for some of the younger children when the story of the Scurlock and Gardner case came up in class discussion and instruction at school.

"For the average kid," James Sr. said to me, "it's a history lesson." Not for his children, of course.

J.T., the brother James worshiped and who had introduced him to life in the street in North Omaha, perhaps bore the greatest grief. He'd let James come with him on the botched armed-robbery crime, an ugly disaster that shaped and shadowed his younger brother's entire life. With me, J.T. was open and willing to take blame. He could be funny and sharp-witted. He seemed durable, if still haunted by his own demons. It was a jail commander who called him to his office to give him the news of his brother's death. J.T. had been out on parole and seen James not long before his killing. But he'd violated a term of his parole, and was taken back to prison. He was in the back of a police car when he said his last goodbye to James. He cried as he told me.

The Scurlock family rarely, if ever, talked about Jake Gardner's alleged racism with me. For them, he'd committed a crime and needed to pay for it. But publicly the Scurlock family also never hid their anger. At one point, James Sr. had shirts made for the family to wear. "These Racists Killed My Brother," read the front. On the back: "Fuck Jake Gardner. Fuck OPD. Fuck Don Kleine. Fuck Pete Ricketts. Fuck Jean Stothert."

Ja Keen Fox, the activist who had organized the protests at Don Kleine's home, said he was awed by the Scurlock family's resilience and their refusal to do the all too familiar thing—forgive their son's killer.

"I love them. I love their honesty. We are hurt and continue to hurt, and we won't say a different thing," he said, summarizing the family's position. "So often Black families who are victims of white supremacist violence are called to forgive, and are pursued to call for some kind of peace they can't ever enjoy."

I spoke with James about the family's anger. For so long, both during the summer of 2020 and in conversations with me, James Sr. had been insistent his interest was only in seeing justice done, not in settling whether or not Jake Gardner was a racist. He suggested the lasting nature of the family's anguish had eroded their ability to draw distinctions or to resist some of the crazy conspiracy talk, such as how Gardner had not killed himself but was alive and under the care of neo-Nazis.

He told me that if the shirts his kids were wearing called out Gardner, he was not alone. The police, the mayor, the governor, the white prosecutor were all named, too.

"I judge hard," James Sr. said of his mood at the moment. "I had hoped all along race wasn't a part of what happened to my son and his killer. But at some point, I was just overwhelmed. I didn't sue anybody cause I thought maybe laws would be changed or something. But nothing has happened. The whole judicial system to me just seems racist. All of it."

In early 2022, I got a text from James Sr. I had wanted him to catch me up on what his children were doing. Qwenyona was working for the Girl Scouts, and running her nonprofit sports organization, the James Scurlock Sports Academy. Rajeanna had got a job with a local armored vehicle company. Marissa was working at a nursing home. Nick had a gig with the restaurant The Cheesecake Factory. Fat Boy and Dre were at home with James Sr.

But then he told me the family members, once so durably tight, had grown more distant from one another after James's death. The money that had been raised in his name, roughly $250,000, was shared among everyone, and James Sr. didn't think that it had played a role in the growing apart. He still babysat for Rajeanna's child, and his house in North Omaha was welcome to anyone. But there was less hanging out, fewer joint shopping trips.

"Just not the same," James Sr. told me.

I talked with Qwenyona and Rajeanna about what their dad had told me, and they did not disagree. They were still a family grieving, and each had found their own way to wrestle with their hurt. That such a process could produce a fracturing of sorts was not a surprise to them. And, they said, it did not have to be forever.

Rajeanna, blood sister to James and the only sibling allowed to see him at the hospital, wrote to me as I was finishing up my reporting. She shared a diary entry. The second anniversary of losing her brother was drawing near:

Dear Self,

It's almost that time of year again. I can't say I'll ever be used to my brother being gone, but then you get used to how you feel when you lose someone. You get used to not being able to listen to that song right now because it might trigger your emotions. You get used to that pain in your chest when you drive by a street that you'd walk to school together along. You get used to the sudden surges of sadness after realizing you can't call him to hang out anymore. You get used to the bipolar roller coaster of one day being more manageable than the next. Through this journey I've learned you will never get used to that person being gone. You just get used to having to deal with it.
Gina S.

At a dinner with some of the family members in the summer of 2022, James Sr. told me he and several of the children had decided to, as the Gardner family had before them, get out of Omaha for good. His son's death and the protests around it had led to no meaningful change. Don Kleine, who had chosen not to prosecute his son's killing as a crime, was on his way to an easy reelection as county attorney. He said the family just couldn't escape their history and felt stigmatized. They had set their sights on Arizona.

"We can't stay here," James said. "Omaha's not for us any longer."

Today, a mural of James can be found at 24th and Camden in North Omaha. A. D. Swolley, a brother to James, had done it. He wonderfully captured his brother's generous, slightly gap-toothed smile. Roses are draped across his shoulders. His cherished hair is exploding extravagantly around his head, a black and curly crown.

When Swolley was young, he told me, he became fascinated with mortuary science. He found a solemn, distinctive beauty in the dead, he said. He saw it in his brother, on the table at the funeral home and now painted on a building in North Omaha.

"They can't," he said of the dead, "be hurt anymore."

"You Stand Relieved"

THE RAIN CAME DOWN SIDEWAYS AT Arlington National Cemetery just after 2:00 p.m. on July 8, 2021. Some who had gathered inside Hatfield Gate popped open umbrellas and held them against the downpour; others, dressed in pressed suits or baseball caps and shorts, seemed to willingly get soaked, the hard rain on a warm day a kind of comfort.

Inside a white trailer, those who had come to bury Jake Gardner lined up to have background checks run before they'd be given a pass to enter the grounds of the cemetery. It took forever, and there was dark joking about whose felony convictions were holding up the line. Jake must be smiling, someone said.

Arlington, of course, exists in the American imagination as a sacred national space. The vast, perfect rows of white grave markers; the Tomb of the Unknown Soldier; John F. Kennedy's final resting place. But it's a site run by the living, and so the humans in charge of it over the decades have rendered it an imperfect place, as American in its failings as in its majesty.

Arlington, declared a national cemetery in 1864, until 1948 was also a segregated cemetery. Sections 23 and 27 were where African American soldiers were buried. When Arlington needed to expand in the 1880s, it did so by effectively seizing land that had become a village made up of freed slaves. There were, too, more recent embarrassments. In 2010, the Department of Defense's inspector general found that cemetery officials had put the wrong headstones on graves, inappropriately buried soldiers on top of one another or in shallow graves. The cemetery, it was found, was both understaffed and burdened with inadequate equipment.

But its immense solemnity is undeniable. Some four hundred thousand soldiers and prominent others are buried across its acres of heartbreak and dignity. Revolutionary War heroes; Tuskegee Airmen; John Glenn; Thurgood Marshall. Arlington holds them all.

The rain quit as quickly as it had been unleashed, and Gardner's family and friends—high school pals he'd learned to drink with, Marines he'd learned to fight alongside, cousins he'd been a hero to—drove on to the Old Post Chapel. At the back, there were two baskets of distinctive pins created for the occasion—one with Gardner's initials, *JG*, the other with a Superman *S*. Everyone took a handful.

Gardner's parents, Dave in a black suit that hung loosely on his frail body, Sue in a simple navy blue dress, made their way to the first pew. A former Marine walked carefully, almost gingerly, down the aisle, his service dog bearing a red Nebraska collar and a MAGA vest. The urn with Gardner's ashes, along with a perfectly folded American flag, were walked by a pair of Marines to the altar.

An organist played the Naval hymn, but because COVID concerns still limited the number of people who could attend, there was no choir. Those in the pews more spoke the lyrics than sang them:

"Eternal Father, strong to save,
Whose arm hath bound the restless wave,
Who bidd'st the mighty ocean deep
Its own appointed limits keep:
O hear us when we cry to thee
For those in peril on the sea."

"Corporal Jacob Gardner," the chaplain said, "you stand relieved. You have watched."

Ben Gevorgyan rose to give a eulogy:

"I know that many of you traveled great distances to be here for this service. On behalf of the Gardner family, I would like to extend their thanks to you for taking the time out of your schedule to be here.

"Sometimes there are people in life that shine more brightly than others. It might be a unique laugh, or a ray of sunshine that comes down from heaven to illuminate their silhouette and make them stand out in a crowd. There is something special about them, and whatever it is, you notice it immediately.

"Jake was one of those people; Jake stood out in a crowd. He was hilarious. The good Lord bestowed upon him the gift of comedic delivery, and thankfully, he used it often. He was a man full of piss and vinegar, and light, and humor. The life of the party—and more still, the guy that threw the party in the first place. The first party I ever saw him throw was about a week after I met him. It was a pizza party. Jake ordered pizza for everyone and had it delivered to the barracks after lights-out, which was a big no-no. Come to think of it, I think he was selling the pizza by the slice. Have I mentioned that Jake was also a capitalist?

"Shined brightly, hilarious, capitalist entrepreneur. He could work hard, but those that really know him, know that he could cut a couple corners too when needed. The mark of a skilled captain. He truly evolved into a skilled captain on this wavy ocean we call life. His ship cast a big wake. In life, and in death. But what a voyage. . . .

. . . "He was a good Marine, and was able to somehow be that while still always mercilessly questioning authority. There were so many questions largely because he had a thirst for knowledge. But he also liked to ask questions to make you think. . . .

. . . "Besides the Superman emblem on his chest he had some other tattoos as well. A Led Zeppelin album cover, a warrior's cross for our dearly departed friend Ron Payne, and another. It said: 'Death Before Dishonor.' At different times in his life I believe it meant different things to him, but in the end it was quite literal.

"There were people that were going to dishonor him, an innocent man, and he didn't see a way out of that. Make no mistake,

the city of Omaha made a deal they knew was wrong, to sacrifice an innocent man, so the city wouldn't burn. A decorated combat veteran with a physical brain injury from his time in service, and they leveled a terrorism charge against him on September 15, 2020. A man who had sacrificed his health and his youth to fight terrorism for our country was sacrificed, because he had the audacity to protect his own life when someone was trying to take it away from him. The weight of the circumstances he found himself in overwhelmed the strength that he had left to deal with the situation . . .

. . . "Here are some of the lessons that Jake Gardner taught me:

> *"If a dog works for treats, he works for himself; if the dog works for praise, he works for you.*
>
> *"If someone asks you about a subject you've studied extensively, loan them a copy of the book you learned it from. If they don't take the time to look at the book, save your breath when they ask you for more advice on the subject.*
>
> *"When running a nightclub, play music that will make women want to dance, and do everything you can to make them be, and feel, safe.*
>
> *"Being able to listen is a virtue.*
>
> *"Whenever possible, do the right thing.*

"Jake is with God now. Let us go forth from this time and reflect on the last lesson I heard him impart to his brother who was about to be a father. On the very night before Jake died. He told his brother, 'Teach your son to solve his problems with his words; teach him to avoid conflict if he can, and to fill his heart with love for his neighbors in this world. . . .'

"Semper fidelis, God bless Jake Gardner, and God bless America."

The doors of the chapel were opened, and for a moment, the Marines carrying Gardner's remains stood in a sudden bit of sunlight. "God Bless America" played, and Gardner's parents followed the urn out the door.

Gardner's family had chosen the Trump International Hotel in Washington to be the site of the reception. They did it because their son would have wanted it. But they also did it, it seemed, as an act of enduring defiance—a raised middle finger to the people who had condemned their son.

The hotel, in the historic Old Post Office, is a glorious building, boasting 263 rooms and thirty-eight thousand square feet of event space. On a Thursday afternoon seven months after Trump had left office, it felt subdued and underpopulated.

But in its grand lobby—a nine-story atrium, with a bar at the center of it—is where the Gardner party gathered for drinks. Aaron Flynn, who fought with Gardner and with whom he'd worried about the war's legitimacy, was there. Don Olson, the military neurosurgeon who'd offered Gardner work in Oregon after the killing, was there. Lee James, Bravo Company's first sergeant, was there.

Jennifer Dunckley-Gable stood in the group as well. Her husband James, a member of the units that saw combat with Gardner in 2003, had been killed in Iraq in a later mission. She'd remarried another Marine. Whiskey was poured. Fox News played on the television.

Gardner was toasted.

"To Jake."

Dave and Sue Gardner wound up staying in Oregon after their son's suicide, buying a house for themselves and their surviving son, his wife, and infant child. They would not let me divulge the town they bought in. They had lost their oldest boy, and their place in the city where they had raised their family. They were not willing to risk the modest sense of safety they had found. It took eighteen months before they would agree to let me use their living son's name—Kyle.

Dave and Sue and other family members reconstructed events for me, and chased down people I should talk to. They gave me their son's medical records from the VA. They showed me their son's autopsy report listing every one of his many tattoos or body markings to debunk the online claim he had a swastika tattoo. There was the year the U.S. Marine Corps was born, and a Marine Corps cross. There was the memorial tattoo for the dead Ron Payne. There was a "Death Before Dishonor" tattoo, as well as the famous series of numbers that played a role in the hit TV series *Lost*. There was no swastika.

I have covered as a reporter tragedies of all kinds, spent time with the parents of murder victims, with children of parents lost in plane crashes, with grandparents torn apart by having to bury grandchildren lost in a fire or a gunfight. Rarely have I seen someone as broken by grief as Sue Gardner. She spoke with me, texted me, sent me material. She cooked brisket Sunday dinner, showing me the kind of time she loved best with her son. The recipe was her mother-in-law's, the grandmother Jake Gardner had been so devoted to. She showed me, hands trembling, pictures of her son with people of color, begging me to see her child didn't hate people because of their race. She staggered through the Sundays with the giant hole in them, as well as through her boy's birthday, and the anniversary of his death. She told me she'd found a pastor at the church near their new home in Oregon who was trying to assist her. There was not a single interaction with her over the months that did not produce tears.

It seemed like every few weeks brought fresh grief. LeBron, the dog Gardner had taken more than thirty-two thousand pictures of across their eleven years together, came undone after his death, chewing his own tail to the point that it was almost lost. He was put down. One of Jake Gardner's friends who had attended his service at Arlington took his life weeks afterward. Dave was beset by one medical nightmare after another, a series of infections, two bouts of COVID, shingles, continued cancer treatments. He was hospitalized multiple times. In November of 2021, Kyle Rittenhouse, the young white man who had shot dead two men during protests over police brutality in Kenosha, Wisconsin, was acquitted on all charges after a trial marked by Rittenhouse's emotional testimony. He feared for his life, he said, and the jury agreed. It was impossible for the Gardner family not to think their son might have been similarly cleared had he gone to trial.

Over the two years I got to know Dave and Sue Gardner, neither had any desire to even visit Omaha, painful as it was to be away from other family members. On the first anniversary of Jake Gardner's death, Dave and Sue found yet another reason to stay away. Friends and family had raised money to buy space on two giant electronic billboards in Omaha to mark the anniversary.

All Gave Some; Some Gave All; Rest in Peace, Jake "Superman" Gardner.

Within twenty-four hours, a campaign to get the billboard owners to take the message down prevailed. Dave and Sue were torn apart anew. I called the billboard company; they refused to talk with me.

Then, in June of 2022, the family's lawsuit against Kleine and Franklin, as expected by many, was dismissed. The federal judge handling the case was respectful of the Gardner family's grief but was not persuaded by the arguments made by their lawyer.

In the blunt language of a court opinion, the judge rendered a verdict, one that felt like it addressed more than just a legal outcome.

"Gardner's parents are undoubtedly bereaved, and of course they have every right to be," the judge wrote in his thirty-five-page evisceration of the lawsuit. "The events that led to this case were tragic for Gardner's family and for Scurlock's, and the loss of a child is devastating under any circumstances. But not all tragic circumstances lead to legal liability. This is one of those instances."

EPILOGUE

"Every Day I Wonder: Did I Do the Right Thing?"

I HAD QUESTIONED AT THE START OF my reporting whether the notion of pure tragedy existed in America anymore. Had our divisions and suspicions and resentments and obscene racial history vanquished that inadequate but meaningful quality of true tragedy—the ability of everyone, from those torn apart by sadness to the wider public, to recognize and honor and even draw strength from shared grief?

I considered the question with both hope and doubt, my worry and pessimism driven chiefly by the online accusations, vitriol, and vigilantism that broke out with James Scurlock's death.

The expert researcher I'd hired to help document and understand the online behavior and its consequences tried to make sense of it. The Omaha tragedy, she said, was an example of how social media users can help shape and determine the narrative in the aftermath of newsworthy events.

The most obvious way social media users do this is by posting and discussing the story on their accounts, spreading awareness about an incident, and presenting information that supports their views on it. They can amplify campaigns and put pressure on local officials to support the outcome they wish to see. They can start and spread misinformation and disinformation campaigns, which can seep quickly and permanently into the mainstream news reports.

Social media users can gather and disseminate open-source information about the people involved. Personal information of the targets is gathered, including social media accounts, property information, court records, financial information, voter registration, etc. This personal information is sometimes then disseminated, a practice known as doxxing.

There are varying degrees of this behavior. Some online vigilantes are loosely affiliated with organizations that focus on exposing specific groups (e.g., the far right), while the far right has long used doxxing and online campaigns to target their opponents.

Social media is immediate, helping to set hard narratives before all the facts are known. Caricatures are created quickly and complex situations are shoehorned into preexisting narratives of right and wrong, guilty and innocent. Different identities were constructed online for both James Scurlock and Jake Gardner after the shooting. For James Scurlock, he was an innocent Black man demonstrating against racism, or he was a violent thug who provoked Gardner. For Jake Gardner, he was a racist, Trump-supporting business owner, or he was a Marine veteran who acted in self-defense. The version you got depended on what platform and websites you visited.

As well, social media and news organizations have a symbiotic relationship. Journalists, who are often working under a tight deadline from behind a computer screen far away from the event, look to social media to understand the story.

Proponents of these kinds of online operations, the researcher told me, will argue that it is a nonviolent response to violence. Opponents have argued that online vigilantism should be seen in the context of mob violence. Online vigilantism is undoubtedly useful and effective, she said, but it is dangerous and ethically complicated.

Often, she told me, regular people step into the role of online activist or investigator or vigilante when they want to see people held accountable. She directed me to an article by a writer named Jon Ronson that explored the psychology of regular people getting swept up in a feeling that they have a role in distributing justice.

"The collective fury felt righteous, powerful, and effective," Ronson wrote of early episodes of online shaming and vigilantism. "It felt as if hierarchies were being dismantled, as if justice were being democratized. As time passed, though, I watched these shame campaigns multiply, to the point that they targeted not just powerful institutions and public figures but really anyone perceived to have done something offensive. I also began to marvel at the disconnect between the severity of the crime and the gleeful savagery of the punishment. It almost felt as if shamings were now happening for their own sake, as if they were following a script."

Ryan Wilkins, the lawyer in Omaha who waged an online campaign to have Jake Gardner charged and prosecuted, was a striking example of the phenomenon. But he was hardly an isolated example. I felt compelled to try to contact as many people as I could who had posted similar claims against Gardner.

The first post identifying Gardner as the person who had shot James Scurlock—one calling him a homophobic racist—had come from an account with the username Antifa, the often violent group that frequently showed up to confront those attending right-wing rallies and the like. I wrote to the account. I wanted to know the basis for their claims. I wrote again and again. There was no response. Ever.

One of the other individuals who had posted about Gardner was Alex Kidwell. He had posted in the hours after Scurlock's killing that Gardner was a white nationalist. I wrote to him and asked him how he knew that. He wrote back saying he had read it in an article online—the post by Ryan Wilkins.

"And what if I told you everything in that article was wrong?" I wrote back. He did not answer, and would not reply to subsequent emails.

Another was Isabelle Briar. She'd posted claims that Scurlock had been shot from behind and that Gardner's father had an Iron Cross tattoo. I asked her if she had worried at all about publishing such claims that might be wrong or incomplete. Gardner's father, I'd learned, had no such tattoo.

"I mean I think we always worry about not having the full story, and we knew we didn't, but the more important point was that a young man was murdered for no good reason," she wrote me. "I think the tattoo was pretty common knowledge. I only made the mistake of going to The Hive once, and I didn't repeat it. After the shooting people were debating if it was racially motivated and a bunch of people were pointing out that his dad has an Iron Cross tattoo and he had a history of racist behavior himself. There were even pictures of his dad's arm, but I think a lot of people got forced to remove those posts. But I wouldn't know."

I reached Paul LeClair as well. He'd posted that Gardner was a "far right white supremacist." Again, I asked for his evidence.

"Some friends of mine who have visited his establishment knew him and his behaviors towards people and his strong opinions against transgender people and people of color. They shared that with me when we were deciding where to go," he wrote.

I asked him how he would feel if much of what he'd heard was erroneous or incomplete. He asked why I wanted to know:

> *Because a lot of online misinformation drove a possibly dangerously false narrative that affected the criminal proceedings against Gardner. You contributed to that portrait. Without anything like first-hand knowledge. That strikes me as reckless. Do you think it was?*

LeClair ended our communications.

Ryan Wilkins, the Omaha lawyer who had publicly accused Gardner of being a neo-Nazi and called for his prosecution, refused over many months to reengage with me after our extensive interview. However, I was given some correspondence between Wilkins and Wendy Reed. She had been a high school classmate of both Wilkins and Gardner. It was Gardner who had stood with her when she was otherwise ostracized for dating a Black student. Wendy was enraged by what Wilkins had alleged, and felt it had contributed to Gardner's eventual indictment and death.

"You cheered your ass off 2 days before he killed himself," Wendy wrote to Wilkins.

Wilkins wrote back, saying he stood by his incendiary claims. But Wilkins then seemed to want to distance himself from the legal outcome he'd campaigned for, and maybe even to suggest Gardner might have been something more or different than the virulent racist he had reduced him to online.

"Like most people, I was shocked and disappointed when I learned of Jake's death," Wilkins wrote. "I never wanted or expected anything like that to happen. Once the charges were announced (several months after my blog post), it was my hope that Jake would defend himself and the public would hear all of the relevant evidence at trial—whether that evidence proved his guilt or exonerated him.

"I believe Jake was capable of true kindness and decency," Wilkins wrote in closing. "Most people are not all good nor all bad—neither our worst moments nor our best moments define us."

Of course, there was also the case of Jennifer Heineman, the distant cousin of Gardner. She'd posted his telephone number online. She testified in front of a legislative panel about her family's seething and longstanding racism. When I finally engaged with her, and she admitted she had no examples of any racist behavior by Gardner or his parents, I sensed she wanted to unburden herself a bit, and I proposed meeting in Omaha. She agreed.

We met early in the afternoon on a day in June of 2022. She had picked a bar in her neighborhood, a historic community within North Omaha known as Benson. She told me a number of accomplished Black poets had lived in the neighborhood years back.

Heineman apologized for treating me with such suspicion when I'd first contacted her, and I apologized for a perhaps overly aggressive approach.

Heineman told me she regretted having posted Gardner's telephone number online, although she said she had actually been retweeting what someone else had already dug up. She said she'd suffered a lifetime of trauma—as a sex worker, and as a child exposed to the overt racism of some family members—and had acted as many victims of trauma do.

"Imperfectly," she said.

"I never meant for anyone to be harmed," she added.

She told me she had never known Gardner very well at all. She'd contacted him during the imbroglio over the transgender bathroom issue but admitted she wished she'd been more open to a constructive engagement with him.

We talked again about her claims of Gardner's racism and white supremacist ideology and her lack of evidence for any of it. She said she'd been speaking as a sociologist, placing him in a broader sweep of the country's racial history. And she recalled, through tears, the destabilizing and depressing experience of first hearing of Scurlock's death and instantly assuming it was her distant cousin Jake who was responsible.

Heineman, sometimes trembling, took breaks to compose herself. She said she realized my mission as a reporter was different from hers—the pursuit of very specific facts. And she had none that could implicate Gardner as what she'd called him out to be. She cried more than once.

The next day, I got an email from her.

"I thought a lot about our talk yesterday and fell into a pretty significant bit of broken heart insomnia," she wrote.

She stood by her need to place both Scurlock and Gardner in the painful historical context of racial injustice in America, and in Nebraska specifically. Whatever the particulars of their lives and families, they could never be seen as on equal ground in America today. She said she did not want her real experience of racist trauma at the hands of family members to be minimized or dismissed. She and I, she said, also occupied unequal positions in society and that fact played a role in our perceptions of what had happened and how the public would receive our takes—"you, a respectable (?) white man, and me, a former whore (with white privilege no doubt.)

"I just wanted to articulate something a little better than I did last night," she wrote. "Twitter is definitely disgusting and we should all interrogate our participation in it. If I had acted from a place of empathy and a true desire for justice for James, I would not have used a toxic platform for my 'call out.' Call outs are about virtue signaling and building an identity, always. Not to mention a monster that feeds off of the spectacle.

"Every day," she told me, "I wonder: Did I do the right thing?"

The implications of such online behavior around newsworthy events, the eagerness for participation, the thirst for punishment, registered most lastingly for me in my conversations with the Black Marine who had befriended Gardner. He'd hung out endlessly in Gardner's barracks during boot camp, retrieved Gardner from Camp Lejeune upon Gardner's discharge, enjoyed cookouts with Gardner's family, drank in Gardner's Omaha bar, and appeared on television with Gardner in a segment on their shared service in Iraq.

The former Marine had made a career as a television journalist. He'd worked in cities across the country, including his hometown Omaha. He'd reached out to Gardner after Scurlock's death and tried to buck his friend up.

Of the events on the deadly night in May of 2020, the former Marine said, "The Black man in me wonders what the hell Jake was doing with a gun out there that night. But the Marine in me is open to the idea I might have done the same thing Jake did in firing that gun."

It felt complicated but honest, conflicted but genuine. It felt empathetic and true.

Yet the Marine would not be named. He said he'd lose friends and maybe his job if he was. He said he was sorry but felt he was without a choice. He'd been thoughtful about issues of race, torn about Gardner's choices, dispirited about the state of our country, but in the end, nothing so much as afraid.

To the extent I felt hopeful, that was a gift from the two families. I had entered the lives of the Scurlocks and Gardners as a stranger they had no obvious reason to trust. I was a reporter who each family knew was deeply engaged with the other. And yet they never sought to get me to divulge what I was learning about their counterparts in sorrow and rage. There was no paranoia or suspicion. Their mission, an independent effort but over time a mutual act of daring, was not to dwell on blame or win an argument, but only to have their truths about their children heard. No small thing—for them, for me, for our bruised and bruising country.

Acknowledgments

I HAD NEVER MUCH WANTED TO WRITE a book across my forty years as a newspaperman. Some folks had encouraged me to. A couple of book agents offered me the chance to. But I never felt I had the requisite talent or discipline. Now that I've gone and done it, or hope I have, there are many people to thank. Or blame, of course.

I am most grateful to the Scurlock and Gardner families, who opened themselves to me and my inquiry at a moment of ungodly hurt, confusion, and fury. I warned them that my efforts would undoubtedly disappoint them, in small ways, and perhaps even in major instances. To them, I promise I tried my best.

Other people who appear in this book shared with me their biographies, their perspectives, their explanations, their regrets, and their hopes, often at risk to their careers and/or their safety.

Research help was provided by Lila Hassan, Rhona Tarrant, John Jordan, Joe Galvin, Margot Williams, Doris Burke, A. C. Thompson, and T. Christian Miller, my longtime and steadfast friends at ProPublica. Early and expert encouragement came from Marty Baron and Mike Connor, two distinguished and tough-minded journalists whose approval I've always sought. Carolyn Lessard gave me her inimitable mix of spiritual support and tech help. Raphaela Morais blessed me with her creative genius. Scott Voorhees made a generous and important set of introductions. Jennifer Dunckley-Gable shared her correspondence with her own lost Marine, James. Sean Huze allowed me to make use of his art born of pain. Emily Chen-Newton did me a couple of important courtesies.

To Dan Grady, Sue Robinson, Ian Urbina, Chris Chivers, Simon Ressner, Moy Pang, Mike Schmidt, Chris Borland, and Matthew Galkin, thanks for your companionship and wisdom—the nature of which will stay private but the value of which will never be forgotten.

It took me sixty-two years to get an agent, but in Todd Shuster I could not have found a better one. His associates Allison Warren, Jack Haug, and Daniella Cohen ain't too bad, either. I am indebted to Scribner's Nan Graham, Colin Harrison, Emily Polson, and Jaya Miceli for their daring, faith, and patience.

Steve Engelberg and Dick Tofel at ProPublica generously let me take my initial reporting and run with it.

I need to give thanks to my parents, Joan and Dick, incomparable role models of decency, integrity, love, and forgiveness. Finally, my five indomitable siblings, Molly, Lucy, Michael, Ann, and Kate, afforded me what they have throughout my entire life—loyalty and laughter.